General de Kalb, Lafayette's Mentor

UNC | COLLEGE OF ARTS AND SCIENCES
Germanic and Slavic Languages and Literatures

From 1949 to 2004, UNC Press and the UNC Department of Germanic & Slavic Languages and Literatures published the UNC Studies in the Germanic Languages and Literatures series. Monographs, anthologies, and critical editions in the series covered an array of topics including medieval and modern literature, theater, linguistics, philology, onomastics, and the history of ideas. Through the generous support of the National Endowment for the Humanities and the Andrew W. Mellon Foundation, books in the series have been reissued in new paperback and open access digital editions. For a complete list of books visit www.uncpress.org.

General de Kalb, Lafayette's Mentor

A.E. ZUCKER

UNC Studies in the Germanic Languages and Literatures
Number 53

Copyright © 1966

This work is licensed under a Creative Commons CC BY-NC-ND license. To view a copy of the license, visit http://creativecommons.org/licenses.

Suggested citation: Zucker, A.E. *General de Kalb, Lafayette's Mentor.* Chapel Hill: University of North Carolina Press, 1966. DOI: https://doi.org/10.5149/9781469658759_Zucker

Library of Congress Cataloging-in-Publication Data
Names: Zucker, A.E.
Title: General de Kalb, Lafayette's mentor / by A.E. Zucker.
Other titles: University of North Carolina Studies in the Germanic Languages and Literatures ; no. 53.
Description: Chapel Hill : University of North Carolina Press, [1966] Series: University of North Carolina Studies in the Germanic Languages and Literatures. | Includes bibliographical references.
Identifiers: LCCN 66003536 | ISBN 978-1-4696-5874-2 (pbk: alk. paper) | ISBN 978-1-4696-5875-9 (ebook)
Subjects: De Kalb, Johann, 1721-1780.
Classification: LCC PD25 .N6 NO. 53 | DCC 973 .3470924

To my Friend and Colleague,
Dieter Cunz

I gratefully acknowledge your kindness in associating me to the tribute paid to the memory of a friend who, as you observe, has been the early confidant and companion of my devotion to the American cause.
Lafayette at the tomb of de Kalb in Camden, March 8, 1825.

TABLE OF CONTENTS

Preface		1
Introduction		7
I.	The German Peasant Boy Emerges from Obscurity as a French Officer	18
II.	Apprenticeship under Marshals Saxe and Lowendal	30
III.	Hero in the Seven Years' War	44
IV.	Marriage and a Mission	55
V.	First Visit to America	65
VI.	Lafayette's Mentor	80
VII.	The Broglie Intrigue	94
VIII.	"Victoire"	108
IX.	An Unguided Tour from Charleston to Philadelphia	120
X.	A Cold Reception by Congress and its Favorable Outcome	132
XI.	American Major General	150
XII.	Valley Forge	161
XIII.	Worse than Valley Forge	182
XIV.	Washington Sends de Kalb to Rescue Charleston; Congress Substitutes Gates	197
XV.	The Last Full Measure of Devotion	213
Appendix I		232
Appendix II		232
Appendix III		233
Principal Authorities		234
Notes		241
Index		246

PREFACE

On April 20, 1777, Lafayette and de Kalb, with a dozen other officers, sailed for America in the "Victoire," contrary to the king's orders. Four days later a British agent reported from Paris to his home office: "The Marquis de Lafayette will go despite the king's orders. He has taken with him the Baron, a very noted and able officer, to be his guardian and instructor. The Baron bears the character of being one of the best generals in the service." The Baron de Kalb had introduced the ambitious nineteen-year-old Marquis de Lafayette to the American agent, Silas Deane, and acting as interpreter, secured for the young nobleman an appointment as major general in the American army. Subsequently, de Kalb's advice served Lafayette, and through him the American cause, very well. This "prodigy," as the Baron called him, actually received, on Washington's recommendation, the command of a division, which he led with the "glory" he was so eager to gain. His relationship to the Baron turned into a beautiful friendship that lasted to de Kalb's death on the battlefield of Camden in 1780.

Among the numerous French officers who fought for the American cause in the Revolutionary War, General de Kalb was one of the most distinguished, second perhaps only to Lafayette. What was the attitude of these foreigners toward the commander-in-chief under whom they served? In an essay, *George Washington as the Europeans Saw Him,* Professor Gilbert Chinard says some striking things about the adjustment of the newcomers:

> These French noblemen had apparently slight reasons for admiring the Virginian gentleman under whose command they had been placed. Most of them were career officers; some of them had fought on the battlefields of Europe. They had graduated from military schools; they had studied the campaigns of Frederick II, whom they had been trained to consider the greatest general of the century and a military genius of the highest rank. They had lived at the court of the kings of France and were familiar with the refinements, artificial but exquisite, of French society. They had the highly

critical mind so often found among educated Frenchmen, and were not to be taken in easily by appearances. They might have resented serving under a man who was represented by some of his biographers as a country squire, a gentleman farmer, and at most a rich Virginia planter. And yet all of them, practically without exception, acknowledged in Washington a military genius, a man of sterling character whose manners reflected those rare qualities which cannot be acquired through upbringing but are the expression of an inner life marked by dignity, sterling honesty and mastery of the will.

Such a change of attitude is to be found in de Kalb's letters; from granting Washington good intentions, he changed to according him enthusiastic praise. The vast gap between the two cultures explains in part the fantastic idea of de Kalb's former superior officer, the Comte de Broglie, of having himself appointed by Congress generalissimo of the American army in place of Washington.

De Kalb was sent by the French Government on a mission to America in 1768, in the course of which he became friends with a number of Americans and learned to like their ways. When the Revolutionary War broke out, he wrote a Philadelphia friend, Dr. Phile, on December 26, 1775, "I am such a friend of your country that I could with pleasure devote the rest of my days in the service of your liberty," and offered to Congress his military experience of thirty-two years. Of course his motives were mixed – every French soldier was eager for revenge against England after the humiliating peace of 1763. Through distinguished service abroad, too, he looked for a generalship to crown his long career. But there can be no doubt of his devotion to the American cause – which he sealed with his death on the field of honor at the battle of Camden.

In Lafayette's case, too, there were divided motives. As is but natural, his latest biographer, Professor Louis Gottschalk, shows that this "paragon of liberty" came to America in part to show his disdainful father-in-law that though shy and frail, he *could* "set the world on fire." He longed for glory on the battlefield. He had romantic notions of the natural rights of man, and felt eager to aid the Americans in gaining their freedom from British oppression.

In the France of a dozen years before 1789, there were of course many who believed in republican or liberal principles, even though American rebels were skeptical about this. The widely beloved Peter Du Ponceau was, shortly after his arrival in Boston, so the story goes, at dinner with John Hancock and Samuel Adams, where he upheld republican principles. Samuel Adams asked him where he had found them. He replied, "In France." Adams said this was impossible, whereupon Du Ponceau immediately retorted: "Because a man was born in a stable it is not necessary that he should be a horse!"

As one views de Kalb's career, it becomes evident that what he lacked was "luck." A Bavarian peasant's son, he left home to make his mark in the world in the adventurous life of a soldier of fortune. By his bravery, his zeal and his good judgment he rose to the rank of colonel in the greatest army of the day, the French – but he was a foreigner and a Protestant – consequently often passed over in promotions.

Later, as major general in the American army, de Kalb longed for a chance to gain glory, but though in command for three years of one of the best divisions, he "never so much as heard a gun go off," as he wrote Mme. de Kalb. He somehow missed Germantown, Monmouth, even Stony Point. Finally, in 1780, Washington selected him to command the Army of the South which was to relieve the siege of Charleston. Hardly had he undertaken his independent command when Congress appointed over his head the incompetent Gates, who then led the army into disaster. The gallant soldier's first American battle was also his last; his glory came, but very late in his heroic career from mercenary to patriot.

Testy, crusty, explosive, morose, grumbling, are some of the adjectives applied by historians to de Kalb; he may appear to be so in some letters to his wife and his friend the Comte de Broglie – written from Valley Forge or Morristown! Trevelyan calls him "a keen but friendly critic." De Kalb was sociable; he entertained when supplies permitted. To the claim that he was phlegmatic and had prosaic German tastes, one can oppose Gottschalk's "the thoroughly gallicized de Kalb." Freeman calls him "maladroit," but Greene "a shrewd diplomat." His tact would not allow him to accept the appointment to a major generalship if among the American officers "anyone is distressed." He wanted an account of every sou – perhaps because of his peasant origin. He was abstemious – yet he regretted having no champagne for his guests at the celebration of the victory of Stony Point. He enjoyed mountain climbing and generally preferred walking to horseback riding. He boasted to his wife of his strength and endurance, which enabled him to overcome terrible hardships. His aide, Colonel Nicholas Rogers of Baltimore, writes: "In form and feature he was a perfect Ariovistus, more than six feet tall, and proof against the greatest hardships." James Lovell said that "in manners and looks he resembles our chief." Very humane in his treatment of his soldiers, he was well aware that a frontal attack on a strong position must cost lives, and was himself ready to fight on the front line. He won and held the loyalty of his aides to a remarkable degree, and made many enduring friendships, all of the best. He was, on the whole, French, perhaps cosmopolitan, yet he sent his boys to a German school. He was deeply religious, but did not wear his faith on his sleeve. He was a devoted husband and father at a time and in a land where infidelity was a matter for amusing witticisms, with the King setting the style. He was of rather a serious nature; on one occasion he wrote to the somewhat supercilious Chevalier de Mauroy: "I lay no claim to making epigrams." In his profession he was universally recognized as a capable and experienced soldier.

The whole picture outlined by these details shows a strong personality, direct, self-respecting and devoted to his friends. Like Washington, he had enjoyed very little formal schooling, but he had educated himself in the requirements and standards of true nobility.

Basic to any study of de Kalb is the well documented biography of Friedrich Kapp, published in German in 1862 and in translation in 1884. It is, in fact, the only serious life of the general, and is now long out of print. The author drew upon documents in American and European archives, and also secured copies of numerous letters de Kalb wrote to his wife from America – a most important source. Since Kapp quoted not nearly all the letters, and some only in part, I felt that I must secure them. Kapp was a political refugee of the German Revolution of 1848 who returned to Germany after amnesty had been declared in 1870. Thinking that he might have presented his copies of the letters to an American library, I wrote to all the likely ones, but the regularly negative replies convinced me that the letters were most probably not in America. Miss Edith Lenel, Kapp's great-granddaughter (with whom I had by that time got in touch, and who had herself written a biography of Kapp) informed me that in her researches in Germany she had found no trace of the de Kalb letters. This seemed to shut out one more possibility.

Through Professor Pierre Renouvin of the Sorbonne, I got in touch with the Vicomte d'Abzac, grandson of de Kalb's granddaughter, living at de Kalb's chateau, Milon la Chapelle. He sent me a photostat of a brochure on de Kalb by a one-time tutor of the children at Milon la Chapelle, informing me that this booklet was the only thing of a historical nature to be found in the chateau.

With only one clue left that might be promising, I finally went to Paris. In a five-volume work by Professor Henri Doniol, *La Participation de la France à l'Etablissement des Etats Unis d'Amérique* (1880), there is a footnote to the effect that the author was permitted to use de Kalb's letters through the courtesy of M. Soulange-Teissier. There was no address or other information in the note, which was by that time nearly eighty years old. Since some of de

Kalb's descendants were honorary members of the Society of the Cincinnati, I called at the library of that Society. The secretary, a Marquis de Valous, knew the Vicomte d'Abzac, but even after an extensive search he could find no Soulange-Teissier. The Bibliothèque Nationale and various other archives also failed to give the desired information.

Shortly before I was to leave Paris, I still had on my list a visit to de Kalb's estate, Milon la Chapelle, if only for local color. It is located in the beautiful rolling country some miles beyond Versailles. There I found the Vicomte, now over eighty years old, living with his sister in a small house on the estate, while the chateau was leased to a lady who showed it to me with great pride. I tried my "clue" on her; immediately she said she knew very well a M. Soulange-Teissier, a cousin of the Vicomte, living in near-by Versailles. She gave me his address, and in half an hour I had come to the end of my search. This fine French gentleman, also an octogenarian, told me it was his father who had permitted Doniol to use the letters. After an hour of conversation, he consented to get the letters from his bank deposit box and to allow me to look through them in his livingroom. Four afternoons were pleasantly spent there, selecting letters important for the biography, which were then photostated for my use. During this time I enjoyed the truly French courtesy and kindness of the entire family. This eleventh-hour discovery made possible a true and accurate account of de Kalb's stay in America, otherwise impossible, for which I am deeply grateful.

To my colleague, Professor Dieter Cunz, who urged on me the need for a biography of de Kalb, I am dedicating this volume as one more outgrowth of our common interests.

I wish to thank Dr. Herbert E. Klingelhofer and Mr. John Reed who were kind enough to read the manuscript and to make some very useful suggestions. In the course of a congenial correspondence I received professional advice from Dr. Alfred Vagts, the author of *A History of Militarism*. Professor Douglas W. Alden, on a sabbatical year in Paris, drove me to Versailles, a trip that led to my most valuable find. Two collateral descendants of the Baron, George Kalb and Rudolf Bischoff, gave generously of their time to show me de Kalb's birthplace. Dr. Robert W. Hill of the New York Public Library turned up for my benefit numerous documents from the archives. I am deeply grateful to the American Philosophical Society for a travel grant, and for aid from the Graduate School of the University of Maryland through Deans Ronald Bamford and Augustus J. Prahl.

Special thanks goes to Dr. F. E. Coenen of the University of North Carolina, for his true friendship in seeing my manuscript through the press.

To my wife, Dr. Lois M. Zucker, I am indebted for constructive criticism and for typing and proofreading.

It is one of the great pleasures of writing a biography that the work invariably leads to acquaintance with delightful persons who inevitably make an author's life richer and more colorful. This book has been a boon in my life, and I greet once more all those who have been mentioned as well as many others who deserve a similar cordial salute.

INTRODUCTION

The most civilized countries of Europe during the eighteenth century, comparable to the first half of the twentieth, carried on almost continuous warfare, turning their pruning hooks into swords and their plowshares into spears. In the course of these wars the Duke of Marlborough and Prince Eugene of Savoy won famous victories, the best known probably being Blenheim, 1704, where these two generals put the French to flight, as described by Southey in a poem found in most anthologies of English verse:

> With fire and sword the country round
> Was wasted far and wide,
> And many a childing mother then
> And new born baby died.
> But things like that, you know, must be
> In every famous victory.
>
> They say it was a shocking sight
> After the field was won;
> For many thousand bodies here
> Lay rotting in the sun.
> But things like that, you know, must be
> At every famous victory.
>
> Great praise the Duke of Marlborough won
> And our good Prince Eugene.
> "Nay, 'twas a very wicked thing!"
> Said little Wilhelmine.
> "Nay, nay, my little girl," quoth he,
> "It was a famous victory,"
>
> "And everybody praised the Duke
> Who this great fight did win."
> "But what good came of it at last?"
> Quoth little Peterkin.
> "Why, that I cannot tell," said he,
> "But 'twas a famous victory."

Blenheim was a battle in the War of the Spanish Succession, which was begun in 1702, with England, Holland and Austria allied against France. The war was launched against Louis XIV for placing his grandson on the Spanish throne, vacant due to the death of Charles II. This would have put Spain as well as France under the rule of the Bourbon dynasty. All the important battles went against France until in 1714 a peace treaty was signed which permitted the French prince to remain King of Spain, while France lost some territories to England, Holland and Austria.

The war of the Austrian Succession broke out in 1740. This was a dynastic war, like other European wars of the time, fought to gain territory for the victorious ruler and his dynasty. The Austrian Emperor, Charles VI, issued a decree in 1724 (called a "pragmatic sanction") regularizing the succession of his possessions, under which in default of male descendants in the Habsburg line, his daughter Maria Theresa became his heiress. Most of the European governments recognized this decree, which made Maria Theresa queen upon her father's death in 1740. However, Bavaria under Charles VII, who had married a niece of the Habsburg Emperor, laid claim to some Habsburg lands, as did also France, Spain and Saxony. Frederick II of Prussia claimed that some old treaties entitled Prussia to Silesia, and, without a declaration of war, marched in and seized this Austrian territory. Of course Austria fought back. All of Europe became involved; England, Holland and Saxony on Austria's side, Bavaria and Spain allied with Prussia. After eight years of fighting, a peace treaty was drawn up in 1748 with the result that Maria Theresa, now empress, continued on the Austrian throne and Frederick retained Silesia. Eight years later there was a second contest, the so-called Seven Years' War (our French and Indian War), fought over Silesia, which ended with this territory remaining a part of Prussia. France lost Canada in this war of 1756 to 1763, and embittered by this humiliation, helped the Thirteen Colonies to defeat England in the next decade in the War of the American Revolution, 1775 to 1783.

This last war was different. Of course, it gave the French statesmen an opportunity for revenge, but the fight of the "insurgents" in the British colonies of North America for the establishment of a free people on a free soil aroused sympathy among many French idealists who felt that this was a war representing a cause, namely, human liberty.[1] Neither in Spain nor in Austria was there any interest in the "rebels;" but France was ready for new ideas. To fight for this objective certainly meant glory, and the glory of Lafayette, de Kalb, Steuben, Du Ponceau, Fleury, Pulaski and some others is not forgotten.

Much was different in European armies of the eighteenth century from what is considered proper in the armed services of our day. The following generalizations do not hold true in every place and at all times, but they may serve as an attempt to describe some of the conditions in Western Europe under which General de Kalb, the subject of this biography, spent his first fifty years.

In the eighteenth century, the style of warfare underwent some interesting changes in Europe from medieval chivalric traditions toward conscripted standing armies. In the days of feudalism the knights were the sole warriors – they alone could bear arms, a thing definitely forbidden to the peasants. They fought chivalrously against an enemy equally armed and equipped, and of course they regarded the introduction of the bow and arrow, and later of muskets, as unsporting and disgraceful. In fact, it was ruinous to them as a class. As towns developed, their defense was at first undertaken by the burghers; but as their wealth grew greater they found it profitable to hire fighters from among the peasants who flocked to the cities and who, being footloose, were willing to risk their lives for pay. As organizers of regiments, members of the nobility found this their proper function, and thus the barons and dukes became the officers of fighting forces, establishing a monopoly that continued, with of course some exceptions, up to the nineteenth century. There was thus established a division of labor; the burghers devoted themselves to trade or manufacture, while the nobles conducted the wars. Thus they secured for themselves pleasant "benefices," though perhaps not quite so comfortable as those of the clergy. Officers, mostly members of the nobility, were freed from taxes on the basis that they paid a tax in blood on the battlefield.

The eighteenth century did not know standing armies, by which is meant nationals of a country organized to fight for the defense of their fatherland or the interests of their princes. The officers of those days, as professional soldiers, served any country in a spirit of impartiality, and of course the common soldiers fought for the power that had purchased their services. In this sale of human beings as cannon fodder the Swiss were very prominent, due to economic reasons.[2] Switzerland is an agriculturally poor country and must export to overcome its unfavorable trade balance. Before the tourist business or the manufacture of watches or cheeses could help the Swiss to secure the necessary imports of foodstuffs, they exported human beings as mercenaries to fight for any nation on an impartial business basis. From the middle ages onward this "free and neutral" nation sent soldiers to fight in practically every European war, to such an extent that the very word "Swiss" came to have the connotation ot a valiant and reliable professional soldier. It became proverbial, however, that the thrifty Swiss retained their independence to the extent that they refused to fight unless they were paid; *Pas de sous, pas de Suisses.* (No pay, no Swiss.) German mercenaries (*Landsknechte*) in similar numbers also found service in the French armies. Rivalry between different groups was naturally great. At one time a French soldier taunted a Swiss with "No pay, no Swiss." The Swiss asked, "And what are you fighting for?" "Honor!" replied the Frenchman. "I suppose we both fight for what we do not have."[3]

Figures from the year 1776 show that foreign troops in the French service numbered 13,120 Germans, 18,040 Swiss, 3,260 Italians, and the same number of Irish totalling 37,720. Somewhat earlier, in the War of the Spanish Succession, 1701 to 1714, Swiss mercenaries fought on opposite sides; 20,000 served with the French, and with the Allies against France there were 13,000 under Dutch, 4,000 under Savoyan, 3,000 under Milanese, and 2,000 under Imperial command.[4] There is an anecdote according to which the minister of Louis XIV, Louvois, one time remarked to the king in the presence of a Swiss general, Stuppa: "Sire, if Your Majesty had all the money which He and the kings his predecessors have given to the Swiss He could pave the road from Paris to Basel with five-franc gold pieces." General Stuppa replied: "This may be so, but if it were possible to gather all the blood that our nation has shed in the service of Your Majesty and the kings his predecessors, it would fill a canal all the way from Paris to Basel."[5]

An eighteenth century custom rather startling to the modern reader is the purchase of officer's posts, under the so-called proprietary system. The officer was paid for the number of men he mustered and was furnished their equipment and food, the colonel being the proprietor of the regiment he had formed, and the captain the proprietor of his company. Commissions came to have a high value in European countries; the cost of a second lieutenancy was about $2,000 and the cost of a commission of lieutenant-colonel could be as much as $30,000. Besides the profits from the rights of ownership, the officer could sell proprietary rights when he retired.

This practice is so different from current ways of appointing or promoting officers that it may be well to cite some details. The officer bought a captaincy or some other commission in a regiment from his predecessor in the office or from the government in the case of a newly established regiment. Since an army career was an honorable one for a young man of nobility or of a wealthy family, such officerships were much sought after; in England particularly the transaction was arranged by a broker. Of course, a commission could be bought only when there was an actual vacancy in a regiment. If, say, a captain or a major was promoted in wartime to a higher but temporary post, for example as colonel, he would draw a colonel's pay plus the appurtenances of his regular commission. He would, however, pay out of his own pocket the salary of his substitute. If a higher post seemed impermanent, a cautious officer would not sell his lower commission but would revert to it when at the close of a war many positions were abolished or entire regiments dissolved. (This is exactly what de Kalb did when his regiment was abolished at the end of the Seven Years' War.) The officer would continue to draw his pay as long as he held his commission. If he retired for incapacity or some other reason, it was to his advantage to sell his commission. There was no provision for pensions, and the sale of a commission was supposed to furnish the living for the officer's old age.

There is a passage by Smollett, the English novelist, a contemporary of de Kalb (in fact born in the same year) in his *Humphrey Clinker*, illustrative of this custom. In the course of his travels, the hero, Mr. Bramble, together with his family, meets a certain Lieutenant Obadiah Lismahago who had fought at Ticonderoga and had been "wounded, maimed, mutilated, taken and enslaved" in two sanguinary wars. Mr. Bramble is indignant that this soldier has not attained a higher rank than lieutenant. The latter explains: "I complain of no injustice. I purchased an ensigncy thirty years ago; and in the course of service rose to be a lieutenant according to my seniority." "But in the course of time," resumed the Squire, "you must have seen a great number of young officers put over your head." – "Nevertheless," said he, "I have no cause to murmur. They bought their preferment with their money. I had no money to carry to market. That was my misfortune, but nobody was to blame." "What! No friend to advance a sum of money?" said Mr. Bramble. – "Perhaps I might have borrowed the money for the purchase of a company," answered the other, "but that loan must have been refunded; and I did not chuse to encumber myself with a debt of a thousand pounds to be paid from an income of ten shillings a day."[6]

Just as there were no standing armies, there was no universal military service. The common soldiers were secured by voluntary or compulsory enlistment. Since the pay given soldiers was very meager, their food very poor, and in general their condition as harsh as that of a galley slave, "voluntary enlistment" amounted in most cases practically to kidnaping. A recruiting officer would establish himself at some public place, perhaps a fair, boast to young men about the adventures and conquests of the soldier's life, give them plenty to drink, and then force "the King's shilling" into the fist of the poor fools in their drunken condition. Other recruits came into the army from the debtor's prisons or were released from jail on condition that they become soldiers. A Bavarian law of 1739 ordered that all idlers,[7] vagabonds, etc., be placed in the nearest army group. The British "Act against Vagabonds" authorized the "impressment of any sturdy beggar, any fortune teller, any idle, unknown or suspected fellow in a parish that cannot give an account of himself... anyone who has been in gaol or was known as an incorrigible rogue."

In England, of course, impressment was carried on more for the navy than for the army. It was a legalized practice for ships of the Royal Navy to lie in wait for returning merchant vessels and seize their sailors to be placed on their ships. Often the men were snatched away before they could even speak to their wives or children awaiting them at the dock. Brutality on naval vessels, and of course in all eighteenth century armies, was indescribable. Floggings of hundreds of blows on the bared backs of soldiers or sailors guilty only of minor transgressions were quite common. It has been said that Prussian soldiers found war a relief from the terrors of peace, since in wartime the punishments were lessened. Desertion frequently brought capital punishment.[8]

The well known German poet Johann Gottfried Seume, (1763-1810) as a young man was leaving the University of Leipzig and was traveling on foot to Paris when he was kidnaped by some of the Duke of Hesse's agents. They tore up his identification papers and then sold him to England along with hundreds of other "Hessians" for service against the American revolutionaries. At the close of the war he returned to Germany; his fascinating account offers many details of this sale of human beings – to mention only one item: on the day after his capture Seume found as companions in his misery a rusticated student from the University of Jena, a bankrupt merchant from Vienna, a haberdasher from Hannover, a dismissed postal clerk from Gotha, a monk from Würzburg, a magistrate from Meiningen, a Prussian cavalry sergeant, a cashiered Hessian major, and other similar poor devils.[9]

Voltaire, in his satirical novel *Candide*, second chapter, gives a picture of the brutalities any well-built young man could meet with. The Bulgarians in this account, of course, are the Prussians and their king Frederick the Great:

> Candide, expelled from the earthly paradise, wandered for a long time without knowing where he was going, weeping, turning up his eyes to Heaven, gazing back frequently at the noblest of castles which held the most beautiful of young baronesses; he lay down to sleep supperless between two furrows in the open fields; it snowed heavily in large flakes. The next morning the shivering Candide, penniless, dying of cold and exhaustion, dragged himself toward the neighboring town, which was called Waldberghoff-trabkdikdorff. He

halted sadly at the door of an inn. Two men dressed in blue noticed him.

"Comrade," said one, "there's a well-built young man of the right height." They went up to Candide and very civilly invited him to dinner.

"Gentlemen," said Candide with charming modesty, "you do me a great honor, but I have no money to pay my share."

"Ah, Sir," said one of the men in blue, "persons of your figure and merit never pay anything; are you not five feet five tall?"

"Yes, gentlemen," said Candide bowing, "that is my height."

"Ah, Sir, come to table; we will not only pay your expenses, we will never allow a man like you to be short of money; men were only made to help each other."

"You are in the right," said Candide, "that is what Dr. Pangloss was always telling me, and I see that everything is for the best."

They begged him to accept a few crowns; he took them and wished to give them an I O U; they refused to take it and all sat down to table.

"Do you not love tenderly?...."

"Oh yes," said he, "I love Mademoiselle Cunegonde tenderly."

"No," said one of the gentlemen, "we were asking you if you do not love tenderly the King of the Bulgarians."

"Not a bit," said he, "for I have never seen him."

"What! He is the most charming of kings, and you must drink his health."

"Oh, gladly, gentlemen," and he drank.

"That is sufficient," he was told. "You are now the support, the aid, the defender, the hero of the Bulgarians; your fortune is made and your glory assured."

They immediately put irons on his legs and took him to a regiment. He was made to turn to the right and left, to raise the ramrod and return the ramrod, to take aim, to fire, and to double up; and he was given thirty strokes with a stick; the next day he drilled not quite so badly, and received only twenty strokes; the day after, he had only ten, and was looked on as a prodigy by his comrades.

Candide was completely mystified and could not make out how he was a hero. One fine spring day he thought he would take a walk, going straight ahead, in the belief that to use his legs as he pleased was a privilege of the human species as well as of animals. He had not gone two leagues when four other heroes, each six feet tall, fell upon him, bound him and dragged him back to a cell. He was asked whether he would rather be thrashed thirty-six times by the whole regiment or receive a dozen lead bullets at once in his brain. Although he protested that men's wills are free and that he wanted neither the one nor the other, he had to make a choice; by virtue of that gift of God which is called *liberty*, he determined to run the gauntlet thirty-six times, and actually did so twice. There were two thousand men in the regiment. That made four thousand strokes, which laid bare the muscles and nerves from his neck to his backside. As they were about to proceed to a third turn, Candide, utterly exhausted, begged as a favor that they would be so kind as to smash his head; he obtained this favor; they bound his eyes and he was made to kneel down. At this moment the King of the Bulgarians came by and inquired the victim's crime; and as this king was possessed of a vast genius, he perceived from what he had learned about Candide that he was a young metaphysician very ignorant in worldly matters, and therefore pardoned him with a clemency which will be praised in all newspapers in all ages. An honest surgeon healed Candide in three weeks with the ointments recommended by Dioscorides. He had already regained a little skin and could walk when the King of the Bulgarians went to war with the Abares. (The French-Austrian coalition which fought against Frederick in the Seven Years' War.)

The eighteenth century abounds in stories of the kidnaping of young men for service as soldiers. The following, related by Carlyle in his biography of Frederick the Great, can perhaps be the tale to end all kidnaping tales.[10]

In the town of Jülich there lived and worked a tall young carpenter. One day a well-dressed, positive looking gentleman (Baron von Hompesch, the records name him) enters the shop; wants "a stout chest, with lock on it, for household purposes;" must be of such and such dimensions, six feet six in length especially, and that is an indispensable point... in fact, it will be longer than yourself, I think, Herr Zimmermann; what is the cost? when can it be ready?" Cost, time and the rest are settled. "A right stout chest then; and see you don't forget the size; if too short, it will be of no use to me, mind!" "Jawohl, gewiss." And the positive looking gentleman goes his ways. At the appointed time he reappears;

the chest is ready, we hope; an unexceptionable article? "Too short, as I dreaded," says the positive gentleman. "Nay, your Honor," says the carpenter, "I am certain it is six feet six," and takes out his foot-rule. "Pshaw, it was to be longer than yourself." "Well, it is." "No, it isn't." The carpenter, to end the matter, gets into the chest, and will convince any and all mortals. No sooner is he in, rightly flat, than the positive gentleman, a Prussian recruiting officer in disguise, slams down the lid upon him, locks it, whistles to three stout fellows, who pick up the chest, gravely walk through the streets with it, open it in a safe place and find – horrible to relate – the poor carpenter dead, choked for want of air in this frightful middle passage of his. Name of the town is given, Jülich, as above, date not. And if the thing had been only a popular myth, is it not a significant one? But it is too true; the tall carpenter lay dead, and Hompesch got "imprisonment for life," by the business.

In the generation following that of the Duke of Marlborough and Prince Eugene of Savoy, there were three great generals who fought the battles of France, in what Saint Simon[11] called "the Golden Age of Bastards and Sons of Bastards." Each of the three came from a different country, all were Protestants but overcame this handicap, all illegitimate, all after great victories becoming naturalized French citizens, and all of royal blood.[12] Their dashing careers and consequent fame and wealth may well have served to inspire vigorous young men likewise to "seek the bubble reputation even in the cannon's mouth."

There was the Duke of Berwick (1670-1734). He was the natural son of the Duke of York, afterward King James II, and Arabella Churchill, sister of the Duke of Marlborough. He was born in England, educated in France, fought in Hungary against the Turks, and came to England at the age of seventeen where his father gave him the title of duke. He served in British, Dutch, and French armies, twenty-nine campaigns in all. In 1706 he was created Marshal of France. He showed his chivalric sense of honor when, in 1718, he was forced to fight against Spain, whose King, Philip V, had taken Berwick's son into his service. On his entrance into Spanish dominions, the Marshal wrote his son, the Duke of Liria, admonishing him to do his duty to his sovereign – even though it meant son against father.

Maurice de Saxe, (1696-1750), was the illegitimate son of Augustus II, King of Saxony and Poland, and the Countess Aurora of Königsmarck. His father recognized him fully and accorded him the rank of count. At the age of twelve he served in Polish forces engaged in the siege of Lille, and two years later fought under Czar Peter the Great against Charles XII, King of Sweden. Next he served in his father's army and in 1720 went to France, where he was made brigadier general. Throughout his life he was notorious for his love affairs. He was elected Duke of Courland, but was driven out by the opposition of the Duchess, Anna Ivanovna, whom he had refused to marry. On his return to Paris he had an affair with the famous actress Adrienne Lecouvreur, who sold her jewels and lent him 30,000 pounds in order to permit him to regain his throne in Courland. He failed, and on his return to Paris abandoned Mlle. Lecouvreur for another mistress. In the course of the war of the Austrian Succession, he distinguished himself by his brilliant capture of Prague, for which victory he was named Marshal of France. Perhaps his most famous victory was that at Fontenoy in 1745, conducted in truly chivalrous fashion. The French and British officers met on the day before the battle for friendly fraternizing; the British asked the French to shoot first, to which the French replied, "We never shoot first!" Though on the next day the British did shoot first, the French won the day, through the genius of Maréchal de Saxe, but also in no small part through the courageous action of Général de Lowendal.

This professional soldier was born in Hamburg in 1700, and was, through his illegitimate grandfather, a descendant of the Danish King Frederic III – thus only a grandson of a bastard. At the age of thirteen he served in the Austrian army as a private, and then in rapid succession fought in the Danish, Saxon and Austrian forces. He fought against the Turks at Belgrade, against the Spaniards in Sicily, then in the wars of Augustus II, King of Saxony and Poland, who appointed him General. He was noted for his effective siege warfare, and was for that reason called to Russia by the Czarina Anna, to take part in the siege of Ochakov on the Black Sea. He later played a brilliant role in the war of the Finns against Sweden. Urged by de Saxe to come to France, he agreed to serve under the then most famous European general. His action proved decisive at the Battle of Fontenoy. Later he besieged and took the so-called "invincible" fortress of Bergen-op-Zoom. The looting and brutalities committed against the townspeople by French soldiers, from the General on down, were so scandalous that they shocked even the French king. Louis XV asked Marshal de Saxe what he should do with Lowendal, to which the reply was: "There are only two courses open; either you must hang him or make him Marshal of France." The latter course was followed. Lowendal's biographer Sinety states that this story is apocryphal, even though it is related in the Biographie Universelle and often quoted. It seems however, quite characteristic.[13]

Berwick, the first of this trio, dates considerably earlier, although de Saxe was a lieutenant under him; but the latter two, Saxe and Lowendal, show a remarkable conformity in their lives and careers. Both entered military service at an almost unbelievably early age, twelve and thirteen respectively; they were boyhood companions and lifelong brothers in arms. Saxe was born four years before his friend, and died five years earlier, in 1750. Both served Austria and fought against Sweden and against France before devoting their valor and their science to the glory of France.[14]

There were soldiers of fortune also in England. Illustrative of the attitude toward such a career is a passage in *The Virginians* by Thackeray, who certainly knew eighteenth century *mores*. In chapter 41 there is a letter, dated October 22, 1756, from Harry to his mother. The American hero, visiting England, was introduced to His Royal Highness, the Captain General (later King George III) "who was most gracious; a fat jolly prince, if I may speak so without disrespect, reminding me in his manner of the unhappy General Braddock whom we knew to our sorrow last year. When he had heard my name and how dearest George had served and fallen in Braddock's unfortunate campaign, he talked a great deal with me – asked why a young fellow like me didn't serve too. Why I did not go to the King of Prussia, who was a great general, and see a campaign or two."

CHAPTER I

THE GERMAN PEASANT BOY EMERGES FROM
OBSCURITY AS A FRENCH OFFICER

In the records of the Evangelical Lutheran pastorate in Kirchenaurach near Erlangen in Bavaria there is, in the third volume of baptismal records for 1721, an entry establishing the facts concerning the ancestry, birth and baptism of Johannes Kalb, who came to be known in history as the Baron Jean de Kalb. The photostat of the church record is accompanied by an official explanation of the Latin terms and abbreviations customary in the eighteenth century. The place of de Kalb's birth was Huettendorf, a village belonging at that time to the Margraviate of Bayreuth, later Prussian, now Bavarian, which formed part of the above mentioned Parish; the date, June 29, 1721.
A translation of the entry reads:

> Sunday, the third after Trinity, festival of Saints Peter and Paul, the 29th of June, at nine o'clock in the forenoon was born Johannes, legitimate son of Johann Leonard Kalb, peasant and resident there, and his wife Margaretha, née Seiz. He was baptized on the following Monday, the 30th. His godfather was Johann Meyer, the legitimate unmarried son of Georg Meyer, peasant and resident of Huettendorf. This was the first child to whom he stood sponsor.

There is a notation in the left margin:

> The wife of Johann Leonard Kalb was the widow of the late Mr. Puz in Huettendorf. Her maiden name was Seiz and she came from Eschenbach.

On the left margin and below the text is a note in handwriting different from the earlier entries:

> † (meaning he died) as Baron de Kalb, knight of the Royal French military order of merit, brigadier of the French Army and major general in the service of the United States of North America on August 19, 1780, at Camden, South

Carolina, in America, of wounds sustained in the battle of Camden.

This original church record is the only positive information regarding de Kalb until, twenty-two years later, he is listed in the records of the Archives of the Ministry of War as an officer in the Lowendal Regiment organized in September, 1743. There is considerable evidence to corroborate this; for example, on August 31, 1779, de Kalb states in a letter to the Minister of War, Prince de Montbarey, that he had had the honor of serving His Majesty as an officer since 1743 when the Lowendal Regiment was created. From this date his record is well documented.[15]

Unsupported by any source is the statement of de Kalb's biographer Kapp that when sixteen years of age de Kalb became a waiter and as such left home.[16] It seems much more likely, in view of his later success, that the young peasant left home to enter upon military service. But where he received the training that qualified him as an officer, where he learned the French and English languages, where he acquired the social training that enabled him to move in officers' circles – these matters present unsolved mysteries.

There is a hint about his activities before 1743 in a notation on his service record to the effect that he had served with the Fischer Corps of Partisans which did considerable fighting in Bavaria during the War of the Austrian Succession.[17] Since de Kalb, like Fischer, rose from humble circumstances to general, a sketch of Fischer's career is pertinent.

Johann Christian Fischer was born January 17, 1713, the son of a bookkeeper in a Stuttgart tobacco factory, or according to other records, a simple servant. He attended the University of Giessen, but to judge from his later career, with very little enthusiasm. Immediately after his father's death, he entered the French military service and took part in the campaigns of the Comte de Broglie in 1741 in Bavaria and Bohemia. While serving under the Comte de Saxe as ordnance officer, he was encouraged to organize a free corps of *Chasseurs*. With these, at the battle of Kempen, June 23, 1758, he saved the French Army, which Prince Charles of Brunswick was about to surprise and encircle. For this alert action, in which he received two wounds, he was made lieutenant general. In 1759 he contributed largely to the French victory at Bergen over the Austrians. In the fall of the same year he was required, on command of his superior, and quite against his will, to levy on the citizens of Northeim a contribution of 6,000 thalers. He tried to alleviate the desperate situation of the burghers, just as he always insisted on rigid discipline among his own troops, by sternly forbidding plundering.[18]

As part of the reward for leaving the Russian and joining the French service in the fall of 1743, Marshal Lowendal was given funds to raise a German regiment. Perhaps here is the answer to the question various writers have found baffling: where did the peasant son of Johann Leonard Kalb learn French and English? Ambitious as he was, he could have picked up languages readily in this wonderfully cosmopolitan environment; even though there were no Englishmen in the group, there were more than a dozen English-speaking Irishmen. What an inspiration Lowendal must have been! In inspecting his troops, he was able to employ the English, German, Swedish, Polish, Danish and French languages. The regiment was organized in Flanders where France was about to strike against Austria.

Officers of the Lowendal Regiment

MM. Le Comte de Lowendal, colonel propriétaire
M. de Bulow, lieutenant colonel, né en Hanover
le Baron d'Elorme, major (Saxon)

Capitaines en pied
(Officers in charge)

MM. de Beauchamp, commandant le 1er bataillon (Français)
de Watteville, commandant le 2e bataillon (Suisse)
de Goze (Flamand)
Lecocq de la Fontaine (d,Ath) (a town in Belgium)
de Müller (Saxon)
de Leonardy (de Phalsbourg)
de Stack (Irlandais)
le comte de Lowendal (fils du colonel)
de Stiebritz (Saxon)
le comte de Linanges (né à Westerbourg)
le comte de Schmettau (né en Bavière)
de Walthausen (du pays de Trèves)

Capitaines réformes
(promoted officers)
MM. du Cherroy (né dans le pays de Luxembourg)
de Weissenbach (Saxon)
d'Illens (né à Lauzanne)
de Slisenski (Polonais)
de Bizot (Suédois)
de Kennedy (Irlandais)
Birckel (Alsacien)

O'Brien (Irlandais)
de Lohenskiold (du Schleswig-Holstein)
de Kalb (aide-major) (né à Nuremberg)
de Haccourt (nè dans le comté de Namur)
de Chabert (né dans l'Amérique anglaise)
de Grüner (Suisse)
Kidlinsky (Polonais)
Keltschevsky (id.)
de Bulow (Frédéric) (Hanovrien)

Lieutenants en premier

MM. Herrmann (Hambourgeois)
Driller (Alsacien)
Laine (du pays de Trèves)
Gomolinski (Polonais)
Biodos de Casteja (de Namur)
de Mahy (id.)
de Straes (Polonais)
de Harte (Irlandais)[19]

Of special interest to us is the mention of "de Kalb, aide major (né à Nuremberg)." Nuremberg is just a few miles distant from the village where he was born. Among the *"capitaines réformés"* he is the only one whose rank is listed *"aide major."* This title (discarded at the time of the French Revolution) corresponds, according to Larousse, to *officier de détail*, selected from among the lieutenants with the commission of captain, under the direct command of the major. In present terminology it approximates *adjutant major*. It is difficult to say exactly what the fluctuating nomenclature signifies. But it definitely appears that de Kalb at the age of twenty-two was entrusted with a post carrying great responsibility. More about the *officier de détail* will be said in the next chapter.

Up to the time of Kapp's biography of General de Kalb, it was the common belief that de Kalb was a member of a noble family. In fact, in a German work published in 1857 on the heroes of the American Revolution, Kapp in an essay on de Kalb writes that he was descended from a noble family settled for centuries in Franconia where it owned estates in the vicinity of Erlangen.[20]

In this same essay Kapp states that de Kalb's younger brother served in the French Regiment Deux Ponts. Kapp's later researches established the fact that this Henry de Kalb was not even related distantly to Jean de Kalb, but was descended from the ancient noble family, Kalb von Kalbsrieth. He fought in the Revolutionary War, distinguishing himself at the Siege of Yorktown. He was the first to enter the fortress, but in scaling the rampart he lost a shoe. Despite this handicap, he forced a British officer to surrender his sword. After the battle the hero was presented to Washington, who asked him whether he was related to the General de Kalb who had fought so valiantly at the Battle of Camden; Major de Kalb replied that he neither knew him nor had he ever heard of him. In 1783 he returned to Germany and married a Fräulein von Ostheimb who has a slight niche in German literature as Charlotte von Kalb, poetess and friend of Schiller.[21]

In a very interesting preface to his *Life of John Kalb*, Kapp relates that he became fascinated with de Kalb's story because of the mystery in which it was shrouded. Even the spelling of his name was uncertain: "Kalbe," "Colbe," but most commonly "Kalb." The date of his birth varied from 1717 to 1732. His native land was given as Alsace or Switzerland. One authority stated that he had served in the Prussian, another in the Austrian, a third in the French army. Some historians of the Revolutionary War gave only fragmentary and sometimes incorrect accounts of his life. It was through Kapp's thorough-going researches that a well-rounded biography of the General was finally presented, to some extent "piercing the mystery."

After Kapp had published his biography of the Baron von Steuben and was planning to write on de Kalb, a fortunate accident led him to the discovery of hitherto unknown source material. While on business in Washington in 1856, he happened to meet a lawyer, John Carroll Brent, who was representing the interests of the de Kalb family before Congress. From him Kapp learned the address of the Vicomtesse d'Abzac, of Milon la Chapelle, Department of Seine-et-Oise, the granddaughter of de Kalb, who was in possession of his papers. When Kapp wrote to the lady for permission to examine and possibly copy the material, he received a reply from a M. Nachtmann, the tutor of the d'Abzac children. The outcome of an extended correspondence was that Kapp purchased copies of the papers and also M. Nachtmann's projected book on de Kalb, which had advanced to 1775. Kapp states that without these papers he could not have prepared a coherent life of de Kalb.

De Kalb's marriage certificate of April 10, 1764, states that *Jean de Kalb, chevalier, fils du feu Jean Leonard de Kalb, seigneur de Hüttendorf, et dame Marguérite Seitz, né à Hüttendorf dans le margraviat de Bayreuth*, is married to Anne Elisabeth Emilie van Robais in Paris.[22]

The peasant's son had acquired the title "chevalier" and the right to the use of the "de" when in 1763 the King bestowed on him the Order of Military Merit which carried with it these honors. The award came in recognition of his outstanding bravery in the battle of Wilhelmsthal in the course of the Seven Years' War. Thus, more than a decade before his arrival in America, de Kalb had become an honored member of the French nobility. Had he been given to witticisms – which he was not – he might have said with Napoleon's general Andoche Junot, when he was made Duc d'Abrantes: "I am my own ancestor!"

Only one other officer in the American armed forces during the Revolutionary War won the Mérite Militaire – John Paul Jones. When in 1781 he returned to a triumphal homecoming, the French minister plenipotentiary, the Marquis de la Luzerne, had ready the Ordre du Mérite Militaire, which the French king wished to award to the heroic captain of the "Bonhomme Richard." But the Articles of Confederation, which Maryland was at long last about to ratify, and thus make them the law of the land, prohibited the acceptance of any order from a foreign state. But in enthusiasm over the valiant sailor, Congress simply postponed ratification for a few days to permit de la Luzerne to create the admiral "Chevalier Paul Jones."[23]

In the list of officers of the Lowendal Regiment, the General's name appears as "de Kalb," and in his correspondence he signs "Baron de Kalb." Where or how de Kalb acquired these titles of nobility is unknown. Kapp states without documentation that de Kalb had assumed a title not legally belonging to him to facilitate his advancement in the army. While this may have been the case, since there are many such instances to be found in the eighteenth century, there are likewise many instances of ennoblement as an award for acts of gallantry in the face of the enemy. A few case histories may serve to exemplify self-awarded and legitimate titles of nobility.

The Baron von Steuben is sometimes spoken of as "Baron" with quotation marks, as is also frequently the case in reference to de Kalb. According to his biographers, von Steuben's grandfather, Augustin Steube, a minister in the German reformed church and a self-made man, in 1708 inserted the "von" in front of his name. His son, Wilhelm Augustin von Steube, was an officer in the Prussian army, and his grandson changed the name to Baron von Steuben, adding also the given name Frederick, which he had not received at baptism, but which had a good sound in the realm of Frederick the Great.[24]

The eighteenth century is full of self-styled noblemen and adventurous types. Heading the list no doubt is Giovanni Giacomo Casanova, who visited all the capitals of Europe, appearing as journalist, preacher, abbé, diplomat, alchemist, businessman, gambler, and of course, author of his spicy memoirs. He added "de Seingalt" to his name for reasons of prestige.

A certain Giuseppe Balsamo vanished from his native Sicily to escape arrest for a series of crimes. He visited, among other countries, Egypt, Greece, Arabia, Persia and Rhodes. At Malta, where the Grand Master was very much interested in alchemy, he introduced himself as Count Alessandro Cagliostro, an adept in the occult art. He traveled widely, selling love philters and elixirs of youth, gaining considerable money from members of fashionable society, particularly the ladies. In Paris he was implicated in the Affair of the Queen's Diamond Necklace.

Teodor von Neuhof, son of a Westphalian baron, came rightfully by the "von" but adopted the title "king." He served in the French, Swedish and Spanish armies. Later, in Florence, he made the acquaintance of Corsican revolutionaries and became interested in their struggle to free their island from Genoese domination. As leader of the movement he went to Constantinople where he prevailed upon the government to equip him with a ship, ammunition and other supplies. He landed on Corsica on April 14, 1736, and had himself proclaimed King Theodore I, but his glory lasted only briefly.

Pierre Augustin Caron (1732-1799) was born the son of a watchmaker, and distinguished himself in his father's craft. His title "de Beaumarchais," he "took over from one of his wives," as his enemies put it. He became a writer of comedies, among them *Le Mariage de Figaro*, as well as a speculator with great ups and downs of fortune, including some terms in prison. He persuaded the French government to send military supplies to the American rebels, organizing for this purpose a fictitious firm, Rodrigue Hortales and Company, which controlled a fleet of forty vessels. He had many dealings with the American representative in Paris, Silas Deane, and is remembered, among other things, as a benefactor of the Thirteen Colonies.

Mention should also be made of the author of *Robinson Crusoe*, who was born plain Daniel Foe, but for reasons of prestige at the court called himself Defoe.

Fairly close to de Kalb's career in time and place, but very different from the adventurers described above, is that of the famous Prussian General Graf Neidhart von Gneisenau, son of an artillery officer, Neidhart, serving in the Austrian army. In 1777 Gneisenau matriculated at the University of Erfurt as Antonius Neidhart. He evidently did not enjoy his studies, for he entered the Austrian army as a private in 1778. About a year later he had to flee to avoid punishment for being absent without leave. In 1781 he was admitted to an Ansbach-Bayreuth regiment as a cadet. He soon became a non-commissioned officer, and in 1782 was promoted to a lieutenancy. Now he assumed the name Neidhart von Gneisenau, and his prince, Karl Alexander, confirmed his right to nobility.[25]

Gneisenau, who later became one of the most distinguished generals in the war against Napoleon, came to the United States in 1782 with the last transport of Ansbach-Bayreuth troops. He arrived too late to take part in any battle, but he gained a great deal of useful experience from the American manner of fighting "in Indian style": troops did not storm the enemy line in a solid body, but scattered to permit gaining protection from trees or mounds of earth, nor did they shoot simultaneously, but individually with definite aim. On his return to Ansbach, he submitted to his prince a memorandum on new tactics. Karl Alexander scorned such innovations and declined Gneisenau's services, but Frederick the Great eagerly accepted the keen young soldier's application for a post in the Prussian army.

Gneisenau's experience shows that it was indeed possible to rise from a humble origin to a high post in the army, and to be rewarded by promotion to a patent of nobility. Other commoners who rose to high posts and nobility in German armies are, for example, Gerhard David von Scharnhorst, Karl Friedrich von Steinmetz, Yorck von Wartenburg and Karl von Clausewitz. In fact, no contemporary ever seems to have challenged de Kalb's right to the "de," even though he served in a German regiment where he was in daily contact with German officers who knew the various branches of nobility. This suggests his valid right to the title.

Works on the French army give hundreds of examples of bourgeois lads who enlist at a very early age and rise to high rank. The following is picked at random;[26] it could with slight modification have been the career of de Kalb, whose highest rank in the French army was that of lieutenant colonel. "François de Chevert, born in Verdun of poor parents, an orphan in childhood, enlisted at eleven years of age. He was made second lieutenant in 1710 (age 15!) in the regiment of Béauce. Thanks to his exploits he enjoyed the finest career that an officer of his class could expect, since after thirty-five years of age he became lieutenant colonel."

During the eighteenth century there was a shift in regard to the subject of nobility among army officers. Count Argenson,[27] Minister of War in France in 1750, issued an edict approved by Louis XV, creating a "noblesse militaire." Argenson himself was a "noble de race" but he regarded it as impractical that officers in the same regiment should be separated by their origin. He gave it as his opinion that certain categories should receive titles of nobility independent of the favor of their sovereign. Voltaire, in his essay *Sur les Moeurs*, praised Argenson for doing away with "dishonorable conditions." However, in 1781 a decision of the Council of War that every officer must have four degrees of *noblesse paternelle* came as a blow to the *noblesse militaire*.[28]

In his memoirs Argenson mentions[29] that Fischer rose from simple servant to chief of a company of *chasseurs* and to the rank of brigadier general. Hoyer[30] states that soldiers who distinguished themselves in combat were rewarded by promotion or presents, or both. General Tercier[31] tells in his autobiography that his father was a Swiss who entered the French army as a volunteer at the age of eighteen, rising to the rank of captain attached to the staff of Marshal Lowendal where he was created "chevalier." De Courcelles[32] in his dictionary of French generals lists numerous high officers who rose from humble beginnings. Preser,[33] writing on the sale of Hessians to England, cites a long list of officers of bourgeois descent. He shows that there were more commoners than nobles. Leonard[34] relates that the Piémont regiment contained many rich sons of *noblesse douteuse* who made the genuine members of nobility uncomfortable because the latter had but small resources. "Wharton[35] thinks the French accorded de Kalb some sort of title."

If historians speak of de Kalb as the "so-called Baron" or the "self-styled Baron," making his title a reproach of dishonesty, it seems to me that the burden of proof rests with them. Also, for the sake of consistency, such writers should speak of M. Caron, self-styled de Beaumarchais, or "de" Foe, author of *Robinson Crusoe*, son of Mr. Foe. If de Kalb's title of "baron" was spurious, his whole career shows that he acted in every way in the spirit of "noblesse oblige."

To judge from his later career, de Kalb had from early years onward an intense interest in a military career, possibly inspired by the great deeds and glory of Prince Eugene, of whom he must have heard in his formative years, through the tales of his exploits and the extremely popular ballad composed in 1717, *Prinz Eugen der edle Ritter*. As a matter of fact, the military calling was probably the only one in which a Protestant could advance to distinction, honor and wealth.

For a boy with an adventurous mind, there were many reasons for quitting the parental farm. He escaped the dull drudgery of tilling the soil, milking the cows, hauling manure, and the entire round of daily chores that must have been irksome to a young man with ambition. Even though serfdom did not prevail in Brandenburg-Bayreuth as it did in Prussia, yet the peasant was subject to the exploitation and whim of the ruler, the margrave, who exercised the power of life and death over his subjects. In a state a little larger than Rhode Island, there were about a hundred thousand inhabitants.

A flagrant example of the utter contempt in which the common people were then held is an act by the Margrave Karl Friedrich Wilhelm, known to be a keen marksman.[36] One day his mistress observed a chimney sweep on top of a roof, and asked her lover whether he could shoot the man so as to make him topple down head first. The Margrave, with wanton brutality, shot him down, and later on when the distraught widow appealed to his charity, indemnified her with a gift of two thalers.

Karl Friedrich Wilhelm at the age of seventeen became the ruler of Ansbach-Bayreuth in 1729 and died in 1757: thus it was in his era that de Kalb left his home. Karl is known in history chiefly as the husband of Frederick the Great's sister, whom he neglected utterly in favor of various mistresses. As to his brother-in-law, the Margrave first promised Frederick to preserve neutrality in the Seven Years' War, and then sided with Austria. Naturally his subjects suffered from this duplicity when the Prussian army ravaged Ansbach-Bayreuth while their ruler fled the country.

The Margrave was always eager to execute justice.[37] On one occasion when a soldier had stolen an insignificant item from a shopkeeper, he ordered the man to be hanged immediately in front of the store. His wrath turned especially against poachers and deserters from the army, but even higher officials were not immune from his tyranny. When his son, aged fifteen, returned ill from an educational tour of Italy, Karl sent the tutor to the workhouse. One of his court favorites, a certain Schaunfels, the son of an innkeeper, who had been raised to nobility by the Margrave, refused when ordered to marry one of his ruler's mistresses, whereupon Schaunfels fell into disgrace and just managed to escape with his life from Karl's wrath.

Another figure at the court who enjoyed the Margrave's favor was a Jew named Ischerle, dealing in jewels among other business ventures. In 1739 he was commissioned by the Margrave to set with the appropriate jewels the Order of the Red Eagle, intended as a present for the King of England. It was the regular practice for princes to let the recipient of an order supply the jewels, but this gift was to be an exception. Ischerle received 20,000 florins for carrying out the commission. The order was sent to England, but not one word of thanks reached Bayreuth. The Margrave was deeply hurt by this seeming British ingratitude for such a precious gift; he had his representative in London make discreet inquiries, and learned that the jewels were not genuine but only Bohemian glass! Hence the king did not feel bound to send his thanks nor did he care to complain about such a shabby gift. The Margrave naturally was beside himself with wrath, particularly when it became known that Ischerle shared with his ruler the favors of one of the court ladies. The poor devil was dragged out of his hiding place, brought into a large hall and given a brief trial, after which he was condemned to be beheaded. The executioner tied him in a chair and was about to proceed with his work, but the victim, hopping about the room, began to plead for mercy, saying he could explain everything. At that moment the executioner, reaching across the table, beheaded the screaming wretch.

The Margrave was succeeded by his son Karl Alexander, notorious for his sale, in 1777, of two regiments of infantry and a battalion of *chasseurs* to England for service against the American colonies - 1644 men for $1,527,000.[38] When the war ended in 1783, scarcely a third of these men returned. It is reported that when the troops mutinied against going, the Margrave himself fired on them.

Of course, in imitation of Versailles, Karl Alexander had various mistresses at his court, among them a highly cultured Englishwoman, the daughter of the Earl of Berkeley and wife of Lord Craven. She was the mother of six children, but had left her husband and was traveling widely in Europe and the Near East. In 1784 she settled down in Ansbach, where she soon gained the ruler's favor, usurping the place of his previous mistress, Mlle. Clairon, a French actress who had held the post for seventeen years. Six years later she managed an unheard-of achievement; she induced the Margrave to cede his realm to Prussia for an annuity of 300,000 florins and to leave with her for England where, after Lord Craven's death, Karl Alexander, somewhat like Edward VIII in 1935,[39] married the "woman he loved" after renouncing his throne. Horace Walpole wrote to a correspondent, "Lady Craven received the news of her Lord's death on a Friday, went into weeds on Saturday, and into white satin and many diamonds on Sunday." When Lady Craven learned that the English were shocked that she had married so soon after her husband's death, her reply was: "I should have done it six hours after, had I known it at the time."

Lady Craven was known as a person of great beauty, charm and culture. She wrote plays in English and French, as well as musical compositions. Under her portrait by Romney, Horace Walpole wrote the following verse:

> Full many an artist has on canvas fixed
> All charms that Nature's pencil ever mixed,
> The witching of her eyes, the grace that tips
> The unexpressionable douceur of her lips:
> Romney alone in this fair image caught
> Each charm's expression, and each feature's thought,
> And shows how in this sweet assembly sit
> Taste, spirit, softness, sentiment and wit.

Rule by mistresses was notoriously common at the courts of the eighteenth century rulers, and the expensive tastes of these courtesans induced more than one ruler of a small German state to gain money by selling his subjects to serve as cannon fodder in a war across the sea. The dramatist Schiller in his social play *Intrigue and Love*, Act II, Scene 2, courageously attacks these brutal abuses. The ruler's mistress, like Lady Craven in real life, is an Englishwoman of nobility, called by Schiller Lady Milford. In the scene in question, an old servant delivers to her a gift from the prince, a chest containing some priceless jewels. She exclaims that these gems must have cost an enormous amount. The servant replies that they did not cost the prince a penny; he had sold seven thousand subjects to England for service in the colonies, two of the servant's own sons among them. The lady says she hopes none were sent against their will. With a bitter laugh the servant replies: "O God no – all of them volunteers. To be sure, several loud-mouthed lads stepped out of the ranks to ask the colonel at what price the prince was selling a yoke of human beings, whereupon the benevolent father of our country ordered all the regiments to assemble on the parade ground, where he had these *Maulaffen* shot down by a firing squad. We heard the crack of the guns, saw brains sprayed on the pavement, and heard the entire army shout "Hurrah! To America!"

Lady Milford is shocked that she has heard nothing of all this.

"Yes, my lady, why did you have to go hunting at the very time the troops were to depart? Too bad you missed the splendid scene when the drums announced the time for departure; weeping orphans followed a living father; a mother, quite beside herself, tried to spear her suckling infant on a bayonet, and bride and groom were torn asunder by sabre blows, while we old graybeards stood in despair..."

Schiller's scene is by no means an exaggeration of events brought about by the conscienceless brutality of the princes of petty German states of his day. De Kalb's native state was particularly active in hiring out troops to Austria or other nations engaged in wars, and had he not left home, he might very well been among those sold, as Frederick the Great expressed it, "like cattle."

When in 1777 Colonel Carl von Donop, commander of a corps of Hessian troops, met his death in an attack on the Americans in Redbank, de Kalb reported in a letter to his friend the Comte de Broglie: "Colonel Donop has died, deeply mourned by his soldiers. His last words were that he died a sacrifice to the cupidity of his sovereign."[40]

CHAPTER II

APPRENTICESHIP UNDER MARSHALS SAXE AND
LOWENDAL

The young peasant who had chosen a military career as his profession served his apprenticeship under the very best generals of the middle half of the eighteenth century. It was most fortunate for Jean de Kalb that from 1743 to 1748 he could witness and take part in the numerous sieges which General Lowendal conducted with amazing skill and monotonous success. Even more instructive was the opportunity he had of observing Marshal de Saxe, the greatest general of France before Napoleon, especially at Fontenoy, the most famous battle of the eighteenth century.

When de Kalb entered the services of France as lieutenant in the German regiment organized by General Comte de Lowendal, the War of the Austrian Succession had advanced to the point where France entered the conflict definitely and vigorously. Flanders was a Habsburg possession at the time, and offered a convenient spot for the French to strike their arch-enemy Austria while at the same time driving the British out of the Netherlands. This was accomplished by a series of splendid victories; most glorified by poets in barrack-room legends is the Battle of Fontenoy, fought in Flanders on May 11, 1745.

This battle was chiefly a contest between the French army under Marshal de Saxe and a British army commanded by the Duke of Cumberland. Characteristically, the French force also had some German and Irish regiments, while the allies of the British were Dutch, Austrians and Hanoverians. Saxe, who had excellent military intelligence that kept him well informed as to every move of the British, assumed a strong defensive position on rising ground, with his right resting on the River Scheldt and his left on a wooded region. Before this line he erected a series of redoubts intended to place advancing British formations under crossfire; this precaution disgusted the regular French officers who patriotically believed that their infantry could always hold the line, even in the face of persistent attacks.

The battle began at daybreak, and the redoubts proved very effective against allied attacks. About noon Cumberland decided on a desperate measure. He formed his infantry into a tight oblong, about 500 by 600 yards in size, numbering approximately 14,000 men. This compact mass of red-coated soldiers advanced up the slope in the style of the day, with colors flying and drums beating, in stately parade step, on the command of the Duke of Cumberland, who placed himself at the head of the front line. From the redoubts the fire was now in full enfilade. When the British arrived at about thirty paces from the French line, there was a pause. Lord Charles Hay stepped to the front of his battalion and made a sweeping salute with his plumed hat. Then he took out a pocket flask and mockingly drank to the health of the French, shouting: "We are the English Guards and we hope you will stand till we come up to you and not swim the Scheldt as you did the Main at Dettingen." Then, turning to his men, he called for three cheers, which were given with enthusiasm. The French, surprised by this unexpected chivalry, responded with a rather feeble cheer. Then they fired a volley which proved not very effective, while the British gunfire at such close range proved to be so deadly that the French infantry broke and fled in confusion.

Voltaire's version of this famous episode has perpetuated a legend: The English officers saluted the French by doffing their hats. The Comtes de Chavannes and d'Auteroches, then the Duc de Biron, who had come forward as well as all the officers of the French, returned the greeting. Lord Charles Hay, Captain of the English Guards, shouted, "Gentlemen of the French Guards, fire!" The Comte d'Auteroches, then Lieutenant of Grenadiers, called back, "Gentleman, we never fire first – fire yourselves." This version is fictitious, according to modern historians.[41]

Such amenities were not so feckless or eccentric as they may seem, for one of the objects sought in warfare of the day was to induce the enemy to fire first. Since the range of the muskets was rather short, the first volley would be relatively harmless. The foe could then only reload while awaiting a return volley at even closer range, perhaps followed by a bayonet attack. "Don't fire till you see the whites of their eyes." It is instructive to test this famous rule, Walter Mills proposes, by walking down a populous city street and noting the distance at which one can distinguish the whites of the eyes of the approaching throng. The results, he adds, will be an impressive demonstration of the ranges at which eighteenth century battles had to be fought.

The Marshal de Saxe was terribly afflicted by dropsy at this time, which rendered him unable to ride his horse; he had himself conveyed about the battlefield in a kind of wicker bed-chair drawn by four horses, while he would bite on a bullet to make himself forget his thirst, which the doctors had forbidden him to quench. At the moment of greatest danger, as the dense column of the British advanced slowly and steadily despite French cannon fire, he had himself lifted onto his horse and rode up and down the line of battle, grouping all his reserves at one point for a smashing flank attack that shook the British column, forcing it to retreat. General Lowendal was in command of the infantry, whose action proved decisive. Likewise distinguished for notable bravery were the Irish regiments fighting on the French side – exiles from their home country because of their religion.

Credit for the victory goes to Maurice de Saxe.[42] His choice of the battlefield showed consummate strategy, and he extracted every advantage from his favorable position. The construction and use made of the redoubts was a break with traditional methods. The stoicism with which he disregarded his pain, and the calmness with which he gave his orders were phenomenal. Since St. Louis, about the middle of the thirteenth century, no French king had won a decisive victory over the English. The glory of this defeat over the British induced the young Pretender to the English throne, Bonny Prince Charlie, to make a landing on Scottish soil in the very same year, with, however, disastrous results for the Stuart cause.

Voltaire had met the sick Marshal just a few days before his departure for the front, when Saxe's death was daily expected, and asked the General what he could do in so miserable a plight. Saxe's reply was: "It is not a question of living, but of leaving," – that is, one more task to be accomplished! Voltaire wrote a lengthy poem in Homeric verse glorifying the deed, an invocation to the Muses, with allusions to Scipio, Hannibal and other heroes, not omitting some flattering lines to Louis XV. This epic, called *Fontenoy*, was published six days after the battle, and within a few days 21,000 copies were bought by the enthusiastic French.

Saxe, rude, coarse and illiterate as he was, wrote a book in 1732,[43] with the striking title, *Mes Reveries*, in which he set down his strategic principles:

"I am not in favor of pitched battles, especially not at the beginning of a campaign, and I am convinced that a really skilful general might wage war all his life without being compelled to give battle. Does this mean a return to a defensive and 'waiting' strategy? By no means! It is necessary to engage in frequent combats and, so to speak, 'soften up' (fondre), the enemy; after that, then can be undertaken the great battle that will crush him. The work of the piques before the descabello of the matador."

Just as Napoleon after him, Saxe considered the essential in a soldier, after a military spirit, to be his legs; in the legs there rests the entire secret of manoeuvre and battle. "Whoever is of a different opinion is a dupe to ignorance and a novice in the profession of arms."

Saxe had a proposal for raising troops in great numbers and of better quality than kidnaped vagrants or debtors released from prison – advice that was not followed until the nineteenth century. His solution was universal military service; the poor bourgeois would be consoled by watching the rich serve, and the rich would not dare complain as they followed the nobles, and all would be wonderfully elevated in mutual esteem. He favored a law obliging men of all conditions of life to serve their king and country for the space of five years.

"It would create an inexhaustible fund of good recruits, and such as would not be subject to desertion. In course of time everyone would regard it as an honor rather than a duty to perform his task; but to produce this effect upon a people, it is necessary that no sort of distinction be admitted, no rank or degree whatever excluded, and the nobles and rich rendered in a primary degree subservient to it."

Benjamin Franklin, disagreeing with the policy of impressment of seamen, wrote: "When the personal service of every man is called for, then the burden is equal. Not so when the service of part is called for and others excused. If the alphabet should say, let us all fight for the defence of the whole, that is equal and may therefore be just. But if they say, let A B and C and D go and fight for us while we stay home and sleep in whole skins, that is not equal and therefore cannot be just."

Saxe's strictures on the current system of raising troops indicate a certain amount of humane feeling. Troops were raised either by voluntary engagement or by capitulation (i.e. an agreement between the troops and the ruler who hires them) sometimes by compulsion, but mostly by artifice. "When you recruit men by capitulation," he felt, "it is barbarous as well as unjust to go back on the agreement. The method of raising troops by artifice is likewise altogether scandalous and unwarrantable; such, among other instances, as that of secretly putting money in a man's pocket and afterwards challenging him for a soldier. That of mustering them by compulsion is even worse."

Saxe on military discipline: "Next to forming of troops, military discipline is the first object that presents itself to our notice: it is the soul of all armies, and unless it be established amongst them with great prudence and supported with unshaken resolution, they are no better than so many contemptible heaps of rabble which are more dangerous to the state that maintains them than even its declared enemies. It is a false notion that subordination and passive obedience to superiors is a debasement of a man's courage, but it is generally conceded that those armies which have been subjected to the severest discipline have performed the greatest deeds. It is best to give few orders, but those should be carried out with great care, and failure to obey punished without respect to either rank or personality; all partiality must be completely avoided; otherwise you expose yourself to hate and resentment. By enforcing your authority with judgment and setting a proper example, you may make yourself at once loved and feared. Severity must be accompanied by great consideration and moderation, so displayed upon every occasion as to appear without design and entirely due to a natural disposition."

The following dialogue is attributed to a colonel and a sergeant on the night of Marshal de Saxe's conquest of Prague: "You are going to scale the wall." – "Yes, my colonel." – "The sentinel will shoot at you." – "Yes, my colonel." "He will miss you." – "Yes, my colonel." – "You will kill him." – "Yes, my colonel." – This was on the night of November 25-26, 1741. No disorder followed the fall of the city, thanks to the good discipline that ruled in Saxe's army. "There is not another example" he wrote to Folard, "of a city ever taken by the French, sword in hand, without pillaging."

Regarding spies the Marshal had a practical viewpoint. "One cannot be too careful in the procurement of spies and guides... Money therefore should never be spared on proper occasion, for the acquisition of a good man is cheap at any price."

Another reform introduced by Saxe was having soldiers shoot individually, not in volleys. "Although I have been protesting against concerted firing, yet in certain situations, it is both serviceable and necessary, such as in enclosures and rough grounds, and also against cavalry, but the method of carrying it out ought to be simple and unconstrained. – The present practice is of little or no effect, for the men are so taken up with waiting for the word of command that they cannot fire with any certainty. How is it to be expected that, after presenting arms, they can, in such a position hold their aim till they receive the command to fire?"

Great wealth, titles and honors were heaped upon the victor of Fontenoy, among them an invitation to membership in the French Academy. Saxe wrote to a friend about it, in his famous orthography: "Ils veule me fare de la cademie; sela m'iret come une bage a un chas." ("Ils veulent me faire de l'Academie; cela m'irait comme une bague à un chat" – "They want to make me a member of the Academie; that would be as suitable to me as a ring to a cat.")

In 1749 Saxe visited Frederick the Great at Sans Souci, and the king, contrary to his methodical routine, sat up till dawn discussing things military with his illustrious guest. He wrote to his friend Voltaire on July 15, 1749, "I have seen here the hero of France, the Saxon, the Turenne of the age of Louis XV. I have gained instruction from his talk, not in the French language, but in the art of war. The

Marshal might be the professor of all the generals of Europe."[44]

Lowendal in his later years embraced the Catholic religion and tried to convert Saxe when the latter was on his deathbed. Saxe replied: "We have been good friends for many years. Do me one more favor! Don't talk to me." His soul was full of reveries. At the last he said to his physician, "Doctor, life is only a dream; mine has been a beautiful dream – but it is too short." His excesses are said to have shortened his life. Barbier reports: "Saxe is at Chambord with many guests, women and lords. The Marshal has a troupe of comedians, and German dancers, musicians, equipages. It is said he entertains like a lord." He died at fifty-five.

Marshal Lowendal was the only contemporary general who in any way approached his master in generalship.[45] He had the same dash and willingness to take an unorthodox tack, the same gigantic physique and strength, but in intellectual accomplishments, mathematical and linguistic skills, he far outstripped Maurice de Saxe; as a matter of fact, he was elected a member of the Academy of Sciences and became an ornament of that scholarly body.

The regiment organized September 1, 1743, by Count Lowendal, in which Jean de Kalb served, was stationed in Flanders and took part in the glorious successes of French arms under Marshal de Saxe in that theater of war. In the campaign of 1744 Menin was besieged and quickly taken, as were soon afterward Ypres and Furnes. When an Austrian army invaded Alsace, the French rushed an army under the command of Lowendal to its defense, drove the Austrians back and ended the campaign in November with the successful siege of Fribourg. The Lowendal Regiment took part in all of these engagements, so that de Kalb experienced four sieges in the course of one year. Count Lowendal, like Washington, habitually, with great temerity rushed into the thick of the fray, but not having the latter's luck, he sustained a severe bullet wound in the fighting before Fribourg.

Scarcely healed of his wound, Lowendal returned to Flanders in time to take part in the battle of Fontenoy, May 11, 1745. During the entire action he could be seen rushing into the most dangerous places, riding along the front despite the terrible fire of the English which felled at his side some of his bravest officers. He changed the direction of a battery in order to secure greater effect against the enemy. At the moment when the French seemed about to be overcome by the weight of the steadily advancing mass of British, he judged they would not reach the sector he had been ordered to defend, and, on his own initiative rushed to the rescue of the French center, placing himself at the head of the Normandie Brigade, together with the King's Household, uniting these two crack units into a smashing flank attack which contributed mightily to the piercing of the enemy column. The Irish regiments also covered themselves with glory – as might be expected when they faced the British.

The French successes in the Netherlands were due in large part to the development of the art of siege warfare, which was Lowendal's forte. He relied not only on skilfully planned zig-zag trenches, but combined this tactic with the concentration of the heaviest cannon fire, so intense that no single defensive force could withstand it. As the armies fell before Saxe, so all the towns yielded to Lowendal.

His masterpiece was the taking of the fortified town of Bergen-op-Zoom in North Brabant in the Netherlands, situated on both sides of the river Zoom near its confluence with the Scheldt. This small town has quite an extensive war history, back even to Norman times. In 1576 the town joined the United Netherlands and was fortified. In 1588 it was successfully defended against the Duke of Parma. In 1622 the Spaniards again failed to take it. In 1725 the fortifications were extended and strengthened by the famous Dutch siege engineer Menno Cohorn, giving it the reputation of being impregnable.

The Allies had done all they could to defend this place in the belief that it would surely hold out. They had reenforced the garrison with ammunition and food, and the port was full of warships. 16,000 Austrians defended the lines. Reenforcements arrived continually by water, for this town could not be blockaded. Lowendal saw all these difficulties, but he was undismayed. He began to dig trenches in the middle of July, 1747. Sorties from the town attacking the trenchworkers were regularly repulsed. The famous Austrian general von Schwarzenberg came to aid the defenders, but was forced to withdraw, and the warships were likewise driven away from the port.

The French troops camping in the low ground were stricken by a contagious disease and 20,000 men had to be replaced. Despite all Lowendal's energy and ingenuity, the siege did not advance, and after three months the breaches were not yet ready for assault. As the fall season found only three points somewhat weakened, the general decided that there were occasions when one must discard the rules and take bold risks. In the night of September 15-16 he lined up his army in strictly maintained silence while the Austrians were sleeping in supposed security. At the break of day, on a given signal, the French fell upon the weakened points, carrying one fort and two bastions, thus entering the city. With fixed bayonets they took the gate to the seaport. Its commander surrendered, and other forts soon followed suit. Two regiments, one Scotch and the other Swiss, offered some resistance but were cut to pieces. Thereupon a panicky flight began, in which arms, provisions and baggage were abandoned. The town was given over to pillage by the victorious soldiers. Seventeen barks were seized, loaded with ammunition and supplies sent to the besieged town by other Dutch cities. On the boxes of supplies was written in bold letters, "To the invincible army of Bergen-op-Zoom." Thus the title of Marshal of France was earned by the Comte de Lowendal.

About him, too, there is told a story of a meeting with Frederick the Great. The King had invited Lowendal and a number of other military men to dinner. Toward the end of the banquet, when the dessert was served, he questioned the guest of honor as to what means he would employ to take the city of Luxembourg if he were ordered to do so. To Lowendal it probably seemed inadvisable to discuss his methods before such a gathering, in which there would undoubtedly be many who were indiscreet. He appeared thoughtful for a while, then replied: "Luxembourg is not a town that can be conquered between the pear and the cheese."

This fighter, who had exposed himself to death in many battles, died at the age of 55 as a result of a little wound on his foot; he neglected it, gangrene set in, and thus brought about his death. An epigram on this able general makes this striking allusion: "He lived like Achilles, and it was his fate to die like him."

> C'est par le talon qu'aujourdhui
> La mort vient de saisir un Général habile
> Lowendal vecut comme Achille;
> Il devait mourir comme lui.

De Kalb naturally profited from his excellent military schooling under the two generals, at the same time using his leisure for private study of modern languages as well as mathematics, particularly applied to the art of siege warfare. Recommendations written for him by his superiors frequently praise his "efficiency." This determination to carry out his work well attracted the attention of those above him, who entrusted him with responsible tasks, also giving him rapid advancement. He received a captaincy and was named *aide major;* at the same time he was entrusted with the duties of an *officier de détail*.[46] His selection for this post indicates that he must have shown great administrative ability. An *officier de détail*, a post peculiar to the French armies of the eighteenth century, combined the duties of a regimental manager and a judge. As the title indicates, the regiment's requirements down to the minutest detail were his to oversee, from simple matters of routine service to vital questions of discipline. The colonel gave his name to the regiment and commanded it in battle; the *officier de détail* was in charge of its needs and maintenance of its effectiveness. He carried on the correspondence with the commanding general and the war ministry, reported on the condition of the soldiers, listed their requirements, protected their rights vis-à-vis their superiors, ordered punishments and rewards – in short, he was practically the colonel of the regiment. The official colonel generally amused himself in the capital or at the court, leaving the *officier de détail* to do the work, especially in times of peace or winter-quartering.

This was a very responsible post for a captain twenty-six years of age. The fact that he filled the position for the entire period of peace between the war of the Austrian Succession (1741-1748) and the outbreak of the Seven Years War (1756-1763) indicates his executive ability. During the interlude between wars, his regiment was garrisoned in Cambrai in northern France, near Lille. He thus lived in a French environment and corresponded in that language with his fellow officers, even though the commands of his regiment were issued in German. When the King or some high commanding officer came to inspect the regiment, he was given a slip of paper with the orders in phonetically written German; the officer would read them off while keeping the paper half hidden under his saddle.

The mercenary regiments in French service were of course organized at different places and at different times, and given varying subventions or contracts. The terms of the agreement between the regiment and the country that engaged its services depended of course on how badly the particular power needed the troops and offered generous or miserly terms – the so-called "capitulations." This great variety existed also in regard to rules and punishments. De Kalb was eager not only to fulfill his duties as *officier de détail*, but also to introduce unity into the procedures in the various foreign regiments and to avoid inhumanity in the judicial regulations. For example, a court martial of his regiment had ordered the death penalty for a deserter who had gone across the border, sold his uniform there, and then had returned to France where he was caught. A minority of the judges voted for the penalty of running the gauntlet because the regulations stated that only those deserters taken in foreign parts would be condemned to death. De Kalb submitted the case to the minister of war, Comte d'Argenson, who on September 20, 1751, decreed that the milder penalty should apply.[47]

In matters of police regulations de Kalb sought to achieve some reform where extreme brutality prevailed, namely in the case of prostitutes caught in the barracks. In general, the matter of their punishment was left to the whim of the colonel, who usually, had them whipped publicly by the soldier with whom they had been discovered. Naturally soldiers rebelled at changing from lover to executioner and were hanged for insubordination. De Kalb wrote to the *officiers de détail* of other foreign regiments and received varying replies. In Toul prostitutes were punished by having to run the gauntlet, in which the whole regiment took part, except the corporals and grenadiers, who were not forced to participate. In a regiment stationed at Colmar, prostitutes were never made to run the gauntlet. They would be compelled to walk for an hour before the parade, or perhaps to sit on a "wooden horse," or in severe cases to be whipped by the hangman.

In a Maubeuge regiment, prostitutes were made to run the gauntlet, but grenadiers were not required to take part in the punishment. In Cambrai, the regulations were somewhat complicated, but in substance prostitutes were punished by a detachment from the particular troop where they had been caught. De Kalb's efforts at abolishing the brutal punishment of the unfortunate women were not successful, but he did gain the point that the soldiers were no longer required to execute the punishment.

Washington had the same problem. In orders issued from his quarters at Darby, Pennsylvania, August 24, 1777, he insists that the general officers prevent straggling of soldiers and likewise "an inundation of bad women from Philadelphia." On August 18, 1779, he orders that the women "now detained may be released" under strict injunctions "never to do the like again." If they persist in the practice they "must be confined in the provost"[48] disagreeable as this may be.

Records show that de Kalb insisted on and obtained the rights accorded to the regiment in important as well as in minor matters. For example, the proper number of beds had at first been withheld from his troops; some deserters from the regiment had been incorporated in a French regiment, and he secured their extradition; at the same time he secured a humane ruling to the effect that a soldier could change his regiment without being guilty of desertion.

Despite the endless details de Kalb had to attend to, he did not neglect careful study of the strategic requirements of the times. The settlement of the Peace of Aix-la Chapelle in 1748 was the result of general exhaustion after a long war, leaving so many matters unsettled that another war was imminent. Convinced of the inadequacy of the French maritime defense, de Kalb gave considerable thought to methods by which France might thwart the ever-growing power of her rival England. When in 1744, in an effort to force the British to withdraw their troops from Flanders, Marshal de Saxe together with the Scotch Pretender, Bonny Prince Charlie, made preparations at Dunkirk to land French troops on British soil, this diversion alone brought about the desired effect. This success of de Saxe probably gave de Kalb the idea for his plan of a landing in England, or a weakening of the

British by attacks on her colonies, where constant friction between the colonial powers in Canada, on the Ohio and the Mississippi was leading to the coming war. The French at first scored a number of successes, e.g., the defeat of Braddock. Plans for dictating in London peace terms to the hated enemy were a popular subject frequently considered by the French.

Numerous attempts to invade Britain were made during the eighteenth century, but none was successful.[49] In 1715 the Chevalier St. George, called the Pretender, attempted an invasion, but the insurgents were defeated. Twenty-five years later Charles, called the Young Pretender, grandson of James II, arrived in Scotland, gained some victories, but was defeated at Culloden. In 1756 and 1757 there were rumors of great preparations on the part of the French. Similar rumors were abroad again in 1779, 1782 and 1783. In 1796 the French Directory, on receipt of an invitation from malcontents in Ireland, equipped seventeen vessels, carrying an army of 18,000 men, and sent them to the west coast of Ireland; but this invasion force accomplished nothing. In the same year, 1200 men in black uniforms, called *La Legion Noire*, proceeded up the Bristol Channel and made a landing, but were forced to surrender. In 1798 there was a rebellion in Ireland which Napoleon saw as an opportunity for striking a deadly blow at his arch-enemy by following Julius Caesar's example of an invasion of Britain. When it became known that a large force was being collected at Boulogne, the danger was recognized and every British seaman was armed. The suspense was terrible until Napoleon's expedition sailed for Egypt, causing all alarm to die away.

De Kalb now prepared a carefully worked out plan to be submitted to the Minister of War in Paris:

> A regiment of foreign marines would be of undoubted advantage to the king. It should number from eight to twelve hundred men, and would have to serve on land, on the coast, in the colonies, and on board the navy, and be composed of Germans, Danes, Swedes, Englishmen, inhabitants of our own seaboard provinces, but above all, of Irishmen. The latter are universally known to be the best sailors and marines of the English navy; besides, they are Roman Catholics. Their concourse to our flag might make it possible for us to people a considerable part of our colonies with them. By making this disposition of them we might secure the adherence of numbers of Irishmen in any undertaking against the naval power, the colonies, or the provinces of England, and might keep ourselves well informed of all the hostile movements of the British. All the world is

aware of the hatred cherished by the Irish against the English. The former have never served the latter for any other reason than the want of better employment. It is remarkable this project has not been broached before. How invaluable would such a corps have been to the State at the time when the king had sixteen thousand Irishmen in his service! For six and forty years France has had no more trusty soldiers, none who served her, on all occasions, with greater zeal and efficiency. But they would have been much more useful at sea than on land, for the former must be regarded as their native element.

After detailing the advantages to be derived from the adoption of his plan, de Kalb proceeds to discuss the disposition of the force to be raised:

Detachments should be sent to Quebec and Louisburg, and recruited in Nova Scotia, which colony is almost exclusively inhabited by English and Irish Catholics. By this means we should be furnished with every information which it would be to our interest to receive from that portion of America. Other detachments could be usefully employed at Martinique, Guadaloupe and Marie Galante, as these islands command all the other French and all the English possessions in that quarter, in consequence of the easterly winds prevailing there from year's end to year's end, and which would enable us in twenty-four hours to reach Barbados, Antigua, and the remaining English Antilles, which carry on considerable commerce. The same advantage is offered by Cape Français, the best harbor in that portion of San Domingo, subject to the King, which lies to windward of Jamaica, the most important English possession in America. A strong detachment of the regiment posted there, might secure the fullest and most reliable intelligence about the strength of the English, their movements, their weak points, and the best means of surprising them.

If the regiment is to render the service fairly to be expected, it must be formed and instructed in time. Soldiers reared in a discipline of years may be depended on for implicit obedience in any enterprise, while ignorance of the country and of the hostile resources will always expose an army to the misfortunes which befell the fleet commanded by the Duc d'Antin in 1740 and 1741. His attack upon Jamaica failed from utter want of knowledge of the country. Had he been in command of soldiers such as I propose to raise, he would have been sufficiently apprised that the English had not a tenth part of the force attributed to them in his calculations. Besides, it is notorious that the British succeeded in taking Fort St. Louis on San Domingo only on account of the cowardice of the garrison; they could never have reduced it, had it been defended by a well-disciplined force such as I have suggested.[50]

De Kalb accompanied the plan with detailed specifications, regarding the regiment's organization, composition, pay, equipment and discipline. He also set down the proposed rights and duties vis-à-vis the Crown. This, the earliest preserved project of de Kalb, is very directly written, with no flattery for higher officials. He writes as a man convinced of the merits of his case, anxious to do all in his power to aid his adopted country in the struggle with England that seemed inevitable in view of developments in America and the French desire for revenge.

In view of Mme. Pompadour's squandering of millions in her sway over Louis XV, the request of a mere captain for the organization of a new type of regiment would probably receive short shrift. However de Kalb succeeded in interesting a lieutenant colonel in his project. The latter was to be the colonel of the marine regiment, while de Kalb himself was to be the senior major. When he submitted his plan to army and navy officials in Paris, he met with friendly interest, but was told that funds for defense were very low; the suggestion that he offer special inducements to some of the favorites of la Pompadour went absolutely against his grain. Rather than stoop to such sycophancy he dropped the plan and returned to his garrison at Cambrai, where in May 1775 he was promoted to a majority in his regiment.

In the summer of 1776, at the battle of Long Island, Colonel Glover's Amphibious Regiment[51] of Massachusetts fishermen saved Washington's retreat by seizing every small boat in the harbor and ferrying the entire army of 9,000 men across to Manhattan. The circumstances of this retreat were particularly glorious to the Americans, wrote Stedman, a British historian. When Washington's army was practically bottled up on the narrow island, "a latter-day Thermopylae" took place on October 18, when four British brigades disembarked at Pell's Point to turn the American position from the rear. In desperation Washington posted Glover and 750 amphibians to resist until his imperilled forces could withdraw. The fishermen stood behind a stone wall, inflicting a terrible defeat on the regulars. Loading their smoothbores and three fieldpieces with nails, broken glass and rusty scrap, they beat off the assaults of five times their number. From dawn till late afternoon the redcoats and the Hessian mercenaries persisted in spite of much heavier losses than they had suffered at Long Island. Even in the hand to hand fighting, their bayonets could not make way against the boathooks wielded by the defenders. At the end of that bloody day, one of the most decisive combats of the war, the amphibians had saved the army at the cost of only seventeen casualties.

Shortly before this battle, Congress had authorized two battalions of American marines. Five years after de Kalb had made his proposal for French marines, the French garrison at Quebec was surprised by a night attack made by troops ferried down the St. Lawrence River. During the Seven Years' War France lost almost all her colonies in America and in Asia.

Well drilled, alert marines might have saved the day for France.

CHAPTER III

HERO IN THE SEVEN YEARS' WAR

Miserrimi belli causa cunnus: This legend was secretly painted by some irate citizen on the wall of the Marquise de Pompadour's palace; it might be translated, "the cause of this horrible war is a whore." It refers to the ruinous meddling in international politics by the mistress of Louis XV, certainly one of the causes of the Seven Years' War. This conflict, 1756-1763, ended after almost continuous defeats of French armies, in the loss of Canada, India, and other French colonies. Through Pompadour's influence on the King, France gave up her traditional policy of enmity toward Austria to enter on an alliance with Austria, Russia and Saxony aimed at Frederick the Great of Prussia, who had deprived Austria of Silesia. The Austrian Empress, Maria Theresa, with her astute chancellor, Kaunitz, was eager to win back this province.

Through his spy service, Frederick learned of the secret plans for a coalition encircling his relatively small country, so he concluded an alliance with England known as the Treaty of Westminster, signed January 16, 1756, for mutual protection. King George II desired protection for his Duchy of Hanover, while Frederick very much needed an ally because of the gradual rapprochement of France and Austria. Kaunitz knew that Mme. Pompadour hated Frederick because of his witticisms at her expense; the King referred to her as "the petticoat queen," and scorned to deal with the "favorite little bitch that slept in the king's bed." Kaunitz felt too that this treaty was definite proof of warlike preparations, so he induced France to enter into an alliance with Austria. In order to prevail on la Pompadour to induce Louis XV, he persuaded Maria Theresa to do "the utmost," namely to address a personal letter to the favorite with the salutation "dear cousin" – thus an empress to a "whore"! Accordingly, the Empress sent through the Austrian Ambassador in Paris a lacquered desk with golden inkwells, adorned with a miniature portrait of Maria Theresa made with inlaid precious stones; the value of the gift was estimated at 77,280 livres. Some historians have denied that there was a letter; but whether the great lady blots her escutcheon by writing a letter or sending a portrait to a wanton seems a subtle distinction. With or without a letter, the courtesan accepted the gift with overflowing gratitude, adding that the present was so precious that she could not allow people to see it, lest it call forth unpleasant remarks. She wrote to the Austrian Ambassador that no one could surmise what had gone on in her heart when she first saw the portrait of the empress. In fact, she would have preferred to receive the portrait without all the costly ornamentation. Austrian diplomats had flattered this vain person by speaking of the alliance of three queens, Maria Theresa of Austria, Elizabeth, Czarina of Russia, and the Marquise de Pompadour, the virtual ruler of France. The Czarina likewise hated Frederick, whom she never forgave for his joke about her taste for vodka and her body odor. He referred to her as "cette infame catin du nord."

To follow the rise of a woman of bourgeois background to the point where she could dismiss chancellors and make her favorites the commanders of French armies is an amazing story. Jeanne Antoinette Poisson was born December 29, 1721, in Paris. Her father, François Poisson, son of a peasant, was the chief clerk in a firm that furnished flour for the army. When some vast irregularities were brought to light, his superiors made him the sacrificial goat. M. Poisson was adjudged the guilty one and condemned to death by hanging. But through the influence of his wealthy friends and patrons, he was allowed to escape to Hamburg, where he lived for fifteen years. Thus the executioner could hang only his effigy. His wife, a very beautiful woman, remained in Paris, had various affairs, and about the time of Jeanne Antoinette's birth became the mistress of a very wealthy and cultured man, Charles François Paul le Normant de Tournehem. He had fallen in love with Mme. Poisson and took pains to offer her daughter the best possible education, first in the Ursuline Convent at Poissy and later by private teachers. It was widely believed that he was the father of Jeanne Antoinette, though he never acknowledged it. On the day she left the convent her mother took her to a fortune teller who predicted that the little girl would one day become the great friend of the king. When, one day fifteen years later this event came to pass, Mme. de Pompadour did not forget the clairvoyant, but granted her a yearly pension out of her own private purse.

The child destined for great things was learning rapidly, tutored by a famous tragedian in declamation, by the ballet master of the Opera in dancing, by a noted tenor in music, by an artist in sketching, in all of which fields she distinguished herself. She was also taught horsemanship and became a fearless rider.

When she was twenty years old, with her rare beauty fully developed and her many accomplishments enhancing her charm, Jeanne Poisson won the heart of a young man twenty-four years of age, Charles Le Normant, son of a wealthy father and nephew of M. Tournehem, the lover of Mme. Poisson and her daughter's benefactor. The four persons just mentioned were all eager for the match; only M. Tournehem's brother was by no means eager that his son should marry a girl whose father was under sentence of hanging and whose mother was notorious for her love affairs. But these scruples were overcome when M. Tournehem secured a lucrative position for his nephew and promised to remember him in his testament.

Still required was the father's consent, namely, that of François Poisson, who was of course still in exile. Once more through the influence of M. Tournehem the matter "arranged itself" as the French say. Poisson's former employers had become in the course of the War of the Austrian Succession extremely powerful profiteers who with very little trouble procured a decree from parliament dismissing the charges and restoring Poisson to full citizenship.

When this Enoch Arden returned after fifteen years, he was surprised to find his wife more attractive than ever in her mature beauty, his daughter most ravishing, with a devoted suitor, and in the bosom of the family a devoted and extremely helpful friend, M. Tournehem. He gladly gave his consent to the marriage, which was performed in the Church of Saint Sulpice.

Mme. le Normant was now at the peak of her beauty; wavy chestnut hair framed a face with regular features and a pearly complexion, dominated by dark gray seductive eyes which could at times appear black. She had a charming smile; her naturally red lips were flanked by two dimples which played in and out in her soft cheeks. Her expression was extremely mobile and vivid. To judge by the paintings of Boucher, she was of more than average height, with a very good figure.

The marriage contract gave the young lady a dowry of 120,000 livres, while the groom received from his uncle 83,000 livres and a promise of 150,000 after his death. Moreover, M. Tournehem promised to let the young couple live in his house on the rue St. Honoré, where there were five servants as well as horses and carriages at their disposal. Finally, the young man received a country home at Etiolles which enabled his wife to assume this name and become the lady of the manor. "Mme. Le Normant d'Etiolles," wrote Barbier in his famous *Journal*, "has a fine figure and is very beautiful. She has received all the education possible, rides horseback marvelously, sings perfectly and knows a hundred amusing little songs."[52] While Voltaire wrote poems in praise of her beauty, Rousseau said "The wife of a charcoal burner is more worthy of respect than the mistress of a prince."

Though she moved in rather frivolous society, Mme. Le Normant was faithful to her husband and became the mother of two children. But she had set for herself a high goal, namely, to become the ruler of France and the official mistress of Louis XV. With great singleness of purpose and firm tact, she managed to attract the attention of the king, and two years after their first meeting, Louis entered upon a liaison with her. Her husband, still very much in love with her, begged and threatened, trying to induce her to return to him, but she did not even reply to his letters. Instead, she showed them to Louis and demanded his protection. In a tearful scene she told the king of the frightful situation into which the sacrifice which she had been weak enough to make for him, had led her; she had been honored and idolized in her family, and now she was despised and hated just because of her love for him. The king wiped away her tears by according her a title and a coat of arms, – la Marquise de Pompadour. This removed the stigma of her bourgeois origin as demoiselle Poisson – Miss Fish.[53]

Louis XV was lazy and easily bored. The Marquise saw to it that affairs of state did not trouble him, and that he would not be bored. There was her company, and hunts, balls, theatricals, even young girls whom she selected and supplied for the king's pleasure when her own charms no longer held him.

The Marquise de Pompadour had ample reason to fear that the sensual Louis XV would tire of her and elevate a rival to the post of official mistress. To prevent this she established "the Deer Park;"[54] she selected a house in an isolated location on land that had formerly served for deer hunts. There the king went incognito, supposedly a Polish gentleman, friend of the Queen, and on returning to the palace reported to the Marquise the details of his romantic adventures. La Pompadour had no fear that any of these uneducated young girls would alienate the king, but she dreaded any interest that he might develop for a lady of the court. The "Deer Park" lasted more than a decade and the number of "pensioners" there is estimated as from 40 to several hundred.

From 1745 to her death in 1764, this remarkable woman was in effect the ruler of France.[55] It was not only by her beauty that the Marquise bewitched Louis. She managed to weave around him a peaceful and enjoyable existence that caused the indolent prince only too easily to forget the cares of state. All the time that was not devoted to hunting, his family, or to affairs of state, he devoted to his mistress.

Early in the morning he went to the Marquise's bedroom, unless he had spent the entire night with her. He left her then only to attend the mass which he never missed. Then he would return to her, and the entire forenoon would be spent tête-à-tête, unless he was called away to the Council of Ministers. Time never seemed long as she told with considerable humor little anecdotes and scandals of the court or the city, which the king enjoyed very much. She would also read him secret reports submitted by the police, describing the vices of prominent personages, which caused the king to laugh heartily. While they observed court etiquette quite conscientiously in public, they lived much like a bourgeois couple in private. However, the Marquise never failed to treat the king with the respect due his position. She was always a good listener and followed with seeming interest when the king told about one of his hunting exploits, even if it was for the fourth or fifth time.

A remarkable feature of this relationship was that the Marquise suffered from frigidity,[56] despite various drugs she swallowed to change this condition. Louis gradually lost interest in this aspect, and six years after its beginning the intimate relationship came to an end. But though no longer mistress, she continued as friend and confidante for fourteen years.

The Marquise modelled herself on Mme. Maintenon, Louis XIV's mistress and confidante. She looked into the files with insatiable curiosity, even the most secret ones. In foreign affairs she felt that she could accomplish great things. She had herself instructed in matters of diplomacy by one of her favorites, the Abbé Bernis. Then she began to grant audiences to important personages, magistrates, counselors, generals and financiers. She listened to their requests with great solemnity, at times cut them down to some extent and promised to refer them to His Majesty.

A magistrate, M. de Meinières, has left a description of such an interview[57] in which he tells how she received him. "Mme. Pompadour was alone, seated before the fire. She looked at me from head to foot with such haughtiness that it will remain all my life long engraved on my soul. Her head rested on her shoulder and she offered not the slightest gesture of greeting. When I had approached her, she said in an angry tone to her servant, who seemed uncertain as to what sort of seat to offer, 'Bring a chair.' He placed it opposite her and so near that my knees were only one foot from hers. During the whole interview she had her eyes fixed on me so as to disconcert me as much as possible." De Kalb had no stomach for that type of interview.

Her influence made one of her favorites, l'Abbé Bernis, minister.[58] As her puppet he signed the treaty that led to the Seven Years' War. For eight years after the peace of Aix-la-Chapelle (1748) armies faced each other tensely across the frontiers. Then the first shot was fired in the wilderness of America by an obscure provincial officer named George Washington. Within a few months Europe had gone to war again, and the tramp of marching men could be heard from the plains of Bengal to the forests of Pennsylvania.[59]

When, after Frederick's victories at Rossbach and at Leuthen, Bernis wished to make peace, Pompadour pulled the strings to have him replaced by probably the only competent man she ever sponsored – Choiseul. Frederick commented: "Poor Bernis, his folly elevated him and his wisdom caused his downfall!" Concerning this famous reversal of alliances, Voltaire wrote that it united the houses of France and Austria after "two centuries of hatred considered immortal." What numerous treaties and marriages could not accomplish, the displeasure of the King of Prussia and the hatred of some highly placed persons whom this prince had wounded by his pleasantries accomplished in a moment." Bernis bitterly complained that it was impossible to serve king and country under a favorite who treated affairs of state like a child.

Earlier in the war, in 1757, Marshal d'Estrées, who had distinguished himself under Saxe and was placed in command of the French army, displeased the Marquise because of his careful strategy. She then had the effrontery to meddle in military affairs by writing d'Estrées a letter on the operation of his campaign, drawing for him a plan on a piece of paper, marking with beauty patches the different points he was to attack or defend. This appeared to d'Estrées naturally very childish, but nevertheless, stung to the quick, he decided to attack – and (beautiful irony!) he won the famous Battle of Hastenbeck over the Duke of Cumberland.

Later Soubise was placed in command of an army, and was defeated disgracefully in the – for Prussia – glorious battle of Rossbach. In 1762, this incompetent general was again defeated, this time by Ferdinand of Brunswick at Wilhelmsthal, which caused Frederick to write Ferdinand: "God bless Soubise! O how I appreciate the selection made by Pompadour!" But far from being considered in disgrace, this friend of the Marquise de Pompadour was made a Marshal of France. The enormous popular hatred against the King's mistress and her inept favorites found expression in numerous mocking songs sung in the streets of Paris. The satirical ballads of street singers may be compared to the witty criticism of present-day cartoons:

>En vain vous vous chargez, obligeante marquise,
>De mettre en beaux draps blancs le général Soubise.
>Vous ne pouvez lever à force de credit
>La tâche qu'à son nom imprime sa disgrace.
>Et quoique votre faveur fasse
>en tout temps on dira qu'à présent on dit:
>Que si Pompadour le blanchit,
>Le roi de Prusse le repasse.

> Kindly marquise, the more you try
> To wrap Soubise in sheets of white,
> The more the people continue to cry
> Whenever he's washed and hung to dry,
> He's then pressed flat by Prussia's might.

The Marquise was well aware of the hatred of the populace against Louis XV (who in his early years on the throne was called Louis the Well Beloved), but particularly against her as the chief cause of the scandals at court and the misery of the common people. She therefore organized her own police, and many who criticized her in any way, or even stopped to read with appreciation a poster attacking her, were imprisoned in the Bastille. She had an arrangement with the postmaster by which all letters were secretly opened, and all passages unfriendly to the king or his favorite were copied and submitted to her. She certainly did fight for her position with desperate energy, naturally causing the king to become more ridiculed and hated as Louis XV's "deluge" gradually approached. A remark of hers to Richelieu is very characteristic; after some of Frederick the Great's victories, Richelieu remarked that perhaps the Prussian ruler might even come to Paris, to which she replied, "Well, then I shall see a *king!*"[60] The one French general to distinguish himself in the Seven Years' War was the Duc de Broglie. He was born in 1718, a descendant of an old and distinguished noble family, originally Italian (Broglio). He joined the army as a mere boy; at fifteen he was placed in charge of a company of cavalry. His brave conduct at the battle of Guastalla in 1734, where Marshal Coligny defeated the Austrians, caused him to be selected to announce this victory to the king. At the siege of Prague he scaled the walls and seized a gate, through which the French troops then entered and captured the city. Further successes in Bohemia won him the advancement to brigadier in 1742. He took part in victories won by Saxe and Lowendal in Flanders in 1746. Under Soubise he experienced the defeat by Frederick at Rossbach, but Broglie, in command of twenty battalions and eighteen squadrons, kept his command intact and led them into Hanover, a famous retreat in which de Kalb took part. In 1759 Broglie was placed in command in Frankfurt, which Ferdinand of Brunswick attempted to capture with an army that outnumbered de Broglie's forces 40,000 to 28,000; the French general disposed of his forces with extreme cleverness, taking full advantage of the terrain around Bergen, a village on a height near Frankfurt. By a very skilful flank movement, he then forced the enemy to retreat in disorder with the loss of 8,000 men. It was a glorious as well as a valuable victory that gained de

Broglie the very highest honors, including that of hereditary Prince of the Empire, bestowed by Maria Theresa. There were wild celebrations in Paris; the courtiers compared Bergen with the greatest battles of history, the poets glorified it, the fishwives cheered it, and the ladies adopted a head dress "à la Bergen."[61] But his glory as a marshal came to a sudden end when he was replaced as a supreme commander by Pompadour's favorite, Soubise, who had commanded at the inglorious rout at Rossbach. As the news of Broglie's exile to his estates reached Paris, Voltaire's drama on the Sicilian king of the twelfth century, Tancred, was being performed, in which the heroine spoke the lines:

> On dépouille Tancred, on l'exile, on l'outrage;
> C'est le sort des heros d'être persécutés.
>
> Tancred is despoiled, exiled, outraged;
> To be persecuted is the hero's fate.

The audience applied these lines to Broglie, and cheered him wildly, forcing the actress to repeat the lines.[62]

De Broglie has his niche in military history by virtue of having put into effect Saxe's theories of concentrating by divisions.[63] He combined two brigades of infantry and one of cavalry with artillery into a formation intended to be self-supporting in local operations, yet capable of swift concentrations for battle. De Broglie's formation was the forerunner of the modern division.

When the Revolution broke out in 1789, Louis XVI named de Broglie his commander-in-chief, but due to the king's indecision, de Broglie's ability could not save him. The marshal then went into exile and fought with the loyalists. In 1804 Napoleon sent him a message;[64] "The victor of Bergen should not hesitate to return to his native land, which he served so gloriously under the government that raised the statues of Turenne and Condé," – by inference placing de Broglie side by side with the great generals under Louis XIV, when France was the great military power.

Throughout the Seven Years' War de Kalb served under the Duc de Broglie, whose corps in 1757 was under the command of the Prince de Soubise[65] who had received his appointment as a favorite of Mme. de Pompadour. He tolerated unbelievable conditions in his army; discipline was extremely lax; even subaltern officers had their mistresses along during campaigns; on the "marches" the "ladies" rode in wagons, often in the company of their lovers who left their commands in order to spend the time more agreeably. In 1759, when he was commanding an army of 50,000 men, there were with the troops 12,000 wagons belonging to hucksters and camp-followers. Every luxury could be purchased; silks, perfumes, parasols, hair powder, rouge, and more of the like. There was regular theater for the officers, as well as frequent dances. The enormous baggage train slowed up the movements of the army, which goes a long way to explain Soubise's numerous defeats. Although, as mentioned above, de Kalb took part in the rout at Rossbach, his corps had the merit of protecting the French army from total annihilation, and of making it possible for the survivors to go into winter quarters in the vicinity of Frankfurt.

In this defeated army, consisting to a large extent of Germans fighting on German soil against other Germans, there were naturally many deserters. Some of them are said to have gone over to Frederick's victorious forces. Among various proposals made to put a stop to this evil, one was submitted to de Kalb for his judgment, which casts a very interesting light on conditions in the French army at that time. It was proposed that the business of recruiting should be taken out of the hands of the captains, all the German regiments be treated as a unit, centralizing the recruiting of soldiers for all of the 21 German battalions, and at one place – Landau – a common depot for all of the recruitment and equipment, be erected instead of scattering the recruiting stations all over the country, by this means procuring cheaper and more reliable recruits, and also making it easier to check on soldiers assigned to the various regiments.

De Kalb[66] considered such a radical step highly impractical, especially in the midst of war. He pointed out that it would offend the captains in their pride as well as in their recognized rights, as well as exposing the German regiments to complete disorganisation. In the French army organization, the captain is at the same time officer, broker and businessman who furnishes the king for a definite price a definite number of soldiers. He naturally is interested in securing for himself the best recruits, since if there are many desertions, he will get into debt or even be forced to declare himself bankrupt. The proposed centralization might make the recruitment less costly, but this economy would be counterbalanced by the poor quality of the recruits, since the officer in charge of the station would not have the same interest in securing the best soldiers as a company captain. Another weakness of the plan was that it proceeded on the assumption that the German regiments, all very conscious of their particular local origin, as Hessians, Bavarians, Saxons, etc., would no longer be differentiated by varying traditions, rights and customs, but would all have to conform to a common pattern – a measure that would run afoul of the jealous vigilance with which each command watched over the preservation of its special "capitulations" (i.e. the contract), thus making it impractical at all times and suicidal in time of war. In view of these sensible objections, not even an attempt was made at such a change.

In Marshal de Broglie's victory at Bergen, April 13, 1759, de Kalb had his part. The Lowendal Regiment was posted in the village and aided in repulsing the furious onslaughts of the Allies. When, in the following year, the Lowendal Regiment was dissolved and divided among two other German regiments, the Duc de Broglie appointed de Kalb assistant quartermaster general (aide-maréchal général des logis) with the army of the upper Rhine, a staff position which he occupied until the end of the war, and which brought him into daily contact with the commander-in-chief, Marshal de Broglie, and his brother the Comte de Broglie. In a letter written November 18, 1761, to Prince Xavier de Saxe, de Broglie expresses his enthusiasm for de Kalb:[67] "I am sending this letter to you by M. de Kalb, and I am seizing this opportunity to call to your attention my most perfect satisfaction with his zeal and his manner of serving." On May 19, 1761, de Kalb was promoted to a lieutenant colonelcy. The de Broglies selected him for advancement because they found him an excellent officer, no doubt very different from the average French officer who spent as much time as possible away from his command.

De Kalb took part in the movements of the Army of the Upper Rhine which was under the command of the Duc de Broglie. His efficiency and reliability gained him the esteem and friendship of his commander as well as of the Comte de Broglie, who was his brother's subordinate. This intimacy continued throughout the rest of de Kalb's life; he never took an important step without consulting the de Broglies. When Mme. de Pompadour's favorite Soubise was given the command of the army, and the de Broglies were in disgrace, de Kalb expressed his regret and resentment at this injustice in such emphatic terms that he incurred the enmity of Soubise, who made an attempt to have de Kalb removed from his post and assigned to a Saxon Corps in the service of France – which would have meant that he would be discharged at the end of the war without any claim for readmission to the French army. However, de Kalb's immediate superiors, Generals de Vogue and de Salles, interposed and declared de Kalb's efficient services indispensable. Soon afterward the Prince de Soubise found himself in deep trouble because of his incompetent conduct at the battle of Wilhelmsthal, and no more was heard of the proposed punishment of de Kalb. The latter fought with such distinction in the unfortunate battle that he was rewarded by the Order of Military Merit,[68] a French decoration established in 1759 for Protestants, the Order of St. Louis being awarded to Catholics in similar cases.

Still, de Kalb resented the empty promises of high officials in regard to his promotion in rank. As much as a decade later, in August, 1779, when de Kalb was serving in the American army, the Comte de Broglie rather lamely wrote that he had recommended de Kalb's advancement, but that now, having lost de Kalb's code, he advised him to write directly to the minister of war, the Prince de Montbarey. De Kalb followed this advice, noting that the Prince had favored his joining the rebel forces and had led him believe that he would be made brigadier in the royal forces in recognition of the risks and hardships he would undergo. He lists chapter and verse in regard to the hazards he had encountered as major general in the American army. Since France and the United States had become allies, the French officers serving in America should be recognized by the Court and treated accordingly. Such a simple act of justice, no doubt, was now the minister's to perform. Nothing happened.[69]

At this time it may be well to list de Kalb's entire military career: he began his military experience in the Fischer Corps of Chasseurs, became second lieutenant in the Lowendal Regiment September 1, 1743; captain, aide-major, December 20, 1747; major, June 10, 1756; and during the last three years of the Seven Years' War, assistant quartermaster general; lieutenant colonel, May 19, 1761; he was awarded the Order of Military Merit, 1763; attained the rank of brigadier in the French colonial troops, November 4, 1776; was made major general in the Army of the Thirteen Colonies, September 5, 1777.

CHAPTER IV

MARRIAGE AND A MISSION

After the defeat of the Prince of Soubise at Wilhelmsthal, the French once more established their headquarters at Frankfurt, where de Kalb remained stationed to the end of the Seven Years' War. No further battles took place in this region, as a peace settlement was momentarily expected; it was signed February 10, 1763. Voltaire, as usual, made a very pat comment; "France has lost more in money and men through *its alliance with Austria* in six years, than *in wars against Austria* in 200 years."

In 1760 the Lowendal Regiment was dissolved and divided between the regiments of Anhalt and La Mark. De Kalb, at the time a major in the regiment, in a letter to Prince de Montbarey, calls this act an injustice to the son of the famous marshal, against all fairness and contrary to the express terms of the contract accorded to the late General Lowendal. Of course, de Kalb lost his command, but his superior, the Duc de Broglie, appointed him to a much higher post, that of assistant quartermaster general. He held this post to de Broglie's great satisfaction, but unfortunately for de Kalb, this appointment terminated at the end of the Seven Years' War.[70]

One careful move on the part of de Kalb, in conformity with eighteenth century custom, was his purchase in 1760 of a captaincy in the Anhalt Regiment shortly after the Lowendal Regiment was dissolved. His name was therefore carried on the lists of the Anhalt Regiment even though de Kalb as quartermaster general did not command the company. This purchase served to guarantee him a footing in the French army when, with the signing of the peace, his wartime post as assistant quartermaster general was discontinued. With the rank of captain, he moved to Landau in the Palatinate, which at that time was a French fortress.[71]

Naturally, he had no desire to continue in this subordinate rank. He took six months' leave to further his cause in Paris by applying for an appointment at suitable rank in a foreign regiment under French command. He turned for support to influential men who knew his war record. The Duc de Choiseul, then prime minister, and the Prince de Soubise, gave him no support. His former commanders, especially the brothers de Broglie, wrote letters of recommendation and promised to keep him in mind. – But that was all. When a lieutenant colonelcy in the Nassau Regiment became vacant, de Kalb applied for the post, but it was awarded to a favorite of the minister. It was rumored at the time that for each of the three French armies four assistant quartermasterships were to be created. De Kalb turned to the Marquis de Castries, a very distinguished officer who had fought in the same campaigns with him in 1762 and who had been, as quartermaster general, his immediate superior. The Marquis promised him his support for one of the positions, but in the end the whole plan fell through, thus occasioning him one more disappointment.

Disgusted with fruitless waiting in Paris, de Kalb decided to return to the provinces at the expiration of his leave in October 1763, and in lieu of something more worth while, to take over the command of his company. At this point, however, a very happy turn of events saved him from the dull round of peacetime garrison life; his engagement and subsequent marriage to Anne Elisabeth Emilie van Robais.

Among the many acquaintances de Kalb made during his stay in the capital was Peter van Robais, retired cloth manufacturer. He was the grandson of a citizen of Holland whom Colbert had induced to come to France for the purpose of establishing a cloth factory; his enterprise had proved so successful that Louis XIV rewarded him with a patent of nobility. This business founded by Peter van Robais' grandfather had prospered through the years sufficiently to allow him to turn it over to the husband of his older daughter and live in comfortable circumstances with his wife and second daughter in Courbevoye, a suburb of Paris. Probably their common Protestant faith may have brought them together. De Kalb became a frequent visitor at the van Robais home, and fell in love with the younger daughter. They became engaged in the winter of 1763-64, and the marriage ceremony took place April 10, 1764, at the Protestant church belonging to the Embassy of the United Provinces to the French Court, which at this time of the still lingering persecution of the Huguenots and Jansenists was the only Protestant church in Paris, the chapel of the Dutch Legation. Although the groom's age was 43 and the bride's 16, the marriage proved a very happy one. Two sons and a daughter were born to the couple; Frederic, born 1765, Anna Maria Caroline, born 1767, and Elie, born 1769. In contrast to the dissolute manners of the times, de Kalb was a faithful and considerate husband and father, while his wife was equally devoted to her husband and children. When one reads his numerous, lengthy letters to his wife, in which he addresses her as *"ma chère bonne amie"* and closes with *"je t'embrasse"* it becomes apparent that an unchanging affection prevailed from first to last in his marriage. The French historian Doniol calls Mme. de Kalb *"épouse visiblement très affectionnée et mère courageuse de trois enfants dont le souvenir ne quitte guère la pensée de leur père."*

In regard to their pecuniary circumstances also the family was very fortunate. De Kalb contributed 52,000 francs, while his wife received, in addition to a rich trousseau, 135,375 francs. After the death of her parents and grandparents in 1767, she inherited the homestead at Courbevoye and 205,406 francs. Further wealth came to her on the decease of some collateral relatives in 1776: 84,000 francs in money as well as further real estate. The entire property of husband and wife must have amounted to approximately half a million francs, which Kapp estimates as at least $100,000. Under these circumstances it is apparent that de Kalb did not seek service in foreign armies for the sake of money.

Until the age of 43, de Kalb had never had a home, having continually served in the army. Now it was quite natural that he should settle down with his wife in the neighborhood of her parents in a suburb of Paris. He gave up his company and retired in 1764 upon his pension as lieutenant colonel.[72]

But just as little as Homer's Odysseus after twenty years of war and adventure, according to Dante and Tennyson, could rest inactive at his home in Ithaca, could de Kalb settle down to domestic repose after more than twenty years in the army. His profession was that of soldier, and it was his ambition to rise to the top. If he took foreign service as brigadier, he might after several campaigns return to France and to a generalship in the French army. Such an opportunity seemed to be offering in 1764. In the Seven Years' War even so small a country as Portugal had become involved when in 1762 a Spanish army supported by French forces had staged an invasion. With the help of the British and their German allies the invasion was repulsed, but the Portuguese feared further Spanish attacks, and therefore they charged Count William of Schaumburg-Lippe, who had served them with distinction in 1762, with raising three regiments for the Portuguese service. De Kalb decided to offer his services as brigadier. He consulted his old patron, the Duc de Broglie, who approved of the plan and not only gave him a cordial letter of recommendation, but induced the English general, Robert Clerke, to write to Count Lippe in de Kalb's interest. The Comte de Broglie also recommended de Kalb highly. The three letters are of interest as showing the attitude toward the professional soldier at this time, the great regard in which the Duke as well as the Count de Broglie held de Kalb, and the definite assumption among the military that renewed warfare seemed a certainty. As a matter of fact, France and England were embroiled a decade later and de Kalb gained great glory in that contest, the War of the American Revolution.

Duc (Maréchal) de Broglie: Lieutenant Colonel de Kalb is one of the best and most efficient officers of my acquaintance and as expert in the details of the service as versed in the science of war. In the late war I found him extremely useful and reliable and can recommend him unqualifiedly as an excellent general.

The Comte de Broglie (the Marshal's brother): Lieutenant Colonel de Kalb went through the whole of the late war with me as assistant quartermaster general and is deserving of your protection in the highest degree. To what my brother has written in reference to him, I can only add that de Kalb is an officer no less intelligent and well informed than brave and indefatigable. I doubt whether you could find a more fitting man for the organization and instruction of your troops. It is neither the want of means nor the desire for riches that prompts Lieutenant Colonel de Kalb to seek service abroad. His circumstances are very good, but he craves a congenial occupation, his present inactivity having become insupportable to him.[73]

General Robert Clerke from Paris, February 17, 1765: Mr. de Kalb will deliver this letter to Your Highness. He is a German and a Protestant. He served in the late war as deputy quartermaster under Marshal Broglie who has confidence in him and esteems him very much as a good officer; but he has it not in his power at present to serve him as he deserves. He appears to me to be a sensible military man. Money is not his object, and he has fortune sufficient to live at his ease. His ambition is to be made a general officer in Portugal, and Marshal Broglie may have it in his power to get him the same rank in France in another war.

I find here that Count d'Oyeras had made proposals to Closen who did not accept of them and who died a little afterward. I have received here great civilities both from Marshal Broglie and the Count and should be glad to have it in my power to show my sensibility to their kindness and good opinions of me. M. de Kalb having no business at present thinks it is no trouble at any rate of going to Germany and paying his respects to Your Highness. He can inform you of many things as to the French part in the German war. I hope to have the pleasure of seeing you myself this year in Germany. I have a great desire to pay my respects to you in your own dominion. I am with the greatest respect,

Your Highness' most obedient servant, R. Clerke[74]

Early in March, 1765, de Kalb traveled to Bueckeburg in northwestern Germany, the official residence of Count Lippe, to present himself to the Prince. His reception was most cordial, and the Prince did his utmost to induce the Portuguese Government to make the appointment. But after protracted negotiations, the need for the troops no longer existed, because the difficulties had been peaceably adjusted, so the whole matter was dropped. It was not considered strange that a German and a Protestant should be recommended for a post in the army of Catholic Portugal by French, British and German generals.

It may be in place here to mention that de Kalb's independent income was noted by contemporaries, and at times with surprise that a man of his means would willingly undergo the hardships and suffering that he faced throughout years. In 1779 the Baron von Steuben wrote: "Calbe and I are the only foreign generals. He has 30,000 livres a year and will leave soon." (Lafayette was on leave in France at the time.)

De Kalb, despite various disappointments, continued to seek opportunities for gaining advancement and glory. He kept his name before the prime minister Choiseul and in 1767 his opportunity arrived. Choiseul, though appointed through the influence of the Marquise de Pompadour, was a real patriot, bitterly resentful over the humiliating peace treaty forced on France by the victorious British as a result of la Pompadour's meddling in politics and the king's indolence and debauchery. His foreign policy was revenge on England. He built up a powerful navy and fortified many points on the coast. He planned not for another war in Europe, but for a weakening of England by the liberation of her colonies. Of course for this purpose the North American colonies were most important, and reports of friction between them and the mother country interested Choiseul immensely. The Stamp act, imposed on November 1, 1765, due to violent protests of the colonists, was repealed May 1, 1766. Choiseul saw here his opportunity, and decided to organize a staff for the purpose of discreetly furthering the insurrection. All of this would, of course, have to be done in secrecy from the British as well as from the King, who would have given half his kingdom not to be pestered by talk of more wars.

It was quite logical that as a member of such a staff he would think of de Kalb, who had served with distinction in the recent war, was highly recommended by the Prince de Soubise and the Broglies, spoke French, English and German, had shown great zeal on numerous occasions, and was currently recommended by important persons for a post in the service of France.

On orders of the Minister, the chief clerk of the war ministry, M. Dubois, wrote to Kalb on February 2, 1767 as follows:[75] "I am going to place you on the staff of officers who are going to carry out a survey of the frontiers under the orders of M. Bourcet, and when I report to the Minister I shall let him know that you have been proposed by this general officer."

Choiseul sent from Versailles specific orders to de Kalb on April 20, 1767: "You are hereby informed that His Majesty has included you in the list of officers who are to be employed this year in the survey of the country. You will visit the coast from Dunkirk to Calais, and take up your headquarters in the first named of these towns. You will there receive from the paymaster of the forces five hundred pounds monthly for the duration of your services. I rely upon receiving accurate reports on the execution of your mission."

On April 22 de Kalb went to Versailles to receive Choiseul's final instructions. To his great surprise he was told by M. Dubois that his destination had been altered, and that the Minister's private secretary, M. Appony, had been directed to draw up special instructions for a secret mission for which de Kalb was to be appointed. He was therefore advised to see M. Appony before waiting upon the Minister. The secretary then read him the instructions written at Choiseul's dictation, and handed him a copy reading as follows:

> 1. M. de Kalb will repair to Amsterdam, and there direct his particular attention to the rumors in circulation about the English colonies; should they appear to be well founded, he will immediately make preparation for a journey to America.
>
> 2. On his arrival, he will inquire into the intentions of the inhabitants and endeavor to ascertain whether they are in need of good engineers and artillery officers, or other individuals, and whether they should be supplied with them.
>
> 3. He will inform himself of their facilities for procuring supplies, and will find out what quantities of munitions of war and provisions they were able to procure.
>
> 4. He will acquaint himself with the greater or lesser strength of their purpose to withdraw from the English Government.
>
> 5. He will examine their resources in troops, fortified places and forts, and will seek to discover their plan of revolt, and the leaders who are expected to direct and control it.
>
> 6. Great reliance is placed in the intelligence and address of M. de Kalb in the pursuit of a mission requiring an uncommon degree of tact and shrewdness, and he is expected to report progress as often as possible.

De Kalb was prepared by the previous letter to await definite instructions regarding the project of a survey of the French coast with regard to military defenses. His long service in the army had provided him with training along those lines, but he felt totally unprepared for a political mission of this sort. He pointed out various objections for his selection for the task, but Dubois, without arguing the points, simply said, "Speak to the Minister."

Choiseul received de Kalb in friendly fashion and listened to his recital of the difficulties and dangers connected with such a mission, together with the feeling of his own inadequacy for the undertaking. Finally, Choiseul replied: "Do not decline the mission with which I am entrusting you. I know it is difficult and requires great intelligence and prudence. I have fixed my choice upon you after much deliberation, and you will not fail to carry it out well. Ask me for the means you think necessary for the execution of my orders. I will furnish them.[76]

In view of the Minister's confidence and earnest urging, de Kalb accepted the mission. He was given a generous amount of time to arrange his private affairs and to see to it that all needs for his voyage were supplied. Already on May 2, 1767, Choiseul sent him 1200 pounds for traveling expenses and payments to be made in connection with his mission; his passport; letters of recommendation to the French ambassadors in Holland and in Brussels; with instructions to forward all despatches through their hands, enclosing in a second envelope all letters intended especially for the Duke; finally, notification regarding the method of his payments.

De Kalb left for Holland early in June, and visited all the coastal cities in search of information regarding the dissensions in America. On July 18 he sent his first report, dated from the Hague.

> To inform myself of all the occurrences in the American colonies, I have now visited all the seaports of Holland, without being able to come to any definite conclusions as to the state of affairs in that quarter. The English give out that hostilities are entirely at an end, in consequence of the repeal of the Stamp Act and other obnoxious measures; but this may well be said for effect, to conceal the *actual* condition of things. Two or three days ago I conversed with a German who has been settled in Pennsylvania these fifteen years, and who is now recruiting French colonists. By his account, agitation is so far from being allayed that but a very trifling provocation would suffice to drive the malcontents into open revolt. The provincial assembly, he says, have resolved to maintain their privileges at any cost; and twenty thousand English troops, widely scattered over the country, could

hardly cope with the forces at the disposal of the colonists, which number four hundred thousand militia, and could easily be increased. The Germans of this and the neighboring provinces alone – continues my informant – independently of the numerous Irishmen living there, can raise sixty thousand men, nor is there any lack of means for the defense of the liberties of the country. As to other resources for the successful combat of the war, this man could give me no information. Indeed, I am only repeating his assertions without being convinced of their truth.

I therefore await your commands, Monsignor, to betake myself to Philadelphia or to some other point in the colonies, and report to you in reference to all the heads specified in my letter of instructions. It should be observed that the English colonies, or rather the mercantile companies which have large interests there, continue to solicit colonists in Germany, in public and in secret, as before. I have seen twelve hundred of these emigrants at Rotterdam, traveling from Cologne by way of Maestricht and Herzogenbusch, as they were cut off from the Rhine because the King of Prussia has forbidden them to pass through his dominions. These people have been shipped in four vessels, two of which have set sail, while the remainder are only waiting for luggage.

Soon after this letter was sent, news arrived that told of the withdrawal of the Stamp Act and other concessions of Great Britain which led to more peaceful feelings on the part of the colonists, and thus seemed to do away with, or at least to postpone their aspirations for independence. In a letter of August 11, 1767, de Kalb told the Duke that in his opinion, the calm would not last long, as the colonists would only wait for a more favorable time to gain their freedom from England. He regarded a further stay in Holland as useless, and asked for further orders. If he was to undertake the journey to America, and the time, in view of the momentary calm, was indifferent to Choiseul, he would prefer to wait until spring to have months of favorable weather ahead of him for travel and for gathering information.

Choiseul was constantly occupied with plans of a war of revenge on England, so that even if hostilities in America seemed remote, he nevertheless wished to know about the situation in the colonies, because in case of a European war France might want to start a diversion across the Atlantic. He therefore replied from Compiègne on August 19, 1767:

As it is possible, and even probable that this quiet will not be of long duration, it is the will of His Majesty that you should make immediate preparations for a speedy tour to America, in order to satisfy yourself by personal inspection as to the condition of the country, its harbors, ships and forces, resources, weapons, munitions of war, and provisions – in short, as to the means at our command, if disposed, in case of a war with England, to make a diversion in that direction. You will adopt the greatest precautions in sending me your report, and will, immediately upon your arrival, inform me where to direct such letters as I shall have occasion to write to you.

In compliance with this order, de Kalb left The Hague for London. On October 1, 1767, he wrote to Choiseul:

I arrived here after a short, though stormy passage. The packet boat from Falmouth to New York does not leave, as I was told in Holland, on the first but on the second Saturday of every month, so that I could not go by that line before the 10th of October. I prefer, therefore, to take the merchantman "Hercules", Captain Hommet, which sets sail from Gravesend tomorrow for Philadelphia. I shall report as soon as I can do so with any security. Be so good, Monsignor, as to send your commands and answers in the same (my) cypher to Mme. de Kalb; she will forward them to me in pursuance of directions already given and still to be given. It is hoped that these letters will be less likely to arouse the suspicion and curiosity of the various correspondents and agents of whose services I must necessarily avail myself. In conclusion, Monsignor, I would recall to your mind the promises kindly made to me on my departure from France, beseeching you to be a father and protector to my wife and children if it should be written in the book of fate that the journey on which I am setting out should lead directly to my final resting place.

It came very near to being the last voyage of his life, for the passage on the "Hercules" was unbelievably long and miserable. Columbus required for his first voyage to the New World, August 3 to October 12, seventy days. De Kalb sailed on October 4 and arrived about January 12, after one hundred days of contrary winds and stormy weather. In a letter dated January 15, 1768, he informs Choiseul that he had arrived a few days previously and mentions some details of the trip. The food became spoiled and the water very low, so that passengers were happy to receive four pounds of mouldy biscuit each week and a bottle of stinking water daily. He refrains from further description of the voyage, but nevertheless applauds his choice of the merchant vessel, for the packet boat had not yet arrived in New York, and was generally believed to be lost at sea. With this remark he concludes his personal notes and turns to the business of his undertaking.

In concluding this chapter, it may be of interest to cite some comments on de Kalb by the publicist Robert Walsh, who served as consul general in Paris in the eighteen-forties, and who was the first American to have a *salon* in Paris. He came in contact with descendants of de Kalb, who allowed him to see some of the family papers. On coming across a copy of Choiseul's instructions to the general, he was so struck by the *carte blanche*, that he called it to the attention of Congress with the following comment:

> The family papers comprise a copy of the instructions of the French Government to Baron de Kalb, when before our declared rupture with the mother-country, in the year 1767, he was commissioned to visit Holland for information concerning the rumors of American disaffection, and to repair to the colonies in case of ascertainment. The language of the instructions which I have before me implies perfect confidence in his sagacity, probity, judgment and general talents of knowledge. Considerable latitude is left to his discretion and his choice of measures. History tells how ably and faithfully he executed his political mission. His reports served us materially in determining the policy of France.[77]

CHAPTER V

FIRST VISIT TO AMERICA

Etienne François, Duc de Choiseul, born in 1719, had a successful army career, rising to lieutenant colonel. He married a wealthy woman, and with these qualifications, turned to diplomacy. He was a favorite of the Marquise de Pompadour, and as a skilful and wily courtier, managed to have her as an ally to the end of her life. His first diplomatic post was that of ambassador to Rome, where he pleased the Pope by the grace of his conversations. He induced the Pope to make Comte de Bernis, another favorite of Pompadour, a cardinal; at this time Bernis was minister of foreign affairs. Transferred to Vienna in 1756, Choiseul helped change French policy vis-à-vis Austria from arch-enemy to ally; this of course was very pleasing to Mme de Pompadour, who was thrilled to receive a letter from Empress Maria Theresa addressing her as "dear cousin." As a result, he became in 1758 minister of foreign affairs, in which capacity he had to sign at the dictation of the British the bitter peace treaty of Paris in 1763, concluding the Seven Years' War. With a fierce determination to get revenge, he built up the army and created a new navy. At one time, acting on a wish expressed by the Marquise, he removed from the court one of his own relatives who was having an affair with the king. He secured Corsica for the French, and expelled the Jesuits from France. Continuing the policy of friendship with Austria, he arranged the marriage of Marie Antoinette to the Dauphin, later Louis XVI. Choiseul is considered one of France's great statesmen.

After the death of Mme. de Pompadour in 1764, the king had a succession of mistresses, becoming more and more dissipated and blasé. Then there entered on the scene another remarkable woman known as the Comptesse du Barry. Born in 1746 at Vaucouleurs, she was the illegitimate child of a cook Anne Bécu, and a father whose identity has never been determined. Far from suffering from the irregularity of her life, Anne Bécu presented her little Jeanne with a younger brother, also illegitimate. Finding it difficult to support a family of three in the small provincial town, she moved to Paris, where she found a position as cook in the house of a famed demi-mondaine, a mistress of a wealthy army contractor, Billard Dumonceau. Jeanne thus grew up among servants who pampered the remarkably beautiful little girl. M. Dumonceau was also struck by the charm of the child, and was moved to pay for her education in a convent school, which she attended until the age of fifteen. She then found employment in a dress shop where her good looks and gay temperament attracted Jean, Comte du Barry, who had the nickname "Roué." Certainly this once wealthy nobleman deserved the title, his occupation being to find attractive girls for wealthy patrons. His highest ambition was the extremely rewarding coup of creating one of his women the official mistress of the king. For four years Jeanne Bécu lived with the Comte du Barry, going by the name of Comptesse du Barry, and did not object to being lent out by her procurer; this earned for her the name of "du Barry's milk cow." In the house of du Barry great hospitality was displayed, and men of nobility and letters consorted there. The du Barry learned the ways of the world there, so that with her great naturalness she found herself at ease in any company. When the proper moment seemed to have arrived, the Comte du Barry decided to give this beautiful, vivacious girl to the king, a plan in which he was aided by Louis's valet, Lebel, and the Duc de Richelieu. The king was highly pleased with this gay young woman of twenty-three, whose merry laughter dispelled the ennui and morbid gloom of the unhappy monarch. Asked what was the secret that attracted him to the daughter of a cook, Louis replied, "Only the secret of making me forget that I shall soon be sixty."

The king decided to present Jeanne to the court as his official mistress, even though various difficulties stood in the way. For one thing, she had to have a name of nobility. Jean du Barry had a genuine title, but unfortunately he was married, though he had not seen his wife for years. The penalty for bigamy in France at the time was hanging! He had a brother, however, a bachelor and retired naval officer living in the provinces, who was persuaded by the payment of a large sum of money to come to Paris and go through the marriage ritual of the Catholic church, immediately afterward returning to his provincial home, where with his newly gained riches he played the *grand seigneur*. After the formalities had been fulfilled, the beautiful Mme. du Barry was ceremoniously presented to the court on January 25, 1769, as the King's official mistress. Court society, to whom the past of this companion of the king's debauches was well known, was greatly shocked.

The cook's daughter, meantime, had become a person of great elegance, with striking black eyebrows, hair in natural curls, aquiline nose, large eyes kept half closed, a pale rose complexion, and seeminly possessing in every way a gay naturalness. To the king, she came as a great novelty. Prostitution, it has been said by a tolerant Frenchman, is a profession like any other, and the du Barry had served her apprenticeship in its skills. She managed to arouse in the old roué youthful passion once more. Then too, the king had always before under all conditions been treated by his mistresses with great respect, but this young thing treated him like a valet and called him "la France." Louis was deeply in love with this frivolous girl, never in the least wicked or political-minded – though she did use her influence to defend herself against attacks from Choiseul's party. It was she for whom the king called in his agony on his deathbed in 1774. He even took steps for her safety after his demise.

But Choiseul was shocked. He felt this was going too far; a former prostitute in the position held with such distinction by Mme. de Pompadour. There had been many women in the Deer Park – but that had all been in secret. Feeling that he, the great minister, had sufficient influence to drive this scandalous person from the court, he rebuked the king for his ignoble choice, and made him blush. But here the all-powerful minister had underestimated the power of a woman. On December 24, 1770, he received a letter from the King dismissing him from his office and exiling him to his estate.[78]

Choiseul, in his fourteen years as minister, had done great things for France, and had planned to do even more. What this statesman in 1767 hoped and expected was a war of revenge against England, with a revolutionary spirit in the American colonies that would permit France to strike at her traditional enemy by creating a diversion across the Atlantic. In order to gain definite information, he sought out a man of experience and judgment who was to investigate personally the general situation in America, its harbors, ships, troops and weapons, munitions, provisions – in short, everything that a French ruler could count on in case he decided to attack the British in the North American colonies. He wanted to be informed also on the personalties of the prospective leaders who might cooperate with French forces, and of course on the number and position of British troops in America. This highly delicate and highly responsible mission he offered to de Kalb.

Choiseul selected de Kalb as a man ideally suited for this assignment. He was known for his zeal and his ability. He could speak both English and German; thus, he was to travel as a German colonel on business in the American colonies. Since the army of Frederick the Great was the admiration of the British military men, English officers in America would readily receive such an emissary and have no secrets from him. The same would be true of American citizens of both English and German extraction. It would be quite a different matter if a native Frenchman undertook the mission – British officers would see him as an enemy, while the average American loathed Frenchmen and considered them suitable only for the trade of tailors or barbers. Moreover, it was a fundamental belief that one Englishman – or American, could lick three Frenchmen. Their immorality was notorious, their politeness only hypocrisy.

De Kalb landed in Philadelphia on January 12, 1768. It was the time of great excitement over the Stamp Act and its repeal, the Quartering Act, and other causes of violent friction between the colonies and the government in London. De Kalb did not require much time to recover from the ghastly experience of a hundred-day voyage in a wind-tossed sailing vessel.[79] In fact, as early as January 15, 1768, he sent his first report to Choiseul. He was naturally enough biased against England because it had defeated and humiliated France, as well as robbed her of her colonial possessions; however, there runs through de Kalb's reports from first to last a great sympathy for the colonists. He is in agreement with "no taxation without representation," and admires the pluck of the colonists in standing up for their rights. Contrary to reports he had heard in Holland, England did not voluntarily repeal the Stamp Act, but was forced to do so by the refusal of all colonies, individually, to acquiesce in the measure, with the same unanimity as if they had jointly deliberated upon their line of action. Thus, despite reports by the British, the matter was far from settled.

> The most violent of the provincial assemblies are those of Boston and Philadelphia, where the commissioners of the new impost were threatened in their persons with violence. Boston has promptly renounced all commercial intercourse with London, refuses to import any more wares, and expresses determination to content itself with the domestic products and fabrics of the country. The women have decided to do without imported tea and sugar. Ever since the promulgation of the act they have been busily at work with their spinning wheels to enable them to boycott English linens; they will do without silks and other articles of luxury until their country is able to produce them.

De Kalb further reported that it was difficult to tell what the end would be, but his common sense told him how reasonable men would resolve the problem:

> All depends upon the policy of the court, which promises to be a conciliatory one, as the advantage derived by the British people from their connection with the colonies is too great to permit the government to stop short of any efforts

to preserve this invaluable magazine of raw products and this most profitable market for its manufactures.

With a certain satisfaction, he reports on the discomfort of the representatives of the English government:

> During the last outbreaks, the troops have treated the inhabitants with much greater circumspection than before, while the commanders have been most careful to avoid any cause of irritation. The commanding general, who has the power to convene the estates of each province, to preside over them, and to suppress all attempts to impair the authority of the laws, pretends to ignore all the libels and pasquils which have appeared in public, although the names of their authors are on everyone's tongue.

As regards the pet scheme and hope of Choiseul, de Kalb speaks with great frankness, without any of a courtier's suavity. The remoteness of the American population from the center of government makes them free and enterprising, but at bottom they are but little inclined to shake off the English supremacy with the aid of foreign powers. Such an alliance would appear to them to be fraught with danger to their liberties.

De Kalb writes that his plans are to make a tour through all the colonies and to engage correspondents at all important points, in order on his return to France to be kept in continued contact at all times with events in America. He asks Choiseul to send any directives he may have to Mme. de Kalb, who will be kept informed at all times as to how his mail is to be addressed. That she was chosen by de Kalb to make these important arrangements throws a pleasant light on their relationship.

The official correspondence was to be sent in code,[80] which, by the way, was a very simple one. He and his correspondent each had identical French-English dictionaries. Each word was designated by three Arabic numerals, of which the first denoted the number of the page, the second the line, and the third the particular word. Names of countries, not likely to be listed in a dictionary, were designated by letter: thus A was France, FF Pennsylvania, etc.

Five days after his first report, de Kalb wrote again, on January 20, 1768. He is very much disturbed by the news from his wife that his letters from Holland and from London had been opened before reaching Choiseul. He fears that the same thing may happen to his letters from America; in fact, it is likely they may not reach the minister at all, or only after they have been read in Downing Street. This would mean that he would be cut off from all news and directives, placing him in considerable peril. He therefore asks permission to cut short his tour of observation, returning to France at the end of April, after making arrangements with correspondents who will continue to keep him informed of developments.

Meanwhile he continues to report from Philadelphia. The English government has repealed the Stamp Act, but only after discovering that it could not be enforced; they have now taxed tea, paper and glass which the colonists import from the mother country – just a roundabout way of raising the revenues by a change of name. It is contrary to the rights of the subjects of the crown to be taxed without their consent. Evidently de Kalb felt warmly for the American cause, as he continued: "England ought to be content with the profits it derives from selling them worthless goods at high prices and purchasing necessities for a song." The report continues in a style similar to that of the account in the Declaration of Independence of King George's tyrannous acts: The Americans were prevented from working their mines; the manufacture of iron was prohibited by law as soon as the product became almost equal to that of England; the same repression was extended to other branches of industry; the colonies were deprived of their trade with the Spanish colonies; they were burdened with troops, not for defensive purposes but for those of subjugation; the expense of the construction of barracks was imposed on the provinces, which were forbidden to expand their paper money issues, while almost all the gold and silver were being sent across the ocean, causing almost daily business bankruptcies and consequent distress.

But de Kalb, critical observer that he is, adds: "In my opinion, the diminution of specie is real, but there is reason to suppose that it is hoarded on account of the disturbed state of affairs. I cannot believe the statements made in regard to the sums exported to England; it is claimed that the article of tea alone has netted three hundred thousand pounds. As soon as I can gain an insight into this matter, I shall report upon it."

De Kalb sees clearly the outcome of the current course, should it be continued: "If the country adheres to its determination to import no goods from England, the trade and credit of the mother country must inevitably fall off; its manufactures must fail, and its workingmen be deprived of their livelihoods. And if the court should undertake to cure this evil by imposing additional taxes or prohibiting the beginning of new (colonial) manufactures, sedition will follow, and the break be beyond healing."

De Kalb spent a fortnight in Philadelphia, during which time he gained an insight into the mood of the colonists, and arranged for correspondents who would inform him, and through him Choiseul, about developments in America. One of the men he met there, with whom he struck up a lasting friendship, was Dr. Frederick Phile, a German-born physician. The name, spelled frequently also Phyle, is evidently an Americanization of the German Pfeil (arrow). Since the Doctor signed himself "Phile", that form is used here.[81]

Dr. Phile had married an American, Betsy Parish, whose sister Patience was the wife of Charles Marshall, son of Christopher Marshall, the famous diarist and Revolutionary patriot, who had originally been a Quaker, but was read out of the Society because of his political stand. After retiring from business – the largest pharmacy in Philadelphia – he devoted himself to the cause of independence. He attended almost daily the meetings of the "Committee on Council and Safety" held at Philosophical Hall. John Adams spoke of him as a "fine facetious old gentleman, an excellent Whig." He was elected March 17, 1775, "manager of a company set on foot for the making of woolens, linens and cotton." He notes in his diary on Christmas day, 1777: "No company dined with us today except Dr. Phile, one of our standing family. We had a good roast turkey, plain pudding, and minced pies."

For a dozen years Dr. Phile held the post of naval officer of Philadelphia. He was also elected a member of Tammany Hall, a society still flourishing in New York, which had an unusual and interesting beginning during this period. It was a custom of Americans loyal to George III to hold an annual celebration on[82] St. George's or St. David's day. Those who disliked the English sovereign decided that they too should have a celebration and hold some kind of patriotic event. As their patron they selected Tammany, an Indian chief noted for his wisdom. With some amusement they made him a saint – St. Tammany, patron saint of republican America, with May 1st as his festival. "On that day many societies of votaries walked together in procession to a handsome rural place which they called "the wigwam," where, after a long talk, or an Indian speech had been delivered, and the calumet of peace and friendship smoked, they spent the day in festivity and mirth."

It is reported that Dr. Phile and Charles Marshall remained up until midnight to celebrate Burgoyne's surrender, and that when the British occupied Philadelphia the two men with their families moved to Lancaster. They exemplify the type of American de Kalb met and engaged as correspondents in the course of his first visit to America.

On two occasions, shortly after his arrival in Philadelphia in the summer of 1777, and after the winter at Valley Forge, de Kalb was a patient of Dr. Phile, who gave him solicitous medical care, actually twice saving de Kalb's life.

To give an idea of the close friendship that grew up between de Kalb and Phile, it will be useful to cite here a letter written by the

Doctor to Mme. de Kalb (to be sure dated a decade later than the first meeting of the two men, during de Kalb's second stay in America). There is a high regard and a genial warmth in this relationship, as well as a sharing of patriotic American political views. The letter is dated Philadelphia, November 29, 1778:[83]

> Much esteemed Dear Madam:
> I am commissioned by my good and worthy friend the Baron (as he himself is at present stationed at Fishkill, about 200 miles from this city), to write you concerning some rocks and plants which I send by this opportunity. His Excellency Monsieur Gerard, the French ambassador for the United States has been so kind as to send them along with his collection for His Most Christian Majesty; he has also given orders to his correspondent in Paris to deliver General de Kalb's share to you, which I hope he will be careful to perform. I have therefore enclosed the name and address of the ambassador's correspondent, to whom you will please apply for them. I have also enclosed an invoice of all the articles now sent. I hope they will come safe to hand, as the General is very anxious about them. I have the pleasure to inform you that the General is in very good health. I am in daily expectation of seeing him in Philadelphia. He has promised me to live with me this winter, and you may depend upon it, Madam, that I will take good care of him. I have often regretted the great distance between your family and mine as no pleasure would be greater for me than for your family and mine to have a personal acquaintance and intimacy with each other. However, it is not for us poor mortals to have every pleasure we wish in this world, else perhaps we might be apt to forget that there is another.
> I hope this will find you and your dear children all in perfect health and which, I pray God, may be continued to you till you have the happiness of embracing your most worthy and affectionate husband, and my most dear friend. Please to present a half dozen kisses for me to your lovely daughter, and my best respects to your two sons. Mrs. Phile and daughter desire to be with great esteem remembered to you all. I am, dear Madam, with greatest respect, your very humble servant and well-wisher, Fred. Phile.

Undoubtedly the views of these former Quakers turned Whigs influenced de Kalb's reports to Choiseul.

On January 25, 1768, de Kalb set out for New York, bearing introductions to some patriots. His strong constitution had survived the unbelievably long and arduous crossing of the Atlantic, but on the way from Philadelphia to New York he encountered an even more severe trial. He had left Philadelphia with three traveling companions, reaching Princeton three days later after having with considerable difficulty crossed the Delaware and Raritan rivers. Finally, on January 28, they approached the New Jersey shore opposite Staten Island, which he hoped to reach by ferry. The time was seven o'clock in the evening, the weather was very cold and the ground was covered with snow. Nevertheless, the owner of the "Blazing Star Inn," located at the ferry, and the ferryman, considered the crossing of the river not at all dangerous, since there was very little ice in the water and a favorable wind was blowing. Meanwhile another passenger had joined the original four, which, with four oarsmen, made nine men for the crossing. In addition there were four riding horses. By the time the ferry reached midstream, the wind suddenly changed into a violent squall and drove the helpless boat toward a small island about a half mile distant from the ferry. There was time only to cut down the masts, since the gale did not permit the lowering of the sails; this at least kept the boat from capsizing. The oarsmen being unable to direct the boat, the waves drove it onto a mudbank a considerable distance from the shore, where it sank with the horses and baggage. All the passengers succeeded in reaching the island by swimming or wading up to their hips in the mud and blocks of ice. On the entire island there was no house, no tree, nothing to afford protection against the cutting wind, while the ground was covered by two feet of snow. In a united effort, the travelers called at the top of their lungs for help, but in vain, since the wind was blowing from the shore directly against them. Their clothing was frozen stiff, and their boots were filled with water. An effort to advance into the island was given up, as they met with thick growths of reeds covered with frozen snow the wind whipped in their faces. It was now nine o'clock in the evening. The only course to follow was to crowd together as closely as possible and by constant movement fight against sleep.

At about eleven o'clock a young sailor overcome by the long agony fell down into the snow; his companions raised him and held him upright for some minutes, but in vain, for he was already dead. About two in the morning one of the passengers who had all along encouraged the others to keep up their spirits, rolled into the snow lifeless. In view of these two deaths, the others renewed their efforts to keep in motion, but they had seven more hours to suffer.

At nine in the morning, they were observed from the shore and rescued. The survivors and the corpses were piled on sleds and brought to the home of a certain Mr. Mersereau. De Kalb bathed his hands, feet and legs in icewater (his letter to Choiseul says for one hour); then he took some food and slept quite motionless for twelve hours. When a doctor arrived, after hearing of de Kalb's procedure he did not bother to look at him, as he was certain the man must be dead after his "silly therapy."

The others, on entering the house, crowded about a huge fire, consequently worsening the damage done them by the frost. There they sat with their eyes fixed and haggard, their mouths half-open, their faces greenish blue, utterly indifferent to their fate. After two days gangrene set in, and some lost toes, ears, and one even a leg.

Due to his self-discipline, and his strong constitution, de Kalb suffered only slight frostbite on his great toe and right hand, and was able to continue his Journey on January 31. He had lost all his luggage, including a hundred louisd'or and the key to his secret code. "I would have found myself in great embarrassment," he wrote to his wife, "had it not been for a friend whom I have found here who offered me the money I needed with the understanding that I would send him the same sum on my return home to Europe. Despite this loss I cannot be too thankful to Providence for letting me escape from this disaster with so little damage." It is not known who the New York friend was – but probably someone recommended by Dr. Phile or Mr. Marshall.

Naturally de Kalb had personal problems to settle, but he had another report ready for Choiseul by February 25, 1768. He continued use of his code, having by good luck found a copy of the same dictionary in New York. Even though he knew that Choiseul was in possession of news concerning conditions in England, he reported with obvious satisfaction rumors that the boycott increasingly carried on by the colonists was being felt by the London merchants, and that wages were falling off.

Then de Kalb turned to the crucial question, that of taxation, which he evidently had studied intelligently from the British as well as the American standpoint:

> The assembly at Boston have just resolved to remonstrate with the court against the tax, as will appear by the accompanying English documents, which I enclose in the original, in order to excite less suspicion in case the letter should be intercepted. The dissatisfaction with the impost grows out of their aversion to being taxed by the parliament, instead of by representatives of their own provinces. It would seem to me that the Court of St. James mistakes its own interests. If the King would ask the colonists for sums much larger than the proceeds of the imposts in dispute, they would be granted without any objections, provided the colonists were

left at liberty to tax themselves, and as free subjects to give their money with their own consent. During the late war they have paid enormous sums, larger ones than the king demanded, because he approached their assemblies with the same formalities he observed in calling upon Parliament for subsidies. It is a matter of surprise that the court has discarded this advantageous method, and that the people of Great Britain are ready to subvert a fundamental polity of the kingdom by taxing their fellow citizens without their consent, when they submit to the same proceeding only at the hands of their representatives in the House of Commons.

How well de Kalb understood the situation is shown by a prophecy which he made after six weeks in America:

All people here are imbued with such a spirit of independence and even license, that if all the provinces can be united under a common representation, an independent state will certainly come forth in time.

De Kalb attended constantly to what was perhaps the most difficult part of his assignment:

On my return to France I shall report the exact list of the English navy and merchant marine, as well as a summary of the entire forces of England by land and by sea. I am on the point of leaving for Boston and Halifax; my ship is weighing her anchor.

In Boston, he proceeds in the report to Choiseul on the 2nd of March, 1768.

Here in Boston I meet with the same opinions as in the provinces already visited, only expressed with greater violence and acrimony. The four provinces composing New England, Massachusetts, Connecticut, Rhode Island and New Hampshire – appear to be more firmly united among themselves, in consequence of the community of interests, than the remaining colonies. Massachusetts in particular, the most wealthy and populous, gives the impulse and the signal of independence to the rest. In spite of this relative spirit, however, they all, from the leaders down to the humblest citizen, seem to be imbued with a heartfelt love of the mother country. The inhabitants of this province are almost exclusively Englishmen or of English stock, and the liberties so long enjoyed by them have only swelled the pride and presumption peculiar to that people.

As for Choiseul's wishful thinking:

> All these circumstances go to show but too clearly that there will be no means of inducing them to accept of assistance from abroad. In fact, they are so well convinced of the justice of their cause, the clemency of the King, and of their own importance to the mother country, they have never contemplated the possibility of extreme measures.

A second letter from his wife informed de Kalb that his last letters from Holland and England had been opened in transit, which led him to fear that his letters from America had met with the same fate. The fact that he had received personal mail but not one letter from the minister, led him to believe that he had become an object of suspicion. For the delicate task he had assumed he needed frequent instructions. He therefore decided to return to France, to change his correspondents and agents in England and Holland, and to secure from friends in America safer addresses for the exchange of letters.

> In this manner I shall be in a position to protect myself and to guard my secret. The perils and hardships of the journey do not deter me, but I am very anxious to carry out my mission successfully.

From Boston de Kalb went to Halifax, where he received the same replies to his questions. He reported to Choiseul on March 7, 1768, his view that the ultimate separation of the colonies from England seemed inevitable, but that he did not believe they would ever call in a foreign power to aid in their fight for freedom. A surprise to de Kalb was the immense amount of shipping in the harbor of Halifax, comparable to the huge number of vessels he had observed in the harbors of Philadelphia, New York and Boston. Such sources of wealth, he felt, could not long remain at the disposal of a government three thousand miles distant.

The next report was written from Philadelphia on April 19, 1768, and shows that he saw at once what American statesmen learned only some years later, that the Canadians could not be counted on as allies of the French Government.

> There are at this day, he says, but few persons in those immense provinces in sympathy with France. Those most

devoted to our government have left the country since the close of the war, and those who remain are satisfied with their present government, or expect no improvement in their condition from a change in rulers. Their lands have risen in value, they pay but trifling taxes, enjoy unqualified freedom of conscience, as well as all the privileges of the English people, and take part in the management of public affairs. Besides, they have become closely allied with the inhabitants of the neighboring provinces by intermarriages and other ties. I regard it as my duty to speak candidly on all these matters, because I will not deceive you, and do not wish you to be deceived by others. In case of a war with our neighbors beyond the channel, it would be difficult, therefore, to make a diversion in this part of their possessions. I always recur to my belief that the quarrels of the English with their colonies will terminate to the satisfaction of the latter. A war with us would only hasten their reconciliation, and on the footing of restored privileges, the English court could even direct all the troops, resources and ships of this part of the world against our islands and the Spanish Main. A foreign war is less hurtful to England than internal discord, which, however, would at once yield to the necessity of defense against a common foe.

On April 24, 1768, de Kalb notified Choiseul that he was about to return to France for reasons previously given; however, he offered to return to America in case Choiseul thought a second journey would serve any purpose. This time his voyage lasted only about one month. He arrived in England June 1, 1768, and in Paris June 12. When he learned that of his numerous reports only five had reached Choiseul, he asked for an audience to give an account of his mission. Choiseul at first set a date, but then postponed the interview. De Kalb then sent a report on the English forces in the colonies. A few days later he received a reply stating that the figures were certainly too high, encouraging de Kalb, however, to send further reports. He also sent him 6,000 francs to meet the debts de Kalb had incurred in the course of his journey.

On August 6, 1768, de Kalb sent the Duke a lengthy report summarizing political, economic and military data. They were the conclusions of a factual and penetrating observer, and proved to be in agreement with the views of other men of judgment, for example Benjamin Franklin, who at that time believed that foreign intervention would cause the colonials to unite with the motherland, and who as late as 1770 believed that finally the British government would not act so unwisely as to lose her most valuable colony.

At the close of the year 1768, Choiseul became less and less interested in de Kalb's reports. He was engrossed in a plan to strengthen France in the Mediterranean by acquiring Corsica, which England also coveted. The island, nominally subject to Genoa, was at the time autocratically held but wisely ruled by the famous Corsican hero, Pasquale Paoli, the Garibaldi of the eighteenth century, who was enjoying the favor of the British. Choiseul in 1768 risked war with Great Britain by making an arrangement with Genoa to acquire the island for France. Paoli, after a brave struggle against the French forces, escaped on a British ship, to be fêted as a liberal hero in London. The reports of de Kalb had convinced Choiseul that the imminent rebellion of the American colonies was preoccupying England to such an extent that it could not risk taking action to block the French designs in Corsica. By his coup Choiseul had weakened England and partially satisfied his desire for revenge.

The success of the Corsican venture, together with plans to weaken British overseas commerce caused the minister to lose interest in reports on the situation in America coming from correspondents whom de Kalb had discreetly secured from New Bern, North Carolina, to Halifax, including, of course, Philadelphia, New York, Boston, Newport, Rhode Island, Edenton, North Carolina, and various other important points. In conformity with the famous quotation from the German dramatist Lessing, "Is there any action too mean for the great?" Choiseul treated de Kalb in a shabby fashion. To his repeated requests for the promised audience, Choiseul sent the reply that his receptions at the War Department were open to all who had anything to say to him. De Kalb went there to request an hour's interview, but Choiseul interrupted him with a flimsy pretence.[85] "You returned too soon from America, and your labors are therefore of no use to me. You do not need to send me any more reports about that country.

De Kalb of course advised his correspondents to discontinue their reports, but he wrote a forceful letter to the minister pointing out the injustice of this treatment – and de Kalb could state his case masterfully. He had left America[86] after four months, for excellent reasons, and had repeatedly offered to return there, despite the terrible hardships he had undergone. The successful completion of the difficult mission deserved recognition, and not a petty dismissal. Evidently, some months afterward Choiseul thought better of his actions, for on June 4, 1770, he promised to include de Kalb in the list of officers to be promoted to brigadier generalship. This plan, however, was not carried out because at Christmas time Choiseul was dismissed. Mme. de Pompadour had raised him to high office, and Mme. du Barry had brought about his disgrace – a vivid illustration of where the power lay in the time of Louis XV. Incidentally, the King's mistress had delayed de Kalb's rise considerably.

De Kalb's reports on the situation in America had a definite influence on French politics, in that they served to convince Choiseul that England was too much concerned and occupied with the revolutionary temper of the colonists to permit military action against the French seizure of Corsica. It turned out that England went no further than to send a protest, which France ignored. Aware that the colonies were tying England's hands, Choiseul's policy was to strengthen the insurgents secretly by every possible means, while professing publicly an absolute neutrality, lest an Anglo-French war should break out and, as de Kalb had prophesied, the colonists should side with the mother country since blood is thicker than water. Choiseul's downfall delayed the execution of this plan for revenge on England, but when, four years later, the Comte de Vergennes came to power, this policy of weakening England more and more was continued, with a triumphant climax at Yorktown.

CHAPTER VI

LAFAYETTE'S MENTOR

When, after his return from America in 1768, de Kalb was nearing the age of fifty, he bought the chateau of Milon-la-Chapelle, a handsome brick dwelling in the Mansard style, situated in spacious grounds in beautiful rolling country about three miles south of Versailles – a veritable garden spot. For several years he devoted himself to his family and to the improvement of his newly acquired estate; one of his particular interests was the planting of trees of various species, some of them imported. Congenially married, he enjoyed everything commonly regarded as essential for happiness; he lived in great comfort, sometimes in his mansion and sometimes on his country estate; his children grew up healthy, and his fortune of four hundred thousand francs made him, if not enormously rich, at least quite independent.

Peace prevailed in Europe at this time, but war was imminent on many fronts. For example, the position of Poland was becoming weaker and weaker during the years that finally led up to the so-called first division of this kingdom, arranged between Russia, Prussia and Austria in 1772. Though France had many close ties with Poland – for example, Louis XV had married a Polish princess – it was not in a position to take action to prevent the aggressions on the part of the three most powerful states in Eastern Europe. The Government did, however, send some French officers there, as well as some arms and money, to help the Polish patriots – called the Confederates – to fight against Russia. About a year and a half before the partition took place, de Kalb was called upon by the minister of foreign affairs, the Duc de Vrillières, through the minister of war, Monteynard, to join in the fight of the Confederates to save Poland,[87] an opportunity for him to give "further proofs of the zeal heretofore manifested."

De Kalb considered the offer with his usual cool prudence. He had undertaken just recently a very difficult and dangerous mission to America, in which he had acquitted himself with great success. Choiseul had promised him a well-deserved appointment as brigadier general, but the minister's fall from grace had thwarted this plan. Now he was asked to undertake another dangerous mission to fight with Polish irregulars engaged in a struggle against three of the best armies of Europe. He doubted whether the French Government was seriously interested in the struggle in Eastern Europe, especially since the terms offered him were only a vague promise of a brigadiership on his return, with the supposition that his expenses would be paid by the Polish leaders. He was told that, if taken prisoner, he was not to be acknowledged by the French Government. To test the sincerity of the Government's intentions in support of the Polish cause, de Kalb set down some reasonable terms under which a professional soldier of his standing could serve in Poland.

> I have maturely considered the proposal of the Duc de Vrillières, to serve the Polish confederation, as well as the terms offered, by which my promotion is to be postponed until after my return, and my compensation to be confined to what I may succeed in obtaining from the confederation. I pray you, therefore, Monseigneur, if you desire to make use of me, and to give me an opportunity of extending my travels and improving my knowledge of men and things, to grant me two favors: 1. The rank of a brigadier, to which my past services and my rank entitle me, so much the more as various junior officers, M. de Rozière and others, have received it. This honor would redouble my zeal and activity in the king's service; in my intercourse with the confederation it would be absolutely indispensable, as it would convince them that I enjoy the confidence of my sovereign and am entitled to be respected accordingly, and that neither necessity nor love of adventure drives me into the ranks of the patriots. 2. That you would be pleased, either in person or by the Duc de Vrillières, to fix my salary, in order that I may depend solely upon the king and not upon the confederation, who may perhaps treat me well, and perhaps ill, in which latter case, I need not, if thus provided for, resort to the painful expedient of quitting their service.
> A point of no less importance – is that I am not to be acknowledged by the king in case of an unforeseen reverse. I pass this over in silence, because His Majesty may have reasons for this policy, to which I gladly defer; but it should be an additional inducement to grant me the two requests above mentioned, as at least some little equivalent for the risk incurred of the probable consequences of a refusal to acknowledge me.
> Last year M. de Valeroissant was sent to the Turkish army as a brigadier, a rank certainly less his due than it would be mine, if services and seniority were considered. Besides, he

received pay to the amount of thirty housand livres *per annum*. One-fifth or one-sixth of that sum would content me when once appointed brigadier, because I do not serve to enrich myself, but to advance and to deserve the favor of my king and his ministers.

When the minister's bluff was thus called, he declined to consider de Kalb's offer, showing that the Foreign Office did not care to risk anything for Poland. As to being disavowed by the French King, even that risk de Kalb had been willing to take if the ministry had been sincerely behind the offer. All was quite different from the occasion when the great Choiseul pleaded personally with de Kalb to undertake the American mission and added: "Ask me the means which you think necessary for its execution; I will furnish you with them all."

The exile of the de Broglies through the intrigues of Mme de Pompadour and the replacement of the Duke in control of the army by the Marquise's favorite, the incapable Soubise, was an unpopular move. Hence, when in 1764 the death of Pompadour was imminent, the brothers were recalled. Their friendly relations with de Kalb continued, as the Count in particular remained in close touch with him as patron and friend; from now on, however, the Count was asking rather than according favors.

Though the Count had a good war record – he had distinguished himself, for example, at the defense of Kassel – he is more noted for his intrigues and his peculiar relation to the king. Strange as it may seem at the present day, Louis XV had in addition to his regular ministers, agents who reported directly to him,[88] giving him their advice; this secret ministry the king had entrusted to the Comte de Broglie. Louis allowed his regular minister to issue official orders, while also, on the orders of the king, the Comte de Broglie gave out directly opposite ones. Embarrassments naturally ensued for the king, who extricated himself from his difficulty by banishing the Count, but in a second letter asking him to continue the correspondence. This correspondence, secret and contradictory, mostly in the interest of Poland, but continuing also the details about the plan for the invasion of England, was published by a great-grandson of the Maréchal de Broglie as *The King's Secret, Being the Secret Correspondence of Louis XV with his Diplomatic Agents, 1752 to 1774, Paris, 1879.*

One intrigue in which the Count engaged was a result of the king's desire for revenge on Britain: the preparation, with the help of M. de la Rozière, of a plan for the invasion of England and a crushing treaty dictated in London.

At this point, the Chevalier d'Eon, probably the most bizarre character[89] in all diplomatic history, enters the story, to ruin completely de Broglie's invasion plan. This political adventurer had been sent by Louis XV in 1755 on a secret mission to Russia. Here, "la Chevalière d'Eon," as he became known facetiously, adopted woman's dress and actually succeeded in worming his way into intimate court circles, becoming reader to the Empress Elizabeth! The truth of the tale is denied, but if true it would be characteristic. Some time later he was again sent to Russia, this time as secretary of the embassy. On this occasion he appeared as a man, the brother of his other self – everyone remarking on his resemblance to his sister. At the outbreak of the Seven Years' War he gave up his diplomatic career to enter the army, serving with distinction under the Broglies. During this service he was wounded. In 1762 he was sent to England as secretary of the embassy. In England, betting on his or her sex became quite the rage – much later, in 1810, a post mortem established that it was male.

When the Count's plan was finished, he submitted it to Louis XV. The lethargic king, willing to take credit for such an adventure if it succeeded, but equally determined to wash his hands of it if it failed, endorsed upon it his written approval, but refused to take any action to carry it out. When some information about a possible invasion from the mainland leaked out, the British with their usual low boiling point when reminded of 1066, were in high dudgeon at French treachery, just after the king and his ministers had signed a treaty of peace! Somehow the plan, detailing harbors, roads, army installations, and other related items, got into the hands of the secretary of the French embassy in London – the Chevalier d'Eon. This cool scoundrel, at a safe distance from the jurisdiction of France, demanded enormous sums from the king for the return of the dangerous document, threatening to make known the extremely embarrassing contents of the papers entrusted to him unless he were paid. Negotiations with the blackmailer continued for years successively through two ambassadors to Britain whom d'Eon treated with great insolence. Louis XV then decided to send to England one of his secret agents, the widely experienced Durand; accordingly, on July 11, 1766, a memorable interview took place. This time d'Eon acceded. He went down into the cellar of his house, and returned with a musty-looking brick which proved to be hollowed out to contain the document, carefully preserved against the damp by heavy folds of parchment.[90]

Shortly after this transaction, d'Eon received a letter from the king, stating that in appreciation of his diplomatic services in Russia, and his distinction in the army, he was according him an annual salary of 12,000 pounds to be paid every three months in whatever country he might be living, except in time of war with the enemy. After some years d'Eon secured permission to return to France with the proviso that he appear only in women's clothes. The distinguished scholar and keen fencer had to comply with this bitter condition, humiliating and annoying as it was to a lover of hunting and riding. The unhappy man's petitions for permission to appear in male garb were never granted.

The miscarriage of the invasion plan and the blackmailing of the king occasioned a distressing loss of face for the Comte de Broglie. Under Louis XVI, who came to the throne in 1774, many distressing matters were forgotten, including de Broglie's sins. The new king appointed him military commander-in-chief at Metz. In compliance with a rule requiring retired staff officers to do garrison duty from time to time, de Kalb spent four months at Metz during the summer of 1775, in close association with his old comrade at arms. Broglie was very much interested in events in the American colonies. In his conversations with de Kalb, it became apparent that the latter felt a great attachment to the "insurgents" fighting for what he considered a just cause. He had in fact kept up a correspondence with some of the American friends he had made in the course of his travels seven years previously, so that he was somewhat familiar with developments in the colonies. For example, he still kept in touch with Dr. Phile of Philadelphia.

The Count was so favorably impressed with de Kalb's efficiency that on November 13, 1775, in a letter to the newly appointed minister of war, Comte St. Germain, he recommended him for return to active service in the army as an officer whose great talents should be retained. St. Germain's career as a professional soldier was typical of the period. He had begun his military career as a lieutenant in the French army, but due to an unfortunate duel, was obliged to leave France to serve in the armies of the Palatinate, of Austria, and of Bavaria. Through the influence of the Maréchal de Saxe, he reentered the French army as lieutenant general, serving with distinction in Flanders, and later in the Seven Years' War at the battle of Rossbach. He evidently sympathized with de Kalb's desire for active duty.

On December 10, St. Germain replied, expressing his regret that at the moment there was no vacancy in the grade suitable for de Kalb, but added a postscript in his own hand: "When you return here, M. le Comte, we shall see what disposition may be made of M. de Kalb."[91] Since at this time America was once more attracting much attention on the part of the French Government, it was obvious what the note implied. When de Broglie came to the capital he eagerly endorsed St. Germain's plan to send de Kalb overseas to place his experience and military skill at the disposal of the American colonies. This is the understanding Silas Deane, the recently arrived American agent in Paris had concerning de Kalb's decision to fight with the colonists. Thus he wrote to Congress November 7, 1776: "The Baron de Kalb being advised by some generals of the highest reputation and by several other noblemen of the first rank in this realm to serve the cause of liberty in America, accordingly offers his services to most honorable Congress on the following terms, ...," etc., etc.

St. Germain summoned de Kalb for an interview which resulted in his being returned to the army, with a two years' furlough "to go abroad in order to look after his personal business" in the cautious phrasing of the document. On November 6, 1776, he was given the grade of brigadier general for the islands. His resolve to go to America was undoubtedly impelled by a number of motives, such as his desire for distinction in his profession, his love of adventure, and the quest for glory on the battlefield, as well as a chance to do a favor to his patron and friend, the Comte de Broglie. There was, by no means last, the motive of his great sympathy with the American cause, acquired during his visit to the colonies. There are many expressions of this feeling in his letters, most definite in one written to his old friend in Philadelphia, Dr. Frederic Phile, dated December 26, 1775, at the very time when de Broglie and St. Germain were discussing de Kalb's new mission. The letter, partly in English and partly in German, reads:[92]

> I am in great distress about your and your family's health and welfare, not having received any news of you since my letter to you of the first of January 1774; whether it was lost by these troublesome times or some other reasons that hindered me from getting an answer I cannot guess. Whatever may be the cause of it, I should gladly hear from you and be as gladly apprised of a good harmony restored between the Colonies and the Mother Country. I hardly can believe that the English ministry will pursue the rash and unjust measures and push the colonies to violent extremities to preserve their natural and constitutional liberties.
>
> [I am to such a degree a friend of your country that if the war between England and her colonies in America should continue I could with pleasure devote the rest of my days in the service of your liberty and to the utmost of my ability employ my thirty-two years' experience acquired in the military art for your advantage. If I might suppose that I could be of service in the American army and receive a call from their Congress, pray tell me, my sincere friend, whether I may offer such a proposal to the Congress, and give me, if possible, a full answer to this point.]

If I did not write to you again before this time, a long journey to Germany, which I just now ended, to see my sons in the Palatinate, hindered me from pleasing myself on that point, for I look on it as a great pleasure to me to entertain myself with so dear a friend as yourself – if all commerce, correspondence and communication with England is not interrupted, you may direct for me under the cover to Henry Keall, No. 121 Fenchurch Street, London.

I am forever, Dear Sir, Your most obedient humble Servant, de Kalb.

The material in brackets is a translation of the German part of the letter, made for the benefit of Congress; the German original follows:

Ich bin ein solcher Freund von Ihrem Land, dass wenn der Krieg zwischen Engelland und ihren Pflanzstädten in der neuen Welt fortdauern solte, so wolte ich mit Vergnügen meine noch übrigen Jahre zum Dienst Ihrer Freiheit aufopfern und meine 32.jährige Erfahrung in der Kriegskunst zu Ihrem besten und nach aller meiner Tüchtigkeiten anwenden, wenn ich glaubte, dass ich bey dem amerikanischen Kriegsheer könnte nützlich sein, und bey Ihrer Hauptversammlung dazu berufen würde. Sagen Sie mir als mein wahrer und guter Freund, ob ich der Versammlung einen solchen Vorschlag kan machen lassen. Was mich auch Theils dazu verleitet ist das grosse Verlangen, das ich habe, Sie mein werther Freund, noch einmal zu sehen. Geben Sie mir, wenn es möglich ist, eine ausführliche Antwort.

To anticipate a bit, Dr. Phile gave the letter to Robert Morris, who sent it to John Hancock, the president of Congress, with a recommendation. It was read before this body on March 13, 1777. Congress voted to extend thanks to the Baron de Kalb for his offer to serve, but it was not acceptable, – "not at present." The date was almost to a day the time de Kalb and Lafayette left Paris together for Bordeaux and America.[93]

Not only France but Spain also was eager to strike at England by supplying the "insurgents" with shipments of arms; King Charles of Spain sent a million francs for the common cause. In order to further this trade, Congress in July 1776, sent a businessman and member of Congress, Silas Deane from Connecticut, to Paris as its representative. He was given rather vague instructions "to transact such business, 'commercial and political' as would benefit the thirteen united colonies." In the course of only a few months he managed to send to America the whole of the artillery, tents, arms and other stores for the campaign of 1777. From several persons, e.g. Arthur Lee and Beaumarchais, the suggestion came to Deane of engaging some experienced French officers who could be of great assistance to the "embattled farmers."[94]

Naturally, de Kalb decided to make Deane's acquaintance. The introduction was made on November 5, 1776, by the Comte de Broglie, who had personal reasons, as will appear later, for furthering de Kalb's departure for America. Deane was evidently deeply impressed by de Kalb's personality, as well as by the honor of *two* calls by the Count. He felt that engaging the services of so distinguished an officer as de Kalb was in conformity with his instructions – it was an opportunity he should not let slip – De Kalb had been in America and had developed a distinct sympathy for the American cause; very important, he also spoke English. He was a lieutenant colonel with thirty years' experience in the French army, and early in November had been promoted to brigadier general for the colonies, and granted two years' leave from the army. This man was offering his services to the American colonies.[95]

Deane reported to the Congress in a letter the following day that many French officers had applied for service in the American forces, but that he was so much impressed with the qualifications of the Baron de Kalb that he engaged him even though he had not been specifically empowered by Congress to appoint officers.

> The rage, as I may say, for entering into the American service increases, and the consequence is that I am pressed with offers and proposals, many of them from persons of the first rank and eminence, in the sea as well as land service. Count Broglie, who commanded the army of France during the last war, did me the honor to call on me twice yesterday with an officer who served as his quartermaster general in the last war, and has now a regiment in this service, but being a German – the Baron de Kalb – and having traveled through America a few years since, he is desirous of engaging in the service of the United States of North America. I can by no means let slip an opportunity of engaging a person of so much experience, and who is by everyone recommended as one of the bravest and most skilful officers in the kingdom; yet I am distressed on every such occasion for want of *your* particular instructions. This gentleman has an independent fortune, and a certain prospect of advancement here; but being a zealous friend to liberty, civil and religious, he is actuated by the most independent and generous principles in the offer he makes of his services to the States of America.

Deane accordingly engaged de Kalb as major general,[96] his appointment to date from November 7, 1776. Broglie and de Kalb made selections from among officers willing to go to America, and on December 1, 1776, de Kalb signed a formal contract with Deane for himself and fifteen companions. To find professional soldiers at that time was not difficult. The generation before the revolution of 1789 had read eagerly in Voltaire, Rousseau and Diderot about liberty and natural rights. There were so many young officers eager to see France go to war for the "insurgents," and they were so open about their radical views, that the Government forbade discussion of the American war in the coffee houses lest France appear to violate neutrality vis-à-vis England. In contrast to the idealists, there were of course professional soldiers intent on advancing in their calling by gaining honor, there were mercenaries willing to sell their blood to the highest bidder, and of course many who had simply drifted into service in the army as a way of making a living. To the greater part of these men peace was a misfortune. When regiments were disbanded or cut down, the officers lost their means of livelihood. They frequented the coffee houses of Paris, became hangers-on in the capitals of the petty German states, or lived by their wits, gambling in watering places. A fine specimen of the latter type is Ricaut de la Marlinière, a *capitaine réformé* in Lessing's comedy *Minna von Barnhelm* who cheats at cards, but resents the word "cheating;" his term for it is *"corriger la fortune."* While many such men of dubious value had already arrived in the States (as well as in Deane's office) unsolicited, Congress had definitely requested Deane to select and enlist four engineers. These specialists, so necessary to an army of backwoodsmen, proved very valuable: Duportail, Lannoy, Radière, and Gouvion earned high praise from Washington.

In conference with Deane it was agreed that de Kalb should select a suitable number of officers who were to be given appointments by Deane according to their merits. Deane arranged for a vessel to convey them from Havre to America, the sailing date to be December 14, 1776. De Kalb's selection by the French ministry to fight against the British in America was in conformity with the Government's policy to harm the British as much as possible without laying itself open to the charge of breach of neutrality. Louis XVI, for example, ordered the French fleet to protect New England commerce, but to stay neutral![97] In 1776 a Colonel Du Coudray was employed by the French Government to check in the garrisons of France the amount of arms on hand that could be sent to the United States, under the pretext, of course, that they were destined for Santo Domingo and other French colonies; he selected 200 four-pound pieces with 100,000 balls, 30,000 small arms with ammunition, and 4,000 tents. Beaumarchais, best known as the author of witty comedies, and hence referred to by diplomats of the day as "the Barber of Seville," was sending guns, ammunition and uniforms to America through a fictitious commercial firm, Hortalez & Co.

At this point it might be well to return to Metz, in the summer of 1775, where an event of great significance occurred. The Duke of Gloucester, the brother of King George III, was making a tour of the Continent; on his way to Italy he stopped at Metz, where the garrison commander, Comte de Broglie, gave a dinner in his honor. For personal reasons Gloucester disliked his brother cordially, and was quite frank in differing with him concerning his policy toward the American colonists. With evident satisfaction he told of American successes, finding eager listeners around the table, as Lafayette recalled in 1828, fifty-three years later, for the benefit of the American historian Jared Sparks. (Lafayette gave the date, incorrectly, as 1776, narrating the events in the third person.)[98]

> Lafayette was but eighteen years old when he first conceived the project of joining the Americans, and risking his fortune and reputation in their cause. In the summer of 1776 he was stationed on military duty at Metz, being then an officer in the French army. It happened at this time, that the Duke of Gloucester, brother to the King of England, was at Metz and a dinner was given to him by the commandant of that place. Several of the principal officers were invited, and among others Lafayette. Despatches had just been received by the Duke from England, and he made their contents the topic of conversation. They related to American affairs, the recent declaration of independence, and the strong measures adopted by the ministry to crush the rebellion.
>
> The details were new to Lafayette. He listened with eagerness to the conversation, and prolonged it by asking questions of the Duke. His curiosity was deeply excited by what he heard, and the idea of a people fighting for liberty had a strong influence upon his imagination. The cause seemed to him just and noble, from the representations of the Duke himself; and before he left the table the thought came into his head that he would go to America and offer his services to a people who were struggling for freedom and independence. From that hour he could think of nothing but his chivalrous purpose. He resolved to return to Paris and make further inquiries.

When he arrived in that city, he confided his scheme to two young friends, Count Ségur and Viscount de Noailles, and proposed that they should join him. They entered with enthusiasm into his views; but, as they were dependent on their families, it was necessary to consult their parents, who reprobated the plan and refused their consent. The young men faithfully kept Lafayette's secret. His situation was more fortunate, as his property was at his own disposal, and he possessed an annual revenue of nearly two hundred thousand livres.

He next explained his intention to his relative the Count de Broglie, who told him that his project was so chimerical and fraught with so many hazards, without a prospect of the least advantage, that he could not for a moment regard it with favor, nor encourage him with any advice which should prevent him from abandoning it immediately. When Lafayette found him thus determined, he requested that at least he would not betray him, for he was resolved to go to America. The Count de Broglie assured him that his confidence was not misplaced, "but," said he, "I have seen your uncle die in the wars of Italy, I witnessed your father's death at the battle of Minden, and I will not be an accessory to the ruin of the only remaining branch of the family." He then used all his powers of argument and persuasion to divert Lafayette from his purpose, but in vain. Finding his determination unalterable, the Count de Broglie said, as he could render him no aid, he would introduce him to the Baron de Kalb, who he knew was seeking an opportunity to go to America, and whose experience and counsels might be valuable.

Accordingly, on December 7, 1776, de Kalb introduced to Deane a youth of the highest nobility and of enormous wealth, who desired to serve in the troops of the United States because he believed in the justice of their cause. However, he could not obtain the consent of his family unless he went as a general officer; their high position required that. This he stated emphatically.

Deane hesitated; – after all, the total military service this lad had experienced was one summer's manoeuvres; he had never been under fire. However, in consideration of the young man's enthusiasm, and de Kalb's recommendations while serving as interpreter, Deane finally decided as follows:[99]

> His high birth, his alliances, the great dignities which his family possessed in court, his considerable possessions in this

BARON DE KALB INTRODUCING LAFAYETTE
TO SILAS DEANE

> kingdom, his personal merit, his reputation, his disinterestedness, and above all his zeal for the liberty of our provinces, have alone had power to influence me to make him the promise of the rank of Major General in the name of the said United States.

Lafayette added to this his signature:

> On above conditions I offer myself and promise to set forth when and as Mr. Deane shall judge suitable in order to serve said states with all the zeal possible without any allowance or special salary, reserving to myself only the liberty to return to Europe whenever my family or my king shall recall me.

For Deane and de Kalb this transaction meant a diplomatic stroke of great significance, assuring the colonies an excellent general, distinguished from Brandywine to Yorktown, and also a romantic hero. The famous phrase spoken on July 4, 1917: at Lafayette's tomb in Paris, "Lafayette, we are here!" implies that the doughboys of World War I were returning France's aid of 1776. In each case, foreign aid proved to be the turning point of the war. Of course, none of them could know December 7, 1776, would loom in history; surely, in Emerson's phrase, they builded better than they knew.

Lafayette in his memoirs says, à propos this meeting, "I became de Kalb's friend." His appointment signified to him the fulfillment of an ardent wish cherished for more than a year.

A great deal of the drive that went into Lafayette's firm resolution must have come from the attitude of his father-in-law, the Duc d'Ayen. He seemed not absolutely opposed to the desire of his other son-in-law, the Viscount de Noailles, to fight with the Americans, for this latter young nobleman was vigorous and romantically dashing and had already applied to the prime minister Maurepas for permission to go overseas. But Lafayette, by contrast, is described by his friend Theodore de Lameth as "pale, frail, with little energy and giving not the slightest indication of the noise he would one day create." When one day the two young men pleaded with the Duke to use his influence to secure them permission,[100] he said, "It is well enough for the Viscount de Noailles to go abroad, for he is strong, eager, and can undertake everything with decision, "but (to Lafayette) what are you going to do there?" When Lafayette told his paternal friend, de Broglie, about this humiliation and his own adament resolve, de Broglie said "Get even with them! Be the first to go to America. I shall arrange matters for you."[101]

The introduction having been made and de Kalb given to understand that Lafayette had overcome family objections to his plan, the two men saw each other practically every day in November, 1776.[102] With all this planning going on, it is not surprising that the English ambassador, Lord Stormond, was informed by his spies that a prominent and experienced officer was about to be sent to America with the connivance of the French Government. His report to the British minister, Lord Weymouth, despite some distortions of fact and some wrong spellings, contains enough accurate information to indicate the justified suspicions of the British Government concerning French neutrality.

> I am credibly informed, a Mons. Colbé, a Swiss officer formerly in this service, who married a daughter of the famous van Robais, was sent to Fontainebleau and stayed there some days. It was proposed to him that if he would go to St. Domingo and from there to North America, he should have the rank of brigadier, and nine or ten thousand livres a year during the time of his being employed. These conditions he accepted after some hesitation, and set out from hence on Monday last. He is accompanied by a Mons. Holtzendorff, a Prussian by birth, who was likewise engaged by this court, and has the rank of lieutenant colonel given him, with six thousand livres a year. He is not thought to be an officer of any distinction, but M. Colbé is, I am told, a man of ability. He was sent to North America during the ministry of M. de Choiseul, who gave him the "ordre de merite."[103]

It had been arranged with Deane that the group was to sail on December 14, 1776, from Havre on "La Seine." Thus de Kalb had to leave for the port on December 8. Lafayette was to be one of the group but found himself detained by his father-in-law the Duc d'Ayen. Disobeying the Duke was nothing to be taken lightly, for a man commanding his influence at court could have a rebellious son-in-law restrained or even arrested on a *lettre de cachet* (arbitrary warrant.) At parting from de Kalb the unhappy, but firmly determined lad said, "Au revoir in America!"[104]

As things turned out, they were going to see America together. Lord Stormond protested so vehemently against France's flagrant breach of neutrality that the French government found it expedient to forbid the departure of "La Seine."

A page from Lafayette's *Memoires* is interesting in connection with this episode:

> When I presented to Mr. Deane my boyish face (for I was

scarcely nineteen years of age) I spoke more of my ardour in the cause than of my experience: but I dwelt much more upon the effect my departure would excite in France and he signed our mutual agreement. The secrecy with which this negotiation and my preparation were made appears almost a miracle; family, friends, ministers, French spies and English spies, all were kept completely in the dark as to my intentions.[105]

It has been remarked at times, with mild amusement, that citizens of a democracy can wax quite enthusiastic over high nobility. The Connecticut merchant, Mr. Silas Deane, was evidently impressed by Lafayette's blue blood, as was later also Congress, even while engaged in fighting to overthrow royalty. As it turned out, there was great éclat as a result of Lafayette's romantic departure and the favorable public opinion concerning it no doubt played a considerable part in bringing about French recognition of the "United Colonies" on March 13, 1778. However, Lafayette's two close friends, the Vicomte de Noailles and the Comte de Ségur, who had been most enthusiastic for the American adventure, gave up their plans for service in America. Lafayette proved to be the only representative of the high nobility who fought under Washington before France entered the war. But Lafayette's espousal of the cause, with all his youthful enthusiasm, was enough. De Kalb's understanding guidance of the lad's rather vague ideals into the practical political and military course which he followed is a master stroke of quiet diplomacy for which America should be ever grateful. The question as to whether de Kalb brought Lafayette to America or vice versa is an idle one. Both were eager to fight with the "insurgents," and both were equally determined; either would have come independently. That the young man of nineteen and the experienced soldier of 56, the Frenchman of highest nobility and the German of humble origin, worked so well together is certainly a tribute to both.

Meanwhile at Havre, the officers prevented by the French government from departing for America, found themselves at loose ends, and scattered in various directions. Accepting the sharp disappointment calmly, and resolved to try again, de Kalb returned to Paris.

CHAPTER VII

THE BROGLIE INTRIGUE

The dinner given by the Comte de Broglie at Metz in the summer of 1775 in honor of the Duke of Gloucester, as Lafayette tells us, aroused his interest in the fight for freedom of the American colonies. It is also probable that Gloucester's account of the valiant struggle of the American farmers against British regulars gave de Broglie likewise the idea of planning for his own participation in that war – though for very different reasons from those of Lafayette. He wished to become generalissimo of the American forces, and with extreme secrecy plotted to attain that objective.

The records of the "Broglie Intrigue," as this feeble plot, contemporary with the "Conway Cabal" has come to be called, are rather meager. They will be given here in full, with some comments and background. These schemes had two things in common; 1. An aim to supersede Washington; 2. A very rapid and harmless collapse.

The idea of engaging some experienced French officers to train and lead American soldiers developed naturally enough, as France was sending guns, ammunition, uniforms, tents and other supplies to further the cause of the "insurgents" as well as to weaken the archenemy, England. Beaumarchais, on July 26, 1776, in a letter to Deane, reports on the shipment of weapons, and then urges Deane to adopt Arthur Lee's plan "of sending engineers and officers – particularly, it would seem, officers of artillery."[106] Similarly, it occurred to de Broglie that a formidable supreme commander could prove very helpful.[107] In view of his long experience in the Seven Years' War he decided that he, the Comte de Broglie, would be the best suited to lead America to victory. Of course, everything would have to be kept strictly secret; this is very understandable since, through d'Éon's incredible blackmail, de Broglie's plan for the invasion of England had caused him to burn his fingers badly; hence he was looking for some exploit by which he might redeem himself and at the same time secure considerable riches.

The idea that an experienced European general could prove of value to the colonists has nothing surprising about it. Arthur Lee, agent in London for Massachusetts, wrote on February 13, 1776:

> A general of the first ability and experience would go over if he could have any assurance from Congress of keeping his rank; but that being very high, he would not submit to have any but an American as his superior, and that only in consideration of the confidence due an American in a question so peculiarly American.[108]

The writer mentions no name, but it is quite likely that he had de Broglie in mind. On November 5, de Broglie called on Deane to introduce de Kalb, whose wish to fight on the American side goes back at least to December 26, 1775, the date of his letter to his Philadelphia friend Dr. Phile, in which he wrote, "I would with pleasure devote the rest of my days in the service of your liberty" and asked whether Congress would welcome his services. This approach led to nothing; de Kalb succeeded only on the third try. Dr. Phile turned the letter over to Robert Morris who sent it on February 17, 1777, with a rather cool recommendation to John Hancock:

> Sir, this letter and its translation were put in my hands to lay them before Congress. The writer, General de Kalb, was a major general in the last war in Germany, has many years commanded a French regiment and is said to be a man of interest at the Court of Versailles. He writes and speaks English well, is a polite gentleman and an excellent soldier. This character of him is given me by Dr. Phile and Capt. Hasenburg who are personally acquainted with him. He was in this country in the distressed times of the Stamp Act and was then supposed to be sent by the French Court to watch the dispute and its progress. If you choose to encourage him, Dr. Phile will transmit your pleasure.

Congress, overrun by foreign applicants, had passed a resolution March 13, 1777,[109] instructing its agents abroad to discourage officers seeking service in the United States army. Meanwhile, the Comte de Broglie through his secretary, M. Dubois-Martin, imparted to de Kalb his ambition to become commander of the American army. On December 11, 1776, he wrote de Kalb a long letter, detailing his plan; in conspiratorial secrecy he concludes, "I leave this unsigned. You know who I am."

> I have seen with pleasure from the relations of M. Dubois-Martin, as well as from your last letter of the 5th instant, the good progress of your affairs, and hope that all your wishes will continue to be realized. You may rest assured that, on my part, I shall not neglect your interests, which, as you

will not fail to remember, I have at all times advocated, the more cheerfully that I know that the favor of the king could not be better bestowed.

I do not doubt that the plan communicated to you by M. Dubois meets your entire approbation. It is clearly indispensable to the performance of the work. A military and political leader is wanted, a man fitted to carry the weight of authority in the colony, to unite its parties, to assign to each his place, to attract a large number of persons of all classes, and carry them along with him, not courtiers, but brave, efficient, and well educated officers, who would confide in their superior, and repose implicit faith in him. There need not be many grades of a higher order; but there is need of some, because the corps and the country are separate from each other. Not but that there is room enough for a number of persons, from among whom a selection may be made. The main point of the mission with which you have been intrusted will, therefore, consist in explaining the advantage, or, rather, the absolute necessity of the choice of a man who would have to be invested with the power of bringing his assistants with him, and of assigning to each the position for which he should judge him to be fitted. The rank of the candidate would have to be of the first eminence, such, for instance, as that of the Prince of Nassau; his functions, however, would have to be confined to the army, excluding the civil service, with, perhaps, the single exception of the political negotiation with foreign powers. In proposing such a man, you must, of course, not appear to know whether he entertains any wish for such a position; but, at the same time, you must intimate that nothing but the most favorable stipulations would induce him to make the sacrifice expected of him. You would have to observe that three years would be the longest period for which he could possibly bind himself, that he would claim a fixed salary, to continue after the expiration of that period of service, and that on no account would he consent to expatriate himself forever. What should make you particularly explicit on this point is, that the assurance of the man's return to France at the end of three years will remove every apprehension in regard to the powers to be conferred, and will remove even the semblance of an ambitious design to become the sovereign of the new republic.

You will, therefore, content yourself with stipulating for a military authority for the person in question, who would unite the position of a general and president of the council of war with the title of generalissimo, field marshal, etc.

Of course large pecuniary considerations would have to be claimed for the preparations for the journey, and for the journey itself, and a liberal salary for the return home, much in the same manner as has been done in the case of Prince Ferdinand. You can give the assurance that such a measure will bring order and economy into the public expenses, that it will reimburse its cost a hundred-fold in a single campaign, and that the choice of officers who follow their leader at his word, and from attachment to his person, is worth more than the reenforcement of the army with ten or twenty thousand men. You will know the persons who adhere to this leader and the unlimited number of subalterns; you know that they are not courtiers, but excellent and well-tried soldiers; you know better than others the great difference between the one candidate and the other, and will lay particular stress upon this point. You will be equally mindful to dwell upon the effect necessarily produced by such an appointment on its mere announcement in Europe. Even in a good European army everything depends upon the selection of a good commander-in-chief; how much more in a cause where everything has yet to be created and adjusted! It is not easy to find a man qualified for such a task, and at the same time willing to undertake it. If matters down there – *"la bas"* – should turn out well, you should induce Congress immediately to send little Dubois back to Mr. Deane with full powers and directions. These powers should be limited in no respect, except in so far as to remove all danger of too extensive exercise of the civil authority, or of ambitious schemes for dominion over the republic. The desire is to be useful to the republic in a political and military way, but with all the appropriate honors, dignities, and powers over subordinate functionaries; in short, with a well-ordered power.

If you send back little Dubois, advise me at the same time of the true condition of affairs and the state of public feeling, adding your suggestions of what is best to be done. Also inform me of the nature of the power conferred upon the agents of the insurgents. Farewell! I wish you and your caravan a pleasant journey. I shall execute your commissions and shall see M. de Sartines when I get to Paris.

Acquaint me with the receipt of this letter, and with the moment of your departure, and write to me under the direction of the Abbé St. Evrard, at the bureau of M. St. Julien, treasurer general of the clergy. I leave this unsigned. You know who I am.[110]

De Kalb, in the interest of the plan of his friend and patron, sent a letter and a memoir to Deane to be submitted to Franklin, who had just arrived in France.[111] The documents were dated from Havre, December 17, 1776:

I hope that you have received my letters of the 12th and 13th and 14th of December, which I had the honor to address to you, as I have this, under cover to Messrs. German and Girardot.

There arrived here tonight a courier from the Court with orders to delay the departure of the "Amphitrite:" I am very glad that he arrived too late, but I fear lest this may prove a hindrance to the departure of the second vessel, and consequently, to my own departure, and that of the officers.

I shall be much obliged if you will present my respects to Dr. Franklin. I submit to his judgment and yours the mémoire hereto annexed, containing my opinion upon what I hinted to you one day in Paris.

A French vessel which arrived yesterday from Lisbon, has reported that an English frigate has taken in these waters an American vessel of 350 tons, laden with indigo, &c, bound, as is believed, for Bordeaux and Havre. This prize was taken to Lisbon, and two persons of position who were on board, have been sent to Falmouth by the packet. I am, &c De Kalb.

Enclosure – Translation

Project. – the execution of which would perhaps decide the Success of the cause of the Liberty of the United States of North America, without the Court of France appearing, for the present, to have the slightest part in it.

In likening the United States to the States of Holland, when they were yet groaning under the repeated acts of tyranny of their sovereigns, I think that the same conduct which was so advantageous to the republican establishment of the Low

Countries would produce the same effect in the present case.

The beginning of the revolution in North America is a most important and a most interesting event for the majority of the European powers; and especially for France, who would willingly take the measures fitted to bring about a formal separation between the Colonies and England, if it could be done without declaring war against Great Britain if that were not absolutely necessary.

This is to be presumed from the permissions privately given by the Government to a number of distinguished officers of different ranks, to enter the service of the Americans and to buy provisions in this kingdom for transport in French vessels. But to return to my plan, I say it would be necessary to those, as yet infant states to supply them with some foreign troops and especially a leader of great European reputation, whose military capacity may place him in a position to be opposed as the head of an army to Prince Ferdinand of Brunswick or the King of Prussia himself; who, uniting a name rendered illustrious by many heroes of his family, with a great experience in war, and all qualities requisite for conducting such an undertaking with prudence, integrity and economy, under the authority of the States, considered as legitimate and sovereign powers.

The United Colonies are able to put under arms perhaps a hundred thousand brave men, for the most part interested in the defense of a just cause, their freedom and their possessions.

But numerous armies and courage are not sufficient to win success if they are not sustained by skill and experience. In speaking thus I have no intention to depreciate the glory, the leadership and the deeds of the officers who command at present; on the contrary, I think that they have acted very well and bravely, especially General Washington, on all occasions; but my scheme is only to have a man whose name and reputation alone might discourage the enemy.

It appears to me that my reflections upon the advantage which would result to the United States from their connection with France, have been foreseen, at least in part, by Congress, since it has sent hither one of its most capable members to obtain officers, munitions, &c.

All that has been done up to this time, has become public before its execution, by passing through the hands of several persons, not only indiscreet but unskilful, whom only necessity and the force of circumstances could have caused to be chosen.

Amongst the officers who engage for the cause and defense of freedom, men of merit form the minority, noble lords and other patrons not being always so candid as to recommend only brave and capable subjects; so that the majority of those officers are perhaps very mediocre as regards conduct, talents, wit, morals and experience, and only change climate for motives of interest and to get rid of their creditors.

All these inconveniences would no longer occur if the States might choose a leader such as I suggest, with power himself to choose the officers and assistants whom he should judge necessary. He would certainly choose the best of every kind: (for no one in the kingdom better knows all the military than he.) – I say, of obtaining the best officers and of placing each individual in the position suited to him, for his own reputation, which would appear to be so intimately connected with the success of the United Provinces: He alone would ask of the ministers their approval, and all the necessaries for the enterprise; none but himself would be in the secret, and I am sure that he is so universally esteemed for his position, integrity and capacity as a general, that without knowing where or how they were going, everyone would follow him and leave him master of the conditions. Many young noblemen would follow him as volunteers, only for the sake of serving and distinguishing themselves under his eyes. That nobility, by its interest at court, by its own credit or the management of its friends and kinsmen could decide the king in favor of a war with England.

The general would be in a position to obtain at the outset, for money or bills, and perhaps even as assistance rendered by one allied power to another, everything that the United States should require.

He would succeed in doing this better than any other minister; the whole French nation would be interested in the quarrel, and the king might be persuaded to declare himself openly. The result would be a treaty of alliance, commerce and navigation at the end, or before the end, of the war.

He would thus see himself obliged to push on the war for his own honour and that of his country, and consequently, to the advantage of the States, because he ought to regard the loss of his reputation as the greatest of all losses, and the honour of being the chief instrument in the defense and restoration of the freedom of a commonwealth as the most flattering of all honours.

Such a man, with assistants of his own choice, would alone be worth twenty thousand men and would double the value of the American troops.

Such a change in the army would, doubtless, encourage friends and produce an opposite effect upon the enemy.

All the military expenses would be administered by his intelligence and integrity to the greatest advantage of the States. There would be under his administration, neither knavery nor misappropriation of money, and he himself would render his accounts at the first demand to the supreme legislature of the States.

This man may be found, and I think that I have found him, and I am sure that once he is known he will unite the suffrages of the public, of all sensible men, of all military men, and I venture to say, of all Europe.

The question is to obtain his acceptance, which, as I think, can only be accomplished by loading him with enough honours to satisfy his ambition, as by naming him field marshal generalissimo, and giving him a considerable sum of ready money for his numerous children, the care of whom he would have to forego for some time during his sojourn beyond the seas, to be an equivalent to them in case of the loss of their father, and by giving him all the powers necessary for the good of the service.

I will answer in advance the objections which might be made to my project, because they naturally occur to the mind of a free people; namely, that such a man, invested with such extensive power in the army, having the chief officers at his devotion, could not only trample under foot the liberties of the country he was charged to defend, but even make himself its master and tyrant.

First, I shall reply that his power, however extensive it might be, would always be subordinate to the States; that no commander, officer or soldier would be subject to him except as regards military movements and the real service of the country; that, besides, it is not probable that any American subject would lend himself to so illegal an enterprise.

Second, I am sure, and would wager my head that such a thought would never enter his noble and generous heart.

Third, he has a vested property in his own country, honours, and a family held in such respect, and to which he is so tenderly attached, that for all the sovereignties in the world, he would never part from them, especially as he is on the point of being created marshal of France.

Fourth, in order to ensure his return and his residence in Europe in a more precise manner, the States could make one of the capital points of their treaties or dealings with the Court of Versailles, the elevation of their generalissimo to the dignity of Duke and Peer of France.

These ideas are suggested to me by zeal for the cause which I have embraced. I leave to Messrs. Franklin and Deane to extend them, change them, or to carry them out. The only thing which I ask of them is to make no mention of my proposition to any living soul, because of the secrecy which is absolutely necessary whether the project be accepted or whether it be rejected. I repeat once more – the choice of the person when I shall name him will be agreeable and generally applauded. De Kalb.

There is great similarity in the two memoirs. Both stress the need of the United States for a man of influence and a great European reputation who has a following of devoted officers, who might have sufficient influence at court to induce the French king to declare war against England. Such a man, sometimes referred to as "Stadtholder" in analogy to the post of William of Orange in Holland, would not be a threat to the liberty of the citizens, because his authority would be confined to the army and foreign affairs, his term would not exceed three years, and he would be accountable to the legislature. Both letters state that the generalissimo must be given great inducements to undertake the sacrifice; de Broglie speaks a little more about money, while de Kalb stresses honors and the cause of liberty. As models for such a post, William of Orange-

Nassau is mentioned by de Broglie, Prince Ferdinand of Brunswick and the King of Prussia by de Kalb; but of course, neither mentions the name of the great leader who might be induced to help the United States. Once more the emphasis is on secrecy in describing the candidate: "none but himself would be in the secret." Francis Wharton, who edited the Revolutionary Diplomatic Correspondence, gives some historic background:

> From the standpoint of Broglie there was nothing strange in the idea that a European soldier of high social and political rank should be proffered to lead the American colonies in their revolt. Poland, to which Kalb had previously gone on a mission similar to that with which he was now entrusted, had been for many years the object of enterprises of this very kind; Russia and France each in turn proffering subjects of distinction as candidates for the throne, while noble aspirants of various grades entered the contest on their own behalf. Don John of Austria had been spoken of for an oriental sovereignty; Leicester in Queen Elizabeth's time, and Marlborough in the time of Queen Anne, received offers of the Government of the Netherlands; Wallenstein's aspirations to the imperial crown were regarded as but natural in view of his splendid military gifts and daring ambition. In after years, Bernadotte was elected to the Swedish throne, and Maximilian sent by Louis Napoleon to govern Mexico. We have no right, therefore, to be surprised that Kalb, unaware of Washington's character and position, and as yet imperfectly acquainted with the rude independence and impatience of foreign control by which American character was marked, should have looked upon Broglie's election to an American dictatorship as feasible; and it is no more strange that he should have conceived such a project before his voyage than that he should have abandoned it in America when he saw how things really were. But it is a matter of surprise that Deane should have gravely recommended such a project to Congress.[112]

A contemporary historian, Donald R. Chidsey, writes in his *Valley Forge:*

> Today this proposal seems preposterous, an egregious burst of vanity. Yet it was put forward in all seriousness; and as politico-military thinking went at the time, it was sensible and even sound. – It just did not allow for the feelings of the Americans.[113]

Mr. Deane had been given some idea of the plan when de Kalb some time previously "hinted to you in Paris" about it at the time when de Broglie introduced him. Deane had been impressed by a nobleman of de Broglie's high rank and by the forcefulness of de Kalb himself. Therefore, when he was reporting on December 6, 1776, to the Secret Committee of Congress on the agreement he had made with de Kalb and several other officers, he added a very vague paragraph in line with de Broglie's wishful thinking. He gave the latter's original Italian name, and confuses the Count de Broglie with his much more famous brother, the Duke and Marshal:

> I submit one thought to you: Whether if you could engage a great general of the highest character in Europe, such, for instance, as Prince Ferdinand, Marshal Broglio, or other of equal rank, to take the lead in your armies, whether such a step would not be politic, as it would give a character and credit to your military and strike perhaps a greater panic in our enemies. I only suggest such a thought to you and leave you to confer with the Baron de Kalb on the subject at large.[114]

Silas Deane "only suggested" many things of diverse kinds to Congress, to which the men in Philadelphia properly paid very little attention. In a letter written a week before the above, also to the Secret Committee of Congress, he suggests the purchase of Swiss or German mercenaries. He continues, in his lengthy letter:

> I have wrote largely and on many subjects, yet I fear I have omitted something; if so, I must, when I write again, recollect on lesser subjects. I wish I had here one of your best saddle horses of the American or Rhode Island breed, a present of the kind would be money well spent with a certain personage; (does Deane refer to Marie Antoinette?) other curious productions would, at this time, though trifles in themselves, be of consequence rightly timed and placed. I mentioned Mr. Rittenhouse's orrery in a former letter, and I think Arnold's collection of insects, etc., etc., but I must submit any step of this kind to your mature judgment.

One more reference to the "Intrigue" is found in a letter to de Kalb from de Broglie's secretary Dubois-Martin.[115]

> I should be glad if you would come here once more, to see Mr. Franklin. It would greatly further the negotiations you have undertaken, as it is possible that otherwise some

other party may approach this member of Congress with the same views as those we advocate. If you cannot get away, I would like you to write to Mr. Deane, asking him whether or not the arrival of Mr. Franklin will effect any alterations in the form or spirit of his despatches, or in the plan you have submitted to him for the choice of a commander-in-chief.

At all events you might warn him against giving too ready an ear to suggestions of parties probably ill calculated for so important a position, as I am quite sure you will agree with me in opinion that there is not a man in Europe so well fitted for the office as ours (Broglie). I do not entertain this view because of my predilection for the candidate. You would very much oblige me by an intimation respecting your ideas and intentions on this head.

These paragraphs are very revealing regarding the "Intrigue." There is no hint of the use of force, nor of subverting American officers; only a suggestion submitted to the Congress through the duly authorized representatives of that body in Paris, Silas Deane and Benjamin Franklin. There is some doubt as to whether Franklin ever saw de Kalb's memoir dated December 17, 1776, because Franklin himself makes no reference whatever to it; he arrived in Paris December 21, 1776, after an exhausting voyage, and with much more important business awaiting him. Washington never mentions it. Deane's bitter enemy Lovell does not make this one of his accusations against Deane, whom he calls "this weak and roguish man." There is no evidence that de Broglie's secret was known to anyone but his secretary Dubois-Martin, de Kalb, Silas Deane, and later Thomas Paine. The stress on secrecy in the documents makes it appear likely that Lafayette knew nothing about de Broglie's hope, since he never alluded to it. If de Kalb's enemy, the Viscount Mauroy, had been aware of it, he would probably have dwelt on it in his attacks on the Baron. The Committee of Secret Correspondence evidently kept *its* secret. Wharton writes, Congress took no notice of the suggestion, nor, after de Kalb's arrival in America, when he had an opportunity of seeing what the situation was, did it again emerge. On February 13, 1779, more than two years after Deane's suggestion, when de Kalb had been commanding a division for two years, the secretary of the Committee, Thomas Paine, dug it up to accuse Deane of a scheme to make a German princeling commander of the American forces in place of George Washington – Ferdinand of Brunswick – but there is no mention of the Comte de Broglie.[116]

No historian had any inkling of the matter until, nearly a

century later, Friedrich Kapp in his biography of de Kalb published in 1862 quoted the documents relating to de Broglie's scheme, which he had discovered among the Baron's papers preserved in the family archives at de Kalb's estate of Milon la Chapelle near Versailles. This secrecy was required in view of what a failure would have meant to the proud Count whose interests de Kalb was willing to serve; had he been asked his preference at the time, he might have chosen to fight under de Broglie rather than under Washington whom he did not then know. He was reminded in no uncertain terms of the debt he owed the Broglie brothers for favors they had done him. At the same time he was enthusiastic about devoting his "thirty-two years of military experience" to the American cause. On November 7, 1776, he signed an agreement with Deane in which he concluded his part with the following statement:[117]

> On the above conditions I engage and promise to serve the American States to the utmost of my ability, to acknowledge the authority and every act of the most honorable Congress, to be faithful to the country as my own, obey to superiors committed by that lawful power, and be from this very date at the disposal of Mr. Deane for my embarkation and in such a vessel and harbor as he shall think fit.

De Broglie, as his commanding officer, had repeatedly recommended de Kalb for promotion; therefore it was natural that the latter should advocate the former's candidacy for a post which, it might appear, an experienced European general could fill better than an American, a Virginia planter such as Washington, who had not yet proved himself; so he presented de Broglie's "idea", adding "I leave to Messrs. Franklin and Deane to extend them, change them, or to carry them out." That placed the whole matter in the hands of the American representatives of the United States Government. He continues, "The only thing which I ask of them is to make no mention of my proposition to any living soul, because of the secrecy which is absolutely necessary whether the project be accepted or whether it be rejected.[118]

There is a final word on the de Broglie Intrigue in a letter to the Count from de Kalb dated September 24, 1777, from Lancaster, Pennsylvania, in which he speaks kindly but critically of Washington's ability as a general.[119] Then he proceeds in his manly and honorable fashion:

> If I return to Europe it will be with the greatest mortification, as it is impossible to execute the great design I have so gladly come to subserve. M. de Valfort (one of the French

officers who was about to return to France) will tell you that the project in question is totally impracticable; it would be regarded no less an act of crying injustice against Washington, than as an outrage on the honor of the country.

With this decision de Kalb buried the documents in his files. The next letter from the Count shows that he has turned to other interests, and neither he nor de Kalb makes any further allusion to the generalissimo aspirations, nor is there any further reference to the "Broglie Intrigue" in any other contemporary document, so far as I have been able to discover.

An interesting comment on Broglie and his plan is contained in an article entitled "Comte de Broglie, the Proposed Stadtholder of America," published in 1887 by Charles J. Stillé, which begins:

"In the Sixth Volume of Mr. Bancroft's history (ed. of 1879, p. 519) we find the following paragraph:

> The Count de Broglie, disclaiming the ambition of becoming the sovereign of the United States, insinuated his willingness to be for a period of years its Prince of Orange, provided he could be assured of a large grant of money before embarkation, an ample revenue, the highest military rank, the direction of foreign relations during his command, and a princely annuity for life after his return.

This seems at first glance a most extraordinary statement, all the more so because Mr. Bancroft makes no further explanation of it, and indeed never refers to the subject in his work."

Professor Stillé is surprised, not to say shocked, because Bancroft attaches so little importance to what to him is "a most extraordinary statement." Evidently Bancroft thought that in a six-volume History of the United States, the above paragraph was sufficient to cover the subject.

CHAPTER VIII

"VICTOIRE"

De Kalb was naturally deeply disappointed that a prohibition by the French Government had prevented the sailing of the "Seine" and thus ruined his opportunity of joining the American cause. But he returned to Paris more determined than ever to reach America, and within a short time two opportunities presented themselves. One was a repetition of the former offer by Deane to place him on a ship carrying supplies to America; the other was the decision of Lafayette to purchase and freight a vessel at his own expense. In his *Mémoires*[120] he recounts that despite the news of Washington's defeats at New York, Long Island and White Plains, his enthusiasm was not in the least dampened. Deane had advised him, in view of the poor prospects of the American cause, to abandon his project, but the determined young man politely thanked him for his frankness, then added: "Until now, you have seen only my enthusiasm in your cause, and that may prove at present not wholly useless. I shall purchase a ship to carry out your officers; we must feel confidence in the future, and it is especially in the hour of danger that I wish to share your fortune."

Lafayette of course talked not only with Deane, but also with de Kalb, the Count de Broglie, and the latter's secretary, Dubois-Martin. It was decided to take advantage of a fortunate turn of affairs that solved the problem of securing a ship without arousing suspicion. A brother of Dubois-Martin, Lieutenant François Auguste Dubois-Martin, who was attached to a French infantry regiment at Port-au-Prince, had come to France to purchase arms and uniforms for his regiment. After completing his business dealings at Bordeaux, he came to Paris for a visit with his brother before returning to San Domingo. He arrived just as the group was organized which was to sail on the "Seine." On his brother's recommendation he was admitted to this group of officers with the rank of major. When the expedition was interdicted by the French government, he returned to Paris. At this point he proved to be the very man needed, for the next attempt was to be made from Bordeaux, a more distant port than Havre and thus less under surveillance by French officials or British spies. Lieutenant

Dubois-Martin had had dealings with shippers at Bordeaux and had naval experience as well. He was therefore entrusted with the task of purchasing a ship, which he accomplished in short order. For Lafayette he bought the "Victoire," Captain Le Boursier, for 112,000 francs. It was to be ready in the middle of March. The price included also the value of the cargo with which the vessel was loaded. Lafayette was elated. De Kalb decided to join the lad who had said, "I'll see you in America."

To fill the weeks of waiting, and also to dispel suspicion regarding his plans, the eager and impatient Marquis paid a visit to his uncle, the French ambassador to England. With a bit of mischievous amusement he found himself introduced to King George III, and to Generals Clinton and Rawdon who had returned from American battlefields to England for the winter season. This was not particularly exciting for the idealistic "rebel," but probably somewhat preferable to the Parisian balls he was required by his position to attend; these festivities would start at the Queen's with dancing from five to nine, followed by supper and then more dancing till six in the morning. And no gentleman of the court could leave before Marie Antoinette had retired.

After three weeks in England, Lafayette returned to France on March 12, as had been arranged. De Kalb, eager not to have his plans frustrated this time, arranged that Lafayette remain incognito at his, the Baron's, residence in Paris until all arrangements had been completed. This was probably a wise precaution in view of Lafayette's wavering conduct in the weeks prior to the sailing of the "Victoire" on April 20, 1777. When all details had been settled with Deane, as well as with the officers who were to sail on the "Victoire," de Kalb and Lafayette set out in the latter's carriage on the evening of March 16, 1777, for Bordeaux,[121] arriving there on the 19th after having slept only one night en route. This impatient haste proved to have been useless, for the "Victoire" was by no means ready to put to sea.

The prospect was one of waiting idly by for several days. For Lafayette this was particularly painful because of a boyish indiscretion he had committed and now felt would have very serious consequences. In his worry he decided to make a clean breast of it to his friend and mentor; it was not true, as he had repeatedly informed de Kalb, that his family and particularly his father-in-law the Duc d'Ayen, had approved of his going to America; on the contrary, the Duke was decidedly opposed to "such folly."[122] Since in his happy mood at his departure from Paris, he had sent a letter to the Duke telling of his idealistic plans, his angry father-in-law could by this time have appealed to the king to stop the fugitive. The king had a very ready means of bringing to their senses young noblemen who were about to disgrace their families, namely the *lettre de cachet*, an order to imprison anyone for any length of time without any indicated cause. This was no laughing matter for Lafayette.

De Kalb was amazed! During the period of planning for their departure, he and Lafayette had seen each other every day. The Marquis openly came to his house, and he called at the Noailles residence, at times even when Mme. de Lafayette was present at their meetings. He could not have dreamed that under the circumstances the plans were a secret from his friend's family; in fact he was told repeatedly that the Marquis' father-in-law approved.[123] The two talked it over and decided that under the circumstances, with their ship delayed for at least another three days, it would be well to find out just what was being done in Paris about their departure. For that purpose a courier was sent on March 20th to one of Lafayette's friends, the Viscomte de Coigny. De Kalb, in deep gloom at the prospect of a second attempt being frustrated, wrote to his wife:

> Bordeaux, March 20, 1777
>
> The grief in which I left you at my departure tore my heart, and it still afflicts me deeply. I should like to be able to come back to you at once. If I could with decency withdraw I would do it; but although I cannot break my promise there is still the possibility that our voyage will be prevented. I find so many matters still to be arranged here that the ministers surely will hear about the Marquis' departure and orders will arrive before our vessel sets sail. Notwithstanding the ardor with which we are at work, nothing is more uncertain than this voyage.[124]

On March 23 de Kalb reported further delays:

> We are still ignorant whether our departure will be prevented, as our vessel, so long detained already, cannot set sail before tomorrow. When the unfavorable wind will turn God only knows![125]

When on March 25 all of Deane's officers had duly arrived and the ship was ready, it was decided not to wait for the return of the courier. But just as the men had entered the longboat that was to take them to the ship, the courier arrived with the reply from Lafayette's friend. Lafayette read it as the sailors rowed toward the "Victoire." Coigny reported that the King disapproved of the plan, and Lafayette's father-in-law was outraged; he was trying to prevent the sailing. This news left Lafayette thoroughly perturbed.

When he told de Kalb about the contents of the letter, de Kalb, notwithstanding what it meant to him by way of disappointment, did not feel that he could do other than counsel the young man not to disobey the king and not to break totally with his family. Lafayette felt the force of this reasonable and unselfish advice, which was of course supported also by the fact that as an officer of the French army he could not well disobey his sovereign's command if an order from the king should arrive. However, he did not alter the arrangements to sail from a French harbor to the Spanish port of Los Pasajes, a small harbor about three miles distant from the larger harbor, St. Sebastian. On March 29, 1777, the "Victoire" entered Los Pasajes, where the ship remained twenty-three days[126] because of Lafayette's indecision. For de Kalb and the other officers it meant almost three weeks of impatient waiting. Naturally the officers spent much of their leisure time in St. Sebastian, attending mass on Easter day, exploring the vicinity and eating at the hotel. In bad weather they remained in the ship. De Kalb wrote numerous letters to his wife, some from Los Pasajes and some from St. Sebastian. Meanwhile Lafayette, torn between two courses of action, had sent a second courier to Paris, to report at St. Sebastian as to whether his voyage would be forbidden. Then he himself returned to France to attempt to win approval for his course of action.

De Kalb found time to write to his wife en route:

> On board the "Victoire," Cap. Le Boursier,
> of Bordeaux, near the mouth of the Gironde
> March 26, at noon (1777)
>
> I wrote you, my dear Love, on the 20, the 22, and twice on the 24, with a word on the 25 in the latter; in two hours we shall be in the open sea. We are weighing anchor in the most glorious weather; that must presage a happy voyage. We came on board last night and we are all of us already seasick, my traveling companion very much so. I'm taking advantage of a little interval, to tell you, dear Love, how much I love you and shall always love you. I promise to send you news shortly and well before my arrival in America, because I am sure that we shall stop in a European port and that I shall be able to write to you in two or three days, for we are going to await in St. Sebastian in Spain the return of a courier who has been dispatched to Paris.[127]

However, before the courier from Paris arrived in St. Sebastion, there appeared one from Bordeaux. He brought orders from the court commanding the Marquis to go to Toulon, there to await the arrival of the Duc d'Ayen and his sister, the Countess de Tessé, to set out with them on a journey to Italy which was supposed to last for ten months, to cure the lad of his silly notions. The Duc d'Ayen did not think highly of Lafayette, and besides he was outraged by his current behavior. The Countess was an oddity: "While young she had lost her faith and been won over to the philosophical ideas of the age. She was a friend of Voltaire, but though flaunting her agnosticism, she invariably crossed herself within the privacy of her bed-curtains whenever she had to take medicine. She amused her nieces with her mannerisms, her pomposity of speech, and the glaring contrasts between her behavior and her talk.[128] To view the art and architecture of Italy in the company of these two elders for the better part of a year must have been an appalling prospect for the young man who was "drawing his sword for the young republic in the hour of her greatest need." De Kalb wrote to his wife in considerable understatement that the journey to Italy was "not to the Marquis' taste." From St. Sebastian on April 1, 1777, he wrote: "This is the end of his expedition to America to join the army of the insurgents."[129]

Lafayette had set out for Bordeaux and possibly Paris in order to secure approval for his expedition. He wanted to follow de Kalb's advice, not to be disobedient to the king nor to break off with his father-in-law, but at the same time he was determined not to give up his project and not to expose himself to ridicule. De Kalb was sure he would not secure the approval he sought (as turned out to be the case), so with his characteristic good business sense he advised Lafayette to compromise with the former owner of the ship at a sacrifice of twenty or twenty-five thousand francs. All would be much better if the boy only had not claimed that the Duc d'Ayen was in sympathy with his course, if he had omitted sending his father-in-law a letter at the moment of his departure, and if he had not returned to France after he was on the open sea, beyond the reach of the French government!

On April 6, de Kalb wrote to his wife from Los Pasajes:

> I had flattered myself with the hope of receiving news from the Marquis from Bordeaux last evening. If they do not arrive today or tomorrow, our stay here will be a very long one, as in that case he will not write until he gets to Paris, for certainly neither M. de Maurepas nor the Duc d'Ayen will permit him to rejoin us. If the Marquis has not already got a bargain with the ship's owner, his blunders will cost him dear. I call them blunders, for his course was foolish from the moment he could not make up his mind quietly to execute his project, undisturbed by threats. It was the letter of the

Vicomte de Coigny, received by the courier sent to him on his return to Bordeaux, which produced this sudden change of purpose. If that letter had not found him already in the boat which was to carry us on board our vessel, I believe Lafayette would have returned at once, and in my opinion, he would have acted properly. When he asked my advice about what to do, I thought it my duty to dissuade him from disregarding the wishes of his father-in-law and the commands of the king. On the contrary I advised him to give way to his family, and to avoid a rupture with them. Had he not constantly flattered himself that he had the approval of the Duc d'Ayen, I would always have warned him not to go as far as he did. He had always assured me that his family sanctioned his plans, that his father-in-law himself intended at some time to go to America with the Vicomte de Noailles, and that even Madame Lafayette had been made acquainted with his intentions by her parents, and would approve of them. I have always thought him to blame for keeping the matter secret from his wife until the moment of his departure. Had he told me in Paris all that he has admitted since, I would have remonstrated most earnestly against the whole scheme. As it is, the affair will cost him some money. But if it be said that he has done a foolish thing, it may be answered that he acted from the most honorable motives, and that he can hold up his head before all high-minded men.

He says furthermore:

This long delay is intolerable. I shall be too late for opening of the campaign, and am so much the more mortified as Mr. Deane offered me a passage on one of his ships.[130]

Thus he unburdened himself of his annoyances to his understanding Emilie, his *chere bonne amie*.

In this same letter of April 6, from Los Pasajes, he wrote to his wife:

I didn't write you yesterday, my dear love, because I went on an all-day hike in very beautiful weather and for quite a distance, to ascend one of the highest mountains in this vicinity. From the top one views a vast expanse of sea and land. We saw Bayonne, which is about seven leagues from here, and the environs quite a distance beyond. The Pyrenees were covered with snow, while we were quite hot. I say "we" because I had with me Messrs. Bédoulx and Brice (Price) who are our best hikers. You do not know the latter; he is a pleasant, likable fellow, an American, highly recommended to M. Lafayette by Mr. Deane. I am thus obliged to look after him. The others in the group went on a horseback ride to Bayonne day before yesterday. (Note: The name "Brice" is de Kalb's Bavarian pronunciation of "Price," the version of his signature.)[131]

The manner in which de Kalb employed the time that hung heavy on his hands while waiting for Lafayette in a small Spanish port is characteristic of the man. Years later, as a major general in the United States army, he preferred walking to traveling on horseback. It was another habit of his to share all happenings with his wife; for example, in this letter he introduces the rest of the companions of the voyage to her by name, all of them "likable and reasonable men." In Lafayette's absence he had to take charge of the group, and at the Marquis' request looked after the young man's personal interests. On April 17, 1777, Lafayette arrived on horseback, disguised as a postboy to elude the police, in his dashing, romantic fashion. He had decided, for a number of reasons, despite various prohibitions, to sail to America. He was following his projected bold course in conformity with his motto, "Cur non?" – (why not?). He had learned that it was the Duc d'Ayen who had procured from the king the royal order, and that everyone else was enthusiastically in favor of his, Lafayette's, enterprise, and critical of his father-in-law for wishing to interfere with the gallant project. As for the ministers, on being asked their real sentiments in the matter, they answered that they would have said nothing at all but for the complaints of the Duc d'Ayen. A petition for permission to leave for the United States submitted by Lafayette had not been refused, – it had not been answered at all, and Lafayette rationalized that this amounted to permission. He thus felt that he had the approval he wanted. Therefore, Cur non? We sail! On April 20, 1777, the "Victoire" set sail for Charleston.[132]

Meanwhile in Paris, Lafayette's adventurous plan, far from being a secret, was the subject of a great deal of gossip favorable to the Marquis. Naturally Americans in Paris followed developments with great interest. George Lupton wrote to William Eden April 24, 1777, that Lafayette would go despite the king's orders and that he had taken with him "the Baron, a very noted and able officer, to be his guardian and instructor."[133]

It is not at all surprising that a boy of nineteen, faced with a very difficult and complicated problem for decision, hesitated and required almost a month to make up his mind, sorely trying the patience of his traveling companions. What *is* surprising is the firm manner in which he took charge of the command of his ship, the tact he showed in dealing with Congress, his bravery in his first battle, his skill in manoeuvering a division, his diplomacy on his return to France, and all his other acts which have made him a great American hero. He was, as de Kalb puts it, a prodigy!

The ship's papers, in view of the official neutrality of the French government, were made out for the French colonies in the West Indies, but Lafayette ordered the captain to sail directly for Charleston. The Captain replied that he could not do this, as the ship's papers protected them only in going to the West Indies. Any English cruiser apprehending them headed for the United States would make them prisoners and take the ship as a prize. Lafayette then repeated his order to sail straight to North America, informing the captain that in case he refused, the command would be turned over to the second officer. Then the truth came out – the captain had smuggled on board several thousand dollars worth of goods which he intended to sell in the West Indies, and that was the cause of his fear of being overtaken by a British man-of-war. Lafayette then promised that he would indemnify the captain if his goods should be seized as contraband. If Captain Boursier had expected that he would be able to wind the nineteen-year-old boy around his finger, he met with a surprise.[134]

In his Mémoires (written at this point in the third person) Lafayette gives some information concerning the voyage:

> As soon as M. de Lafayette had recovered from the effects of sea sickness, he studied the language and the trade he was adopting. A heavy ship, two bad cannons, and some guns, could not have escaped the smallest privateer. In his present situation he resolved rather to blow up the vessel than to surrender; he concocted measures to achieve this end with a brave Dutchman named Bédoulx, whose sole alternative, if taken, would have been the gibbet. – At forty leagues from shore they were met by a small vessel: the captain turned pale, but the crew were attached to M. de Lafayette, and the officers were numerous; they made a show of resistance. It turned out, fortunately, to be an American ship, which they vainly endeavored to keep up with, but scarcely had the former lost sight of M. de Lafayette's vessel when it fell in with two British frigates – and this is not the only time when the elements seemed bent on opposing M. de Lafayette as with the intention of saving him. After having encountered for seven weeks various perils and chances, he arrived at Georgetown in Carolina. Ascending the river in a canoe, his foot touched at length the American soil, and he swore that he would conquer or perish in that cause.[135]

In one of the letters Lafayette wrote on shipboard to his young wife, he expresses his satisfaction at not having gone to Italy with his elderly relatives for ten months as he had been ordered to do by the King. Then he goes on:

> And consider the difference between my occupation and my present life and what would have been if I had gone upon that useless journey. As the defender of that liberty which I adore, free myself beyond all others, coming as a friend to offer my services in this most interesting republic, I bring with me nothing but my own free heart and my good will, no ambition to fulfil and no selfish interest to serve; if I am striving for my own glory, I am at the same time laboring for its welfare. I trust that for my sake you will become a good American; it is a sentiment made for virtuous hearts. The happiness of America is intimately connected with the happiness of all mankind; she is destined to become the safe and venerable asylum of virtue, of honesty, of tolerance, of equality and of peaceful liberty.[136]

De Kalb was definitely a friend of America, though not so exuberant about it as Lafayette, and so were the other officers, mostly young idealists. But there was one Mephistopheles in the group, the Viscount de Mauroy. He later on became very much embittered when Congress, on September 15, 1777, selected de Kalb instead of him for a newly created major generalship; he gave vent to his spleen in a memoir he later wrote on his experiences in America. This cynical report, among other things, serves to inform us to some extent on the tenor of the conversations on board the "Victoire" in the course of her 54-day voyage:[137]

> My companions on board were in a visible state of enthusiasm, and I certainly did not make it my project to cure them of it; but the Marquis de Lafayette really interested me; his youth, his ardent desire to distinguish himself, his name, his fortune, the pleasures that he was sacrificing for the sword, his constancy in fighting against all obstacles, and the happiness which he experienced in overcoming them all, won me over to him, delighted me at his success. While all the others occupied themselves with the endeavor to foster his sweetest hopes, I tried by my objections to keep him prepared for the disagreeable things that he would probably meet with, lest there be too painful an impression if he experienced them at a time when his imagination was the most highly exalted in his idealization of the Americans.

"Well," Lafayette said to me one day, "you do not believe that people are moved by a love of virtue, of liberty? You do not believe that the simple, good, hospitable men and women prefer well-being to all our vain pleasures, and death to slavery?"

I replied: "If the savages of the new continent had united to live in a society to which some man of genius, of virtue, of talents and constancy, a modern Timoleon, had given laws, such a people could now serve as a living illustration of the virtues you have just sketched for me; but men already civilized (and not at all by such philosophers), are the ones who brought to a savage land the vices and prejudices of their respective mother countries.

"Fanaticism, insatiable greed, and poverty, these are unfortunately the three causes that incessantly drive to these shores masses of immigrants who come to slay the natives and destroy in a wasteful spirit forests as old as the world itself; they drench a still virgin soil with the blood of the aborigines and fertilize it with thousands of corpses scattered over fields seized by force. In this picture, which is only too true, do you see fewer horrors than could be shown you in the continent which we are leaving?

"I know that you are going to cite to me the Quakers and the happiness which Pennsylvania can offer us, but this exception serves only as a contrast unfavorable to the other provinces; and isn't it a fact that the supposedly good people indulge in secret in the projects of their neighbors? – that they desire only peace and plenty, and that in the end any and every power is indifferent to them, since by their constitution, which is truly monastic, no power can bind them together.

"This it is on which I base my conviction; to speak frankly, I expect to find in America only men like those on our continent; I think that because of their prejudices we Frenchmen must be detested by them. When we come as people who offer them enlightenment superior to theirs, we wound their pride in general, and arouse their envy in particular."

Rousseau and Voltaire!

In Appendix A is a table of all the officers who crossed to America on the "Victoire," listing the grades promised them by Deane and those awarded by Congress in cases where they were accepted –

usually identical. The group that was to have sailed with de Kalb on the "Seine" from Havre had scattered, but six of these men joined the "Victoire" expedition. This was a young man's enterprise; the average age was under thirty, and if de Kalb and de Mauroy, the "old men," are omitted, under 27. The last column of Appendix A tells a very tragic story; despite their enthusiasm, their hardships on the sea and on land, and the efforts of Lafayette and de Kalb in their interest, seven officers were refused appointments by Congress, and six were forced to return ignominiously without having gained any glory. However, they were in decency reimbursed for their expenses for the trip to America and their return to France.

In the following paragraphs are some interesting data regarding the men who crossed in the "Victoire."

De Kalb was the only one among the group to fall in battle.

De Mauroy's contract was repudiated by Congress and he returned to France an embittered man.

De Valfort rose from the ranks and became a colonel in 1777. Poor health caused him soon to return to France, where he was appointed director of the military school at Brienne, and thus the chief teacher of Napoleon.

De Lesser: a lieutenant at the age of ten, a colonel by 1777, he was refused by Congress. After distinguished service in the French army, he retired as general.

Dubuysson served in the cavalry regiment of the Duc de Noailles, where Lafayette served in the summer of 1775; he was given the rank of major by Congress and became de Kalb's faithful aide. In the battle of Camden he tried with his own body to protect the wounded general from British bayonets, himself receiving severe wounds. He wrote an interesting account of the group's first experiences in the United States.

Sourbader de Gimat who was given the rank of major by Deane, was made a lieutenant colonel by Congress and became aide-de-camp to Lafayette, with whom he made the trip to France in 1779. He saw considerable action, including the siege of Yorktown, where he was wounded. When he returned to France in 1782, he bore a letter from Washington to Lafayette. Later he received a command in the Antilles.

Cloquet de Vrigny at the age of seventeen served in the Noailles Regiment, then joined the Fischer Corps, where he rose to captain. After crossing in the "Victoire" he became one of Lafayette's aides. After his return to France he fell victim to the French Revolution.

De Capitaine, a topographer, was assigned to work in his specialty.

De Colombe was taken prisoner at the battle of Savannah and was paroled.

Leonard Price, a native of Baltimore, served with Lafayette as his American aide.

De Bédoulx served with the rank of lieutenant colonel under Pulaski.

Congress found that Deane had exceeded his powers in promising appointment to all these officers, most of whom could not speak English; in fact, he is frequently criticized harshly for his ill-advised actions. However, in defense of the Connecticut school teacher, overwhelmed in Paris by bewildering complications, it should be recalled that but for his well-meant bungling, the United States would never have had Lafayette, de Kalb, Steuben and Pulaski.

At the time of Lafayette's "escape" Deane was bitterly attacked for his share in abetting this illegal act. He wrote a letter in defense of his action to the French foreign minister, the Count de Vergennes, concluding: "No country need be ashamed of him, and I am sure he will one day justify to the world that my early prejudice in his favor was well founded.[139]

CHAPTER IX

AN UNGUIDED TOUR FROM CHARLESTON TO PHILADELPHIA

"We have seen today several kinds of birds," wrote Lafayette to his wife from on board the "Victoire" on June 7, 1777, "which announce that we are not far from shore.[140] The hope of arriving is very sweet, for a ship life is a most wearisome one." Almost fifty days had passed in dull monotony, aggravated toward the end by short rations due to unwisely liberal distribution of the food supply in the first weeks. He tells us that after recovery from seasickness he had busied himself with military books and with the study of English. He closes the letter, "Adieu; night obliges me to discontinue my letter, as I have forbidden some days since any candles being used in my vessel; see how prudent I have become!" No British frigates attempted to stop the "Victoire" and therefore Lafayette did not have to follow out his super-heroic resolve to blow up his ship, his friends, the crew, the cargo and himself rather than surrender to an English captain.

De Kalb saw no point in a daily letter to his wife on shipboard, but on American soil he writes her a letter dated Sunday, June 15, 1777, North Island at the entrance of the Bay of Georgetown, fifteen miles from that town, at a port called South Inlet in (South) Carolina.

> Finally we reached land, my dear love, two days ago, after a long and painful voyage, without having stopped at our island, without any bad incidents, but not entirely without anxiety every time we saw some ships, all the more so since we had decided to defend ourselves, though we were poorly equipped for the purpose. A contrary wind prevented us from reaching Charleston where we had intended to land. No one on board knew the coast well enough to say where we were and which port we might enter. The Marquis, Mr. Price and I set out in the yawl from our ship, with the lieutenant and seven sailors, to discover where we could find a pilot. We started on Friday at two in the afternoon and rowed till six in the evening, ascending the river to Georgetown, called the North Inlet, until the low tide caused us to be stranded.

Up to that time we had encountered only some ignorant negroes who were fishing for oysters and who agreed on the way home to guide us to the pilot who lived at the upper end of the island. The confused statements of these four negroes in regard to this region were very unsatisfactory. We did gather that they belonged to a major of militia, but they added at the same time that the enemy (the British) were at times carrying out raids in this vicinity and that they had carried off a week ago several fishermen. Though we did not find out much from these slaves, we left our yawl behind and entered the negroes' oyster boat in order to be conducted first to the pilot and then to their master.[141]

About midnight the negroes set the three men ashore and pointed to their master's house. Guided by the light in the distance, Lafayette, de Kalb and Price set out in that direction. When they approached the house from which the light came, the dogs began to bark and the major, suspecting a British raiding party from some enemy ships, made ready to defend himself and challenged the arrivals. De Kalb, speaking English, explained that they were French officers who had just arrived from Bordeaux to serve in the Continental Army, that their ship was at the mouth of the inlet, that they had set out to find a pilot, and that they were asking shelter for the night. They were then immediately invited into the house, and there learned they were in the summer residence of Major Benjamin Huger, a prominent citizen of South Carolina, who received them with "a cordial and generous hospitality." The next morning the weather was beautiful, and everything conspired to give Lafayette a most favorable first impression of America. The novelty of all that surrounded him, the black servants who came to ask his commands, the beauty and the foreign aspect of the country which he beheld from his windows and the rich vegetation with which it was covered, – all united to produce on the sensitive young man a truly magical effect, exciting in him a variety of inexpressible emotions.[142]

With the high tide, the yawl came up in the morning and took the officers back to the "Victoire." Lafayette had decided to have his ship sail into Charleston while he and de Kalb with a few others would travel overland. Major Huger tried to find horses for them, but was able to secure only three. Lafayette offered the men on the "Victoire" the option of going by ship or overland on horseback or on foot. Practically everyone at first voted to leave the ship, but then, either because of the expense, or the weariness after a very long voyage, or the impossibility of procuring horses for the trip, almost all changed their minds and decided to stay on board. This moved Lafayette to say that if everybody was staying on board he would stay also and face all the risks involved. This decision was the result of his generosity and his inborn nobility, but de Kalb knew how repugnant it was to the Marquis to return to the slow-moving, seasickness-producing ship after he had once reached the American soil.[143] Therefore he said that in his opinion they should all leave the boat. Their aim, after all, was to reach their destination quickly and unharmed; and since now they were in safety so near their goal, it would not be prudent to expose themselves to new risks. "As for me," de Kalb concluded firmly, "I shall go by land; let him who wishes follow me! All who stay on board will have only themselves to blame if they meet with misfortune."

It is not surprising that in a boatload of idealists there should be violent and conflicting voices raised against one sensible and forceful personality.[144] The upshot was that de Kalb, Lafayette, Dubuysson, Lesser, Valfort, Gimat, Bédoulx and Price started for Charleston on foot or on horseback, arriving Tuesday, June 17, 1777. This march of about sixty miles, accomplished in three days, was an extremely strenuous experience. Dubuysson tells[145] that some of those who had been unable to secure horses found they could not walk in their boots, so they discarded them to walk barefoot on the burning sand and through the forests. As a result, his legs were for fifteen days as thick as his thighs. They reached Charleston looking like beggars or brigands and were treated as such; local inhabitants pointed their fingers in scorn, while they were thinking of themselves as officers of the king of France's army brought to their present pitiful state by a desire for glory in the defense of these very people; they were treated as adventurers even by the French, of whom there were many in Charleston. The greater part of these were officers ruined by debts and hence cashiered by their corps, who had flocked to Charleston from the French West Indies. The American governors were in the habit of getting rid of such scum as quickly as possible by giving them letters of recommendation to Washington or to Congress. The first ones were received very favorably, but their conduct soon showed what they were, and now Congress no longer had faith in recommendations, nor any regard for those who presented them. The men from the "Victoire" had ample reason to think back to these reports, first heard in Charleston, about the American attitude toward French volunteers in the American cause.

Aristotle says that in drama a recognition scene frequently leads to a complete reversal in the hero's fortune. So in the dramatic situation in Charleston, when on the day following the officers' arrival, the "Victoire" triumphantly moved into the harbor, there was a revolution in the attitude toward the new arrivals. Now they were cordially received everywhere. Certainly the fine ship proved that its owner was a real marquis! The French officers who had been the first to poke fun at them now came in droves to court Lafayette's favor and to apply for service under his command. The Marquis was paid honors of the sort generally accorded only a marshal of France. A full week was passed in dinners and various other activites.

In a letter to his wife Lafayette gives an enthusiastic description[146] of his days in Charleston:

> My own reception has been most peculiarly agreeable. To have been merely my traveling companion suffices to secure any of our men the kindest welcome. I have just passed five hours at a large dinner given in compliment to me by a gentleman of this town. Generals Howe and Moultrie, as well as several officers of my suite were present. We drank each other's health, and endeavored to talk English, which I am beginning to speak a little. Tomorrow I shall pay a visit in company with these gentlemen to the governor of the state and make last arrangements for my departure. The next day the commanding officers here will take me to see the town and its environs, and I shall then set out to join Washington's army.

He was delighted with everything in the country for which he was ready to give his life:[147]

> I shall now speak to you, my love, about the country and its inhabitants who are as agreeable as my enthusiasm had led me to imagine. Simplicity of manner, kindness of heart, love of country and liberty, and a delightful state of equality are met with universally. The richest and the poorest men are completely on a level, and although there are some immense fortunes in this country, I challenge anyone to point out the slightest difference in their manner toward each other. I first saw and judged of country life at Major Huger's house; I am at present in the city, where everything somewhat resembles British customs except that you find more simplicity here than you would in England. Charleston is one of the best built, handsomest and most agreeable cities that I have ever seen. The American women are very pretty, and display great simplicity without any affectation, and the extreme neatness of their appearance is truly delightful. Cleanliness is everywhere even more studiously attended to than in England. What gives me most pleasure is to see how completely the citizens are all brethren in one family. In America there are none poor, and none even that can be

called peasants. Each citizen has some property, and all citizens have the same rights as the richest individual or landed proprietor in the country. The inns are very different from those of Europe; the host and hostess sit at table with you and do the honors of a comfortable meal, and when you depart you pay your bill without being obliged to pay a tax in addition. If you dislike going to inns you may always find country houses in which you will be received as a good American with the same attention that you might expect in a friend's house in Europe.

The Marquis fitted perfectly into the life in America as he found it in Charleston two days after his arrival. In his letter to Mme. Lafayette he says further:

From the agreeable life I lead in this country, the sympathy which makes me feel as much at ease with the inhabitants as if I had known them for twenty years, the similarity of their way of thinking and my own, my love of glory and liberty, you might imagine that I am very happy – but you are not with me, my dearest love.[148]

From Petersburg, Virginia, on July 17, 1777, he writes to Mme. Lafayette with the same enthusiasm about his "American experience:"

I am now eight days' journey from Philadelphia, in the beautiful state of Virginia. All fatigue is over... the journey is somewhat tiring; but although several of my comrades have suffered a great deal, I myself have scarcely been conscious of fatigue... The further I advance to the north the better pleased I am with the country and its inhabitants. There is no attention or kindness that I do not receive, although many scarcely know who I am. [149]

Lafayette's cheerful view of the United States, in sharp contrast to the impressions of Messrs. Mauroy and Fayolle may in part have been due to letters of introduction for him and de Kalb from their newly made Charleston friends, as well as from Governor Caswell of North Carolina and other hospitable gentlemen along the route.

In writing to Mme. de Kalb, the Baron seems to have had some doubts, in contrast to Lafayette's optimism, regarding their coming reception by Congress, due to what he observed in Charleston regarding the prevailing American attitude toward French officers. In telling of the week's stay in Charleston he does not mention the gay entertainment, but he remarks that one cannot praise too highly the city council for the aid they have offered their guests in equipping themselves for the long journey north. As a professional soldier he is very much interested in the defences of the Charleston harbor. He complains about the high prices and the intolerable heat. But he evidently relished the overland journey of more than 800 miles, as from Annapolis he writes his wife that he is feeling fine, in better health than any other member of the group, that no tiring march harmed or incommoded him, and despite his fifty-six years he feels that he can best any of the young men.

At the start of the journey to Philadelphia, it was decided that, lest the entire caravan, to use de Kalb's expression, should overwhelm inns along the road, it would be better to split up into groups. Lafayette and de Kalb travelled together, because they had numerous letters of introduction in common. Lafayette wished to have with him Messrs. Lesser, Valfort and Bédoulx, as well as his aides-de-camp Gimat and Price. The eighth was Dubuysson, de Kalb's aide-de-camp. Evidently Lafayette did not relish the prospect of having to listen to Mauroy as his captive audience.

In a letter from Charleston, June 20, 1777, to his patron, the Comte de Broglie,[150] de Kalb mentions Mauroy's complaint that all who spoke English were in his, de Kalb's group – what was to become of the rest? De Kalb explained to him that Lafayette would need his aides with him, and naturally also those to whom he was intimately attached. Moreover, de Mauroy would not need to worry, because all, in the course of the preceding three months, had been studying English, and knew enough to get along; certainly de Mauroy could not expect in future to have an interpreter at his side all the time.

Broglie had commended Mauroy particularly to de Kalb, but with his usual directness the baron explains in the letter that he can by no means share his good opinion of the Vicomte's character. "The fellow has an enormous self-esteem," de Kalb writes. He goes on to say that Mauroy is continually complaining that he has been treated unfairly, he never agrees with anyone, he becomes argumentative on every subject, defending his position with stubbornness and, when opposed by several, loses his temper. Sometimes he even claimed that he had been a cavalry officer, then on another occasion he tells of having taken part in some attack that could only have been made by infantry. All this, of course, does not increase confidence in the man. What annoys de Kalb most is the continual stream of complaints against Mr. Deane – why, no one knows. He detests the country for which he is going to fight, even before he has seen it; sometimes he wishes that he had been taken prisoner by the British because then he would have been returned to France promptly. "I want to ask you, therefore,[151] M. le Comte," de Kalb continues, "to understand why I am not becoming intimately associated with him. This will in no way prevent my gladly cooperating with him on every occasion for the general good, and particularly in the service of the King and the French nation."

The 800-mile journey from Charleston to Philadelphia lasted from June 25 to July 26. The procession, led by Lafayette and de Kalb, started out in the spirit of the "Victoire"! At its head rode one of the Marquis' servants in the uniform of a hussar. Next came the carriage of Lafayette and de Kalb, with a groom riding beside it. This was followed by a gig occupied by the two colonels, de Valfort and de Lesser. The third vehicle was for de Kalb's aide-de-camp, Dubuysson (who in a memoir left the fullest account of this journey) and Lafayette's aides, the Messrs. Gimat and Price. Then followed a wagon loaded with baggage. At the end of the procession came a negro on horseback. Tally-ho, so to speak![152]

Another overland group of officers was led by de Mauroy, while de Vrigny, Bédoulx, and Colombe went by sea, despite the danger of being captured by the British. The three groups reached Philadelphia at approximately the same time.

The route taken by the first group led through New Bern and Halifax (North Carolina), Petersburg (Virginia), Annapolis and Baltimore, to Philadelphia. Despite kindly hospitality shown them by the Governor of North Carolina, Richard Caswell, and various others, the trip was described by Dubuysson as much harder than any military campaign in Europe; there, in the course of the war, came pauses, offering time for rest, and even amusement; here hardships continued for more than a month, getting worse every day. The wagons broke down, the horses died or went lame, some of the baggage was stolen, a considerable part of the journey had to be covered on foot, the travelers being forced to sleep in the woods at times, annoyed by insects, suffering from thirst and hunger, fever and dysentery. It proved to be highly ironic that their spirits were upheld through all the hardships by the thought of the glorious reception that would be accorded them on reaching Philadelphia![153] If Charleston had welcomed them so hospitably, how much more warmly would Congress receive them, particularly since they had letters of recommendation from Franklin and Deane!

There are two contemporary documents written by members of the "Victoire" group that form interesting pendants to Lafayette's enthusiastic appreciation of America. One is a journal kept by the Chevalier Pierre de Rousseau de Fayolle; the other, a memoir from the pen of Viscomte Charles Louis de Mauroy. Both men were refused apointments by Congress, both left Philadelphia for Boston, and both months later returned to France. In both accounts one may note the flavor of sour grapes.

Starting from Charleston for Philadelphia on June 26, 1777,[154] our caravan consisted of six officers and four servants or carters, which made ten persons in two wagons drawn by four horses. The wagon in which I rode lost one of the shaft horses on the third or fourth day – it died of colic in a single hour. We were obliged to purchase another, which cost us dearly, but it was in good condition.

We experienced abominable heat in South Carolina, and when at the end of the day we wished to refresh ourselves, we found the inns frightful and the water execrable. Also, one of our companions, Capitaine, fell sick at Charlotte, the second city we struck. It is one of the worst places that one can imagine. However, we found there a doctor who took excellent care of the patient; he lodged him as well as the rest of us, in his home, and I did not leave the house until after the sick officer was quite out of danger. In Charlotte we bought two horses to add to our four overburdened beasts, in hope of making up the time which the sick man had caused us to lose.

The other wagon had proceeded on its course with at least fifteen days start. As for me, I left the nineteenth on horseback, in order to reach Philadelphia more quickly and to secure funds to pay the cost of the wagon that would arrive a long time after me. Our money was running low because of the purchases and the over-night stops we were forced to make.

Up to the present, one thing is certain, we have not found anything that could please us; our only resource was money, and as a rule the people proved not at all helpful. The men are well-built and alert, but the women look very slovenly. I do not know whether the future will prove more agreeable, but things are not by any means as they were described to us in France. The Americans are disunited regarding their common cause, and I do not think that they will ever do anything remarkable. Vanity pricks them; they all want to be officers and not soldiers, and they are not worth anything in either category.

Their army is miserable from every point of view, particularly so as regards officers; one can have no idea how bad things are. There is no sort of discipline whatever; but what is still worse is their ignorance and false vanity, which will make it impossible for them to resist the forces of the British general whenever he makes an effort to conquer the country; his victory will be the easiest thing in the world.

CHEVALIER DE MAUROY'S MEMOIRE[155]

We arrived in Charleston in the month of June... In the middle of the principal square stands the statue of Pitt. It faces the sea, eyes fixed on the people, arms extended toward them. This "situation pittoresque" (does he intend a pun?) might have rekindled the enthusiasm of my companions, which was beginning to require fuel, but unfortunately only the statue extended its arms.

The city council received us with politeness but did nothing to remove obstacles which confronted strangers on a journey as long as the one we still had to make before we reached Philadelphia; therefore we ourselves looked for the means of surmounting them. We bought wagons and horses, we hired guides. We were forced to separate into groups because too large a crowd would have exhausted the resources of the benevolent inn-keepers such as we then still hoped to encounter on our route. It was only by scattering money freely that we were able to set out on our way. And it was only with still more money that we were able to continue on our journey.

The nature of the roads made it impossible for our vehicles to cover much distance daily, and therefore I decided to leave them behind. Then, followed by only one servant, I left the little caravan at Camden, a town eighty miles from Charleston, and left my baggage, which overloaded our carriages, with a local resident, a doctor by profession, who according to report was the most honest man in the country. This honest man promised me to send it on safely, assuring me that nothing was easier, and that it would arrive before me. Actually my trunks arrived in the vicinity of Philadelphia, carefully wrapped in heavy packcloth, but I never saw again my possessions which had been inside – the trunks were empty!

I crossed the Carolinas through continuous pine woods, where at long distances I encountered a few plantations. The inhabitants appeared to me to be afflicted with an absolutely childish curiosity. As soon as I alighted, they threw themselves on everything that belonged to me and went round and round it in every direction, even down to the smallest piece of equipment, and kept questioning me pitilessly without any particular plan. When necessity forced me to stop at some colonist's house, and when he finally decided to receive me, generally I found him, to begin with, a good-natured fellow, a calm soul, occupied in an easy-going effort to care for his family and land. But if I stopped at a tavern, I would find some colonists assembled, getting drunk on a very disagreeable drink composed of rum and water, discussing their public affairs like wild men, with every argument ending in a fist-fight, so that the strongest always ended in winning the argument. They were usually riding cheap nags worth ten or twelve guineas at most, amusing themselves with races in which the bets ran as high as two thousand pounds. I began to consider that they would have to make too many sacrifices for their life of independence.

Doubtless Miss Liberty is a very fine lady, and probably means everything to one who does not possess her, but she is a haughty mistress who absolutely refuses to share her favors. In order to live free one must, like the ancient philosopher, throw one's money in the ocean. Farmers, such as those I describe above, will not rush to their vast coasts to imitate Crates. I suspect that all Americans are cold and lazy, but that assembled to talk about public business while drinking toasts to Washington and other heroes of America, they get excited, for the strong liquor lends them a heat of which they are normally incapable, and that with rum and fisticuffs they can be assembled and kept united so long as their intoxication lends them a false courage.

The population of the two Carolinas does not approach that of the northern provinces because 1. the time of their settlement was later; 2. the cultivation of the land is done by negroes and there are twenty blacks for each white man; 3. the climate is anything but wholesome. I saw on the banks of some rivers splendid locations for plantations abandoned because their owners had all perished.

On entering Virginia I began to find on the right and left a much more settled territory. The dense forest which I had been traversing disappeared entirely on the side by the sea, and on the other it seemed to retreat from one hill to another to crown the summit of a chain of mountains where at intervals I believed I could catch glimpses of the gates of a new universe.

It is in this delightful province that Washington has his superb plantations. Though the work is still done by negroes, their outnumbering of the whites is much less striking and does not sadden the heart of a sensitive observer as in the case of the Carolinas...

Maryland enjoys the same advantages...

Finally I entered Pennsylvania and was not a little surprised on arriving at Lancaster to meet with groups of American officers who were leaving for their home on a three months' leave. I had just learned that the English had moved up to Delaware Bay, and it seemed to me very strange that their threat to Philadelphia could not keep these American heroes at their posts. Those among them with whom I discussed this matter through my interpreter (for at that time I knew scarcely any English) explained to me that they had to attend to their business. I gave an appearance of being satisfied by this answer, but I did not sense either in their conduct nor in the explanations of these gentlemen that spirit found among men who are extremely enthusiastic about liberty and who show an ardent love of the public welfare. Even the first seeds of honor seemed to me to be neglected.

I arrived in Philadelphia in the first days of August... It resembles very much our cities in Flanders. The finest building erected here is the jail, built of stone; it is large and sanitary. One notes several large courts where the prisoners are free to stroll. This monument does honor to humanity; it reveals that there are at least some sensitive men who still recognize their brothers in the unfortunate victims of the law. To lock up one's fellowman in a frightful dungeon, to refuse him the free sight of the heavens, to leave him finally with nothing but his despair, however guilty he may be – does this not in some manner justify all crimes? Fortunately, under a government as mild as ours, this terrible spectacle does not wound our eyes.

It is interesting to observe how the American scene is reflected in the comments of the travelers. Lafayette was determined to find everything wonderful, and his letters glow with enthusiasm. Youthful, friendly, titled and wealthy, his warm personality produced friendliness in all around him, who were eager to recommend him to other hospitable "insurgents" whose entertainment provided bright spots in tedious, wearisome travel. De Kalb, approaching sixty, having fought through several long wars, was prepared to meet further disappointments and hardships. He knew what he had come for, and he pressed forward with firm purpose, not without occasional indignant outbursts about the heat or the insects. Middle-aged Mauroy, rather uncertain about what he was doing in this galley, expected to find everything good in nature but degenerating in the hands of men. He wore blinders that made him critical of a prison in Philadelphia, but totally unaware of the Bastille.

Undoubtedly both the excellences and the defects reported by the several travelers were all there, and very real. The beauty of Charleston, and its hospitality, were celebrated then, as they still are. But Lafayette had the best opportunity to see them at first hand, as well as the spirit and disposition to appreciate them. Mauroy's summing up of the coldness and laziness of the "colonists" in the wooded sections of the Carolinas, who could be roused from their sodden lethargy only by drink, is a fair picture; the lack of patriotism of the officers going on furlough to "attend their own business" while their country was in real danger, represented one of Washington's problems. It is also plain enough that he had no great love for nature, but was extremely bored by traveling through the beautiful woods in the rare days of June. Long days of travel did not seem so fatiguing to young Lafayette as to de Kalb, almost three times his age. As for Fayolle, he announces curtly, "We have not found anything that could please us." So it was, that keen as each observer was, he saw reflected only his own inner self.

Tough-minded as Mauroy was, he was also given to writing sentimental verse. In one quatrain he admits the influence of Abbé Raynal's *New World:*

> Je m'embarquais pour l'Amérique,
> Je quittais mon pays natal,
> Traversant la vaste Atlantique
> Sur le foi de l'Abbé Raynal.[156]

CHAPTER X

A COLD RECEPTION BY CONGRESS AND
ITS FAVORABLE OUTCOME

"We were received like dogs at a game of ninepins" (comme des chiens à un jeu de quille), Lafayette told the Chevalier de Mauroy when the latter reached Philadelphia two days after de Kalb and Lafayette. He said that he had answered Congress with pride, demanding that they read his letters more carefully. When Mauroy called on the Baron, he found him also in a furious temper about the manner in which Congress had received the French officers sent over by Mr. Deane. If they would now offer him a division, he said, he would not accept it. After what he had seen of Congress, he felt that an honest man would disgrace himself by serving in their army.[157] Congress claimed that Deane was not empowered to make appointments and that therefore all members of this respectable body wished eagerly to see him hanged – Deane was in fact about to be recalled.

To understand the hostile reception accorded the idealists who had come so far to fight for the American cause, one must consider what was happening in America while they spent three months in crossing the ocean and trudging north to Philadelphia.

Deane had written to Congress, November 6, 1776, "The rage, as I may call it, for entering into the American service increases, and the consequence is that I am pressed with offers and with proposals, many of these from persons of the first rank and eminence, in the sea as well as in the land service."[158]

On this side of the ocean, Thomas Jefferson in July, 1776, wrote to John Page, "I would not advise that the French gentlemen should come here. We have so many of that country, and have been so much imposed on, that Congress begins to get sore on the head."[159] Robert Morris wrote to William Bingham, February 16, 1777, "Spare me all you can in the introduction of French officers to me. Could I speak the language and had spare time, it would be a pleasure, but now it is too much the reverse."[160]

Congress did "get sore" on March 13, 1777, and resolved that the Committee of Secret Correspondence be directed forthwith to write to all their ministers and agents abroad to discourage all gentlemen from coming to America with expectation of employment in the service, unless they are masters of our language, and have the best recommendations.[161] But James Lovell, member of Congress from Massachusetts, insisted that it be understood that the line drawn against those who do not speak English did not mean a patent for those who do.

On the same day Congress passed another resolution: "that the two German officers mentioned in the letter of His Excellency Governor Henry, not understanding our language, cannot be provided for by Congress in the army of the United States."[162]

On the following day Congress voted along the same lines:

> Resolved, that mons. Faneuil's scheme for offering, arming and clothing a corps of Frenchmen, to be raised in the French Islands, to serve in the United States, as mentioned in General Washington's letter of February 20, 1777, be disapproved.
>
> That General Washington be acquainted, it is the opinion of Congress, no commissions should be granted to foreign officers, to serve in these states, unless they are well acquainted with our language, and bring strong credentials of their abilities:
>
> That a Copy of the Resolution of Congress, passed yesterday, discouraging foreign gentlemen coming over to America to serve as officers in the Army of the United States, without being acquainted with our language, be transferred to General Washington.

On March 16, 1777, John Hancock wrote to General Schuyler: "The number of foreigners already employed in the army of these states is a prodigious weight upon the service, and the evil is like to increase unless a speedy stop can be put to it."[163]

The very next day, de Kalb's letter of December 26, 1775, written to the Philadelphia physician, Dr. Phile, in which the Baron expressed the wish that he might place his thirty-two years of military experience in the service of the United States, came before Congress. The doctor had given it to Robert Morris, who then passed it on to the president of Congress, John Hancock. Congress voted that the Committee of Secret Correspondence write a respectful letter to General de Kalb, thank him for his obliging offer and decline to accept it at present. March 19, 1777, the date of this reply, is the very day de Kalb and Lafayette arrived in Bordeaux to take passage on the "Victoire."[164]

Other business at the same meeting was the appointment of a

Committee on Foreign Applications, with James Lovell as chairman. He had no love for Frenchmen, and he loathed Silas Deane, but since he spoke fluent French, all French applicants were sent to him as counselor. He was also frequently called upon to act as interpreter, all of which duties he considered an annoying waste of time. On June 30 he wrote to Joseph Trumbull, "These Frenchmen have used me up quite."[165] How frayed his nerves must have become through dealing so often with importunate impostors can be seen from the resolution he introduced at approximately the same date of Lafayette's and de Kalb's arrival:

> Whereas, Silas Deane, Esq., when agent under the Committee of Secret Correspondence, entered into conventions with several foreign officers which Congress have declared themselves not bound to ratify and which in the present situation of affairs, they could not comply with, without deranging the army, and thereby injuring at this critical juncture the American cause; And, whereas the credit, reputation and usefulness of Silas Deane Esq., now one of the American commissioners in France, will be greatly impaired by the consequences of his indiscretion in having entered into such conventions, his recall becomes necessary for the interest of these United States: Therefore
>
> Resolved, that Silas Deane, Esq., now one of the American commissioners in France, be forthwith recalled; and that from the day of his receiving this resolve, all and every power with which he has been vested by Congress do cease and determine; and that he take the earliest opportunity to embark to North America and repair to Congress.[166]

Just after the arrival of de Kalb's and Lafayette's group, on July 29, 1777, Lovell wrote to William Whipple a letter full of righteous wrath, of which the second paragraph reads:[167]

> In addition to the perplexities which I have before mentioned to you about French treaties made by Deane, we have a fresh quantity from the arrival of two majors general, two brigadiers, two lieutenant colonels, two majors, three captains and two lieutenants created and ranked seventh of November last and December, to whom have been advanced 16,000 livres, one half gratuity and half pay. Ought not this weak and roguish man to be recalled; if as corresponding agent he did this, what will not he think himself entitled to do as a commissioner?"

The worst of Deane's deeds, in the eyes of Mr. Lovell, was the appointment of the Chevalier Du Coudray. This officer, who with the consent of the French Government, had been collecting cannon from various arsenals in France, had succeeded in sending them to the United States. As a reward for his aid to America, this overbearing, impudent officer demanded from Deane the rank of major general, the command of the whole artillery, and also of the entire engineering services; furthermore, he was to be subject only to Congress and to the commander-in-chief, thus outranking all American officers in these branches except Washington. Du Coudray arrived in June, 1777, and presented his demands to Congress, whereupon "the wrath of Congress rose to the boiling point, while that of several officers in the army boiled over." Sullivan, Greene and Knox threatened to resign if Congress should accede to these impudent demands. Not only American officers, but also four French artillery officers sent over by Franklin refused to serve under him. A compromise was finally achieved after hot debates; Du Coudray was made inspector general of ordnance and military manufactures, with the rank of major general. Mr. Lovell was particularly angry at Deane for having been duped by this supercilious bluffer whom Duportail and the other artillerists regarded as incompetent.[168]

This was the background in Congress and the army, when, on the morning of July 27, 1777, the French officers reached Philadelphia. They brushed themselves up a little, perhaps looking forward to five-hour dinners with toasts to George Washington, in the manner of hospitality at Charleston. It was Sunday, so Congress was not in session, but they delivered their letters of recommendation and their contracts to John Hancock, President of Congress. By the next day presumably their papers would have been read. What actually happened at this fateful rendezvous is told by the Chevalier Dubuysson in his *Mémoire:*

> We were exactly on time the next morning, but they made us wait a long while. Finally Mr. Morris appeared with another member of Congress who, he said, spoke French very well and was empowered to deal with all French applicants, and that we were to refer all our problems to him. He left, to return to Independence Hall. The other gentleman, Mr. Lovell, did not invite us into the building, but received us in the street, where he then left us standing after addressing us in very good French as a group of adventurers. He ended his harangue by saying that Deane had exceeded his powers. Congress had asked him to send over four engineers; instead of that he had sent us M. Du Coudray with some supposed

engineers who were not engineers at all, and artillery officers who had never served in the army. Mr. Franklin had then been instructed to procure four engineers, who had duly arrived. "French officers are very well brought up indeed to come here to serve the United States without first having been invited! Last year, it is true, we needed some French officers, but now we have many of them, and very experienced ones too!" Having said this, Mr. Lovell returned to the Halls of Congress.

Such was our first reception by Congress; we did not know what to think of it; it is impossible to be more stupefied than we were. The Marquis de Lafayette, de Kalb and de Mauroy, with the other officers, all with recommendations such as we had, tolerated, at least, if not openly avowed by the French Government to fight against England in America – how could they possibly expect such a reception?[169]

The officers decided to find out what was at the bottom of such scandalous conduct by a member of the American Congress. They soon learned of scandalous conduct on the part of various French officers. One had been cowardly at Ticonderoga; Mr. Conway (of Irish extraction but an officer of the French army) was detested by the officers of his brigade; but the one who really made all Frenchmen despised was Du Coudray. From the time of his arrival, he adopted a superior tone, claiming to have been a brigadier in the French army, letting it be known that he was an adviser of the ministers in charge of the French Government, and a personal friend of all the dukes and princes, producing letters to prove his boasts. He submitted a contract given him by Silas Deane awarding him the grade of major general, with supreme command of artillery and engineering. He went so far in his impudence as to inform Congress that aid sent by France was due entirely to his eloquent and insistent solicitations. Small wonder that Congress refused to honor Deane's subsequent appointments.

Parenthetically, to close with Du Coudray, it may be said that his end was in character. Desiring to cross the Schuylkill, he entered a ferry boat on horseback, disdaining the ferryman's advice to dismount.[170] In midstream his horse became unmanageable, he fell into the river and was drowned. With a feeling of relief the American army gave him a fine funeral with interment in the Romish chapel in Philadelphia.

Franklin and Deane sent to the Committee of Foreign Affairs a letter of recommendation of Lafayette dated Paris, May 25, 1777:

... The Marquis de Lafayette, a young nobleman of great family connections here and great wealth, is gone to America in a ship of his own, accompanied by other officers of distinction, in order to serve in our armies. He is exceedingly beloved and everybody's good wishes attend him; we cannot but hope he may meet with such a reception as will make the country and his expedition agreeable to him. Those who censure it as imprudent in him do nevertheless applaud his spirit, and we are satisfied that the civilities and respect that may be shown him will be serviceable to our affairs here, as pleasing not only to his powerful relations and to the Court but to the whole French nation. He has left a beautiful young wife, and for her sake particularly we hope that his bravery and ardent desire to distinguish himself will be a little retarded by the General's prudence, so as to not permit his being hazarded much, but on some important occasion.[171]

The authorities were indeed impressed with this new and different sort of French officer, as well as with Franklin's mention of his high nobility and influence at the Court in the interest of the American cause. Lafayette himself, moreover, made only two conditions; that he serve without pay and as a volunteer, i.e., without a command; he also agreed to cancel the agreement with Deane. Congress thereupon awarded him a major generalship, dated July 31, 1777, which, however was to be purely honorary, as Benjamin Harrison stated in a letter to Washington of August 20, 1777. This youth was not to have any pay, nor claim to a pension, nor, worst for the would-be hero – any command or promise of a command. Within two hours after Lafayette's agreement with Congress, he received the major general's sash and was invited to dinner at headquarters, where Washington assigned him lodgings and invited him to eat at the General's table for the rest of the campaign.

By all this Lafayette was "dazzled," as Dubuysson puts it, and caused to forget his comrades for the moment; but only for the moment; he was too good-hearted to forget his friends for long. As he thought over the situation, he could not but feel that the preferment he had received over the distinguished soldier de Kalb was in glaring contrast to their respective merits. This *noblesse oblige* caused him to offer to send back his sash[172] with the statement that he could not accept the appointment unless his comrades-in-arms should also be accorded the grades agreed to by Silas Deane. Dubuysson believed that, had Lafayette held out firmly, de Kalb would have received his major generalship and the others their respective ranks. But he was probably wrong - for the following reasons:

These members of Congress were not the sort of men to accede to an ultimatum; they were inclined to be quite anti-French, especially since their experience with Du Coudray; and three of the best American generals – Knox, Greene and Sullivan – had angrily stated that they would resign if any more French officers were appointed to high posts.

Here was perhaps a turning-point in history, with de Kalb determining its course. He had been rudely insulted on his arrival by a representative of Congress, and now he found that a lad of nineteen, with no military experience, was to be given the place and rank that should have been his by any reasonable standard. Had he been vindictive, he could have urged on Lafayette to refuse the major generalship unless Congress honored all of Deane's contracts. There is little doubt as to what the reaction to such an all-or-nothing proposal would have been. What then of Franklin's hopes, expressed in his letters from Paris, that respect and civilities shown Lafayette would be "serviceable to our affairs here, as pleasing not only to his powerful relations and to the Court, but to the whole French nation?"

What if Lafayette had returned to France in a huff because Congress had met him and his comrades with insults and refused to honor their contracts? Meanwhile his "escape" on the "Victoire" had made him a national hero celebrated everywhere, whom even his formerly irate father-in law now regarded with pride. The alliance with France hung very much in the balance as did, of course, the aid by the French fleet, without which the war could have turned into a stalemate. That Lafayette was the sort to issue an ultimatum is shown by the fact that in a letter to the President of Congress, Henry Laurens, of January 31, 1778, he stated that unless his demands were met by Congress, he was prepared to resign his commission and return to France, accompanied by many of the French officers.[173] By this time Lafayette had gained some distinction, so Congress acceded, the point being of no great importance.

As Lafayette hesitated, de Kalb stepped in energetically. Far from showing any jealousy, he was pleased with his friend's good fortune, but refused absolutely Lafayette's offer to threaten Congress with his resignation in the interest of the group. Instead he urged him to join the army immediately, because, after the éclat caused in Paris by his decision to fight for the freedom of the United States, and his sensational escape, it would appear a ridiculous anticlimax if he were to return without having gained honor and distinction on the battlefield. Lafayette accepted his mentor's excellent and unselfish advice. Thus the United States gained a good general and a noble legend, of a dashing, twenty-year-old

French aristocrat who devoted his life and his fortune to the service of our liberty.

A few weeks later, Lafayette showed outstanding bravery in the battle of Brandywine, where he received a wound in the leg. De Kalb's action was certainly a diplomatic stroke of the first order.

The Baron now decided to take action to clarify his own position. As was said of the Latin poet, "Anger shapes the verse," so there came out of the Baron's wrath a very eloquent letter to Congress. He began by saying that an accident to his leg was keeping him in bed (intimating that he was not lobbying.) He did not come as a humble petitioner, but dealt with Congress on an equal footing, even presenting his case in their language. He mentions, in passing as it were, two painful weaknesses of the American case; the incompetence of Mr. Deane and the boorishness of Mr. Lovell. He insists that Congress fulfill its part of the contract (written in English which even Mr. Deane must have understood) just as de Kalb had fulfilled his. Salary was not important, but left to the decision of Congress, while the rank accorded by Deane was absolutely essential. If Congress did not want his services, he was ready to return, naturally upon reimbursement of his expenses. He showed no jealousy whatever of his friend Lafayette, but made it clear why he could not serve under this lad, since the two of them had come with the same promises and the same purpose. He dropped a hint that a lawsuit against Mr. Deane would not help the American cause in France, and closed with bitterness at the insults inflicted on him.

> An accidental lameness, he says, prevented me from calling on any member of Congress to know what has been or shall be decided in regard to the agreement between Mr. Deane and myself, and not to trouble the gentlemen of the Committee for french officers, or multiply their business by writing in french, I take the liberty of applying to your excellency for information on that account, in explaining myself in english as much as I may be able to do it. I was vastly surprised at my being introduced to Mr. Lovell to hear him (almost in public) exclaim loudly against Mr. Deane's proceedings, and disapprove all the conventions this agent has made for several officers, as being contrary to his powers. To which I answer that a public man ought to know what powers he hath from his constituents or hath not; that Mr. Deane is generally esteemed to be a candid man and a man of sense; that whatever he may have agreed to with others, and this too in a language he did not understand, mine is in english, and so very plain that it can admit of no various

interpretations; for that reason I will strictly keep to the text of it as for the rank; as to interest, I will not be too rigid but rely on Congress' pleasure. As I have now fulfilled my part of that agreement, I wish Congress would do theirs without loss of time, and let me hear of their resolution thereof. I would not be a simple spectator in the scenes prepared for opening.

If you will not ratify Mr. Deane's engagement and appoint me major general in your army, I am ready to return to Europe, but think myself entitled to ask you a sufficient sum for my going home. I received from Mr. Deane 1200 livres French money, and certainly by going to and fro in France under his directions, and all the other expenses until my arrival in Philadelphia, I spent twice as much. And though I ardently desired to serve America, I did not mean to do so in spending part of my own and my children's fortune – for what is deemed generosity in the Marquis de Lafayette would be downright madness in me, who does not possess one of the first-rate fortunes. If I were in his circumstances I should perhaps have acted as he did. I am very glad that you granted his wishes; he is a worthy young man, and no one will outdo him in enthusiasm in your cause of liberty and independence. My wishes will always be that his successes as major general equal his zeal and your expectation. But I must confess, sir, that this distinction between him and myself is painful and very displeasing to me. We came on the same errand, with the same promises, and as military men for military purposes; I flatter myself that if there was to be any preference it would be due to me. 34 years of constant attendance on military service & my station and rank in that way, may well be laid in the scale with his disinterestedness, and be of at least the same weight and value; this distinction is very unaccountable in an infant state of a commonwealth, but this is none of my business. I only want to know whether Congress will appoint me a major general and with the seniority I have a right to expect this (for I cannot stay here in a lesser capacity). It would seem very odd and ridiculous to the french ministry and all experienced military men to see me placed under the command of the Marquis de la Fayette. If, on the contrary, it will not be agreeable to the U.S., I ask your excellency to give me full satisfaction for the purpose of going back, so that I may leave this country as soon as possible. I hope there will be no difficulty in fulfilling my request, for I should

> be sorry to be compelled to carry my case against Mr. Deane or his successors for damages. And such an action would injure his credit and negotiations, and those of the state at court.
>
> I do not think that either my name, my services, or my person are proper objects to be trifled with or laughed at. I cannot tell you, sir, how deeply I feel the injury done to me, and how ridiculous it seems to me to make people leave their homes, families and affairs to cross the sea under 1000 dangers, to be received and to be looked at with contempt by those from whom you were to expect but warm thanks.[174]

In a legal sense de Kalb was in the right, but he was sufficiently broadminded to see Congress' side. In a letter to his wife he states that the group of officers was so large and the ranks granted them so high that American officers would necessarily feel dissatisfied and slighted. Congress was in the difficult position of either having to disavow Deane or to risk resignations from able and patriotic American generals such as Knox, Sullivan or Greene. Certainly Congress chose the lesser evil; as Kapp, de Kalb's biographer, says, "In political and state matters it is frequently better to cut a knot than to untie it." Thus all of the officers, by resolution of Congress of September 8, 1777, with the exception of Lafayette, were rejected. After a report on the French officers' desire to serve the United States the minute continues:

> Resolved: that the thanks of Congress be given to the Baron de Kalb and the Viscount de Mauroy with the officers who accompany them, for their zeal for passing over to America to offer their services to these United States, and that their expenses in this continent, and their return to France be paid.
> Resolved: that Congress agree to the said report and resolve.
> Ordered: that the Baron de Kalb and the Viscount de Mauroy be furnished with a copy of the foregoing report and resolution, attested by the Secretary.[175]

Accordingly, de Kalb asked each officer to list his expenses which were then submitted to Congress for payment. By September the funds of the French officers were pretty low; Dubuysson relates that he and de Kalb had each only two shirts and one threadbare suit. Upon receiving payment, all the disappointed idealists started on their homeward journey. De Kalb, thanks to his strong constitution and the ministrations of Dr. Phile, had fully recovered from the fever resulting from a contusion of his right knee that had confined him to bed or his room for fully six weeks.

In company with his faithful aide Dubuysson and the two colonels, de Lesser and de Valfort, de Kalb started, September 15, 1777, on a northerly route toward Boston, planning to return via that port. He decided first to visit "an extraordinary place," the settlement of a German pietistic sect at Bethlehem, Pennsylvania. It is remarkable and also characteristic that this lifelong soldier was interested in visiting a community whose members refused to bear arms. But it appears even more striking that at a time when the plan that was to crown his career had just come to nought, he described this visit sympathetically in a detailed account to his wife.

> We made a detour to see this extraordinary place. It is a town 52 miles from Philadelphia, founded thirty-three years ago, inhabited entirely by people of the same religion, called the Moravian Brethren, in German *Herrenhüter*, and who call themselves the United Brethren. They follow the Lutheran service, have bishops and preachers who have only a modest income apportioned to their needs and those of their families. The married people live in separate houses, as is the custom elsewhere, but they have public houses, very large and suited to their purpose. There is one for the widows, one for the grown-up women from fifteen to old age, and one for unmarried men; one for the little boys, and another one for young girls. Every house has a governess or governor of the appropriate sex. Each group is distributed in apartments for ten or twelve in each room, where they work. Everybody is busy and everyone is gay in working all day long except during the hours of rest and recreation.
>
> There are men of all possible trades and their products are of reasonable price, resulting from their application and their sobriety, and above all from their fund of probity. Above the apartments of their houses there is a great salon or dormitory where there are all the beds. Each dormitory is lighted by a big lantern placed in the middle, and two persons of the sex of the house serve in turn as guards to watch all night over the tranquility of the others, the danger of fire, and also to assist any who find themselves in some need of help. There are brother and sister cooks who are in charge of expenses, who receive the money from their pensioners; each one working for his account, pays his portion which is regulated. The fathers and mothers pay for their children. Those who lack means are assisted by the Community. The

parents are permitted to keep masters in their homes for children of all ages. Likewise a child may stay in the house of his parents. When a young man wants to marry, he is examined by the elders to determine whether he can support a family, and when this point has been settled, he is led to the Community, where the governesses present their charges one after another until there appears one that suits him. The young girl then has the right to refuse the young man if he does not suit her. The young people of different sexes never take the opportunity of seeing each other or speaking to each other privately, much less in public. The children have all their meals regulated, the grown-ups only dinner. They prepare their breakfast and supper themselves, or ask of the cook whatever they wish, according to taste, the state of their health, or their desire to spend money. There is always plenty in a land of good living, fertile, well cultivated and in a very agreeable situation, near two rivers, abounding in good produce, game and fish. These people observe Sunday strictly, and also every evening of the working days there are prayers at the church at which only a few people fail to appear. They sing hymns there, and the discourses and prayers of the minister are listened to with great devotion. The sexes never mingle; the men have one half of the church, the women the other. They also have separate doors lest they meet on entering or leaving. Their number in this town is between six and seven hundred. There are no poor people here; everything here breathes comfort, cleanliness, decency, good morals and happiness. There have never been any instances of a lawsuit – not even of disputes; there are very few punishments on the part of fathers and mothers; never any disobedience nor misconduct on the part of the children. Here all Christian virtues are practiced as far as human weakness permits. If there can be a dwelling place of peace and innocence on earth, it is here. Nine miles from here there is a similar establishment called Nazareth; in addition there are many brothers scattered through other towns and the Capital. Everywhere they are hospitable and above all honest toward strangers.

I forgot to mention that the men never bear arms and that the women are distinguished by ribbons with which they tie their headgear or bonnets under their chins; the married women have a blue ribbon, the widows a white one, and the unmarried women a rose-colored. Everyone dresses simply but properly.[176]

The Bethlehem Diary of September 17, 1777, contains a reference to this visit [Vol. XXXI, p. 314 (in German)]: "The Baron de Kalb and three other officers of the French Service came to visit Bethlehem. One of the Frenchmen, Colonel Valfort, from Lyon, seemed to be a very pious man, who expressed great pleasure at everything he saw and what he heard of our doctrines." It was characteristic of de Kalb, who possessed a simple faith, that he did not become emotional in his religion.

While he was visiting his fellow-countrymen, a messenger from Congress arrived to inform de Kalb of action taken on the day of his departure: "Monday, 15th September 1777. Resolved that another major general be appointed in the Army of the United States; the ballots being taken, Baron de Kalb was elected."[177]

The reversal by Congress of its previous action was due to the very favorable impression made by de Kalb on members of the Congress with whom he had been negotiating in regard to the settlement of the claims of the French officers. His knowledge of English definitely set him apart from the other French applicants. Lovell, now very favorably disposed, wrote to his friend Whipple, September 17, 1777, praising de Kalb, "who in manners and looks resembles our Chief." He even expressed concern lest de Kalb refuse the major generalship.[178]

A letter from the President of Congress, Henry Laurens, to John Lewis Gervais, dated from York, Pennsylvania, October 9, 1777, presents this view of his character:

> Dear Sir:
> This will probably be delivered to you by the Baron de Kalb, a gentleman who has long been attending Congress with tenders of his service in the army and who a few days before we left was actually voted a major general, to be commissioned one day antecedent to the Marquis de Lafayette. This shows you the high estimation which Congres has made of the abilities and merits of the Baron.[179]

The resolution creating de Kalb's commission was passed September 15, but on October 4 both his and Lafayette's were dated the same day. Congress even offered to date the former back to November 7, 1776, in conformity with the contract signed with Deane, but de Kalb refused this, being satisfied with the arrangement which did not place him in the ridiculous position of ranking under a boy of twenty.

Charles Thomson, secretary of the body, was sent after de Kalb as a messenger to urge his acceptance of the commission. De Kalb asked that he might take a night to think the matter over, since it placed him in a difficult situation. The following morning he wrote a letter of appreciation to his friend Richard Henry Lee, declining the offer.

> Bristol, September 16, 1777
>
> Sir: I am unable to tell you with how much reluctance and even sorrow I must acquaint you that I cannot accept of the honor Congress intended to me, for the various reasons I explained to you, Sir, to several members of Congress, but more particularly to Mr. Lovell, and which I repeat to Mr. Secretary Thomson; they are all of great weight with me. I beseech you, dear Sir, to lay before Congress that I have and always shall retain the highest sense of thankfulness and veneration for the whole of so respectable a body of men and for each of the members in particular. My most sincere vows will ever be for success in all their measures and undertakings and for the general welfare and happiness of your states. I will never forget the private obligations I owe to some of your gentlemen, but especially your kindness to me. I will never be happier than when I hear from you, or when I shall be able to convince you of the esteem and respect with which I have the honor to be, Sir, your most obedient and most humble servant.[180]
>
> Signed: the Baron de Kalb

On the urging of Charles Thomson, however, de Kalb agreed to reconsider the matter and to write to Congress. He was chiefly concerned about the impression his move would make on his superiors and friends, the Broglies, and more immediately on the group that sailed on the "Victoire." His refusal would not help his fellow officers, for Congress had definitely decided against appointing men ignorant of the language of the private soldiers and of the officers above them. He states his dilemma in characteristic fashion in a letter to his wife:

> I have meditated further over the matter, and have considered it in a twofold aspect. If I return, no one can complain of me, for I have done no man harm, and have served everyone to the extent of my powers. But in that case I shall attain none of the objects for which I have undertaken this journey. If I remain, Valfort, who knows all my movements and understands my motives, will undertake my defense on his return. Besides, I am persuaded in advance that the Marshal as well as the Comte de Broglie will approve my seizing the most dangerous and enterprising horn of the dilemma, and preferring to deprive myself for some time

longer of my domestic comforts and my family. The Chevalier Dubuysson will acquaint Congress with my conditions on which I accept their offer. If they are granted, so much the better for me; if rejected, I shall at least have the honor of having declined what was offered to me alone, and shall again salute you and our household gods.[181]

On September 18, 1777, from Bethlehem, de Kalb sent his reply to Congress. He states that the appointment leaves him in an "uncertain and fluctuating situation of mind, between the desire of serving in your army and the apprehension of blame from home." Therefore he asks the Congress to grant him certain points:

1. That he may be free to return to France in case his superiors disapprove his course.

2. That his commission be not previous to Lafayette's but, of the same date, "that it may be in my power to show my regard for his friendship to me, in giving him the seniority over me in America."

3. That Congress grant Chevalier Dubuysson a commission of lieutenant colonel with only the pay of a major as his aide-de-camp.

4. That Congress award Dubuysson a pension for life if he would serve in the next two compaigns.

5. That in case of his death, a suitable pension be awarded to Mme. de Kalb.[182]

Well aware that at times Congress had made appointments without consulting the commander-in-chief, de Kalb closed with an emphatic statement regarding the newly created major generalship and command of a division; in case Washington should prefer some other officer for the post, he would readily withdraw and "gladly and entirely submit to his commands and to be employed as he shall think most convenient for the good of the service."

How strongly de Kalb felt on this point is shown by a letter dated by him "At Peter Wolff's, October 2, 1777." The recipient is indicated only as "Dear Sir" – probably he was a member of Congress interested in furthering de Kalb's appointment:

By the letter of this day you honored me with, I plainly see that what you thought on, and spoke of to me at Lititz, can in no way be effected, no proposals having been made to Congress for such a purpose. I am not the less obliged to you for your intended kindness. I should have been glad of its having taken place as a proper means to remove many difficulties which are likely to increase rather than subside, as I guess by a letter received from Colonel Lee, to whom I repeat once more that if Congress or some of their members were in the least distress of removing any uneasiness my stay should give to whomsoever, I would decline the favor Congress have a mind to confer on me. I would have nobody displeased for my sake.

It may perhaps seem odd that I do not reside at Yorktown (York, Pennsylvania) where Congress were meeting at this time, and sue in person for an answer from Congress to my letters to Colonel Lee of 18th September and 18th October. But I would not be charged, in case I was to stay, of having solicited the influence of friends to be employed.

I have the honor to be, with great esteem and respect, dear Sir, your most obedient and very humble servant.

The Baron de Kalb[183]

The Baron was determined to be assured that Washington wanted him. He writes in a letter to the Comte de Broglie of October 11 that a member of Congress (in fact the secretary, Charles Thomson, was entrusted with this mission) persuaded him to join the army, which he then did, on October 13, 1777. Christopher Marshall notes on that day: "After dinner, Gen. de Kalb set out for the camp."[184] He was cordially received by Washington and the other officers. Shortly afterward he was placed in command of a division.

The peace and otherworldliness of Bethlehem were rudely interrupted after Washington's defeat at the battle of Brandywine, September 11, 1777. In the days following, hundreds of wounded arrived at the house of the single brethren, which was requisitioned as a hospital. There was apprehension that General Howe might pursue Washington's army as it withdrew to Bethlehem. "At the same time, amid wild rumors that the main army was approaching, General de Kalb, with a corps of engineers, was engaged in surveying the higher points in the vicinity, with a view to planning defenses if necessary."[185]

In this chapter many a harsh word has been quoted in regard to the Connecticut schoolteacher, Silas Deane. It seems only fair to allow his biographer, George L. Clarke, to say a few words in his defense. Along with this is quoted a masterly defense of the man by Benjamin Franklin, addressed to Mr. Lovell. Note the final words, which should have made Lovell blush.

Clarke's Defense of Silas Deane

One would suppose that Silas Deane might naturally expect an ovation equally cordial with that of the Frenchmen (d'Estaing's fleet), for through his energy, address and watchfulness, combined with the friendliness of Vergennes and the French Court, and the activity of Beaumarchais, eight shiploads of military supplies had been forwarded to the American army for its campaign of 1777-78. He had commissioned Pulaski, de Kalb, Lafayette and Steuben as Major Generals; he had signed the treaties of amity and commerce with Franklin and Lee; last of all, he had persuaded Vergennes to send d'Estaing with a fleet of fourteen ships of the line and several frigates, a force sufficient to announce to the world that France was willing to do her utmost to carry out the provisions of the treaty.[186]

Franklin to Lovell

Sir:

I see in a Vote of Congress shown me by Captain Franval, that Mr. Deane is disowned in some of his Agreements with Officers. I, who am on the spot, and know the infinite difficulty of resisting the powerful solicitations here of great men who if disoblidged might have it in their power to obstruct the Supplies he was obtaining do not wonder that, being a Stranger to the People and unaquainted with the Language he was at first prevailed on to make some such Agreements, when all were recommended as they always are, as *officiers experimentés, brave comme leurs épées, plein de Courage, de Talents, et de Zèle pour notre Cause*, etc., etc., in short mere Caesars, each of whom would have been an invaluable Acquisition to America. You can have no conception, how we are still besieged and worried on this head, our time is cut to pieces by personal Applications, besides those contained in the dozens of Letters, by every Post, which are so generally refused that scarce one in a hundred obtains from us a simple Recommendation to Civilities.

I hope therefore that favorable Allowance will be made to my worthy Colleague on account of his situation at the time, as he has long since corrected that mistake, and daily proves himself to my certain Knowledge as an able, faithful, active and extremely useful Servant of the Publick; I think it my duty to take this Occasion of giving to his Merit, unasked, this tribute as, considering my great Age, I may probably not live to give it personally to Congress, and I perceive he has Enemies.[187]

CHAPTER XI

AMERICAN MAJOR GENERAL

Baron de Kalb, understandably still smarting from the humiliating reception he had received from members of Congress on his arrival in Philadelphia, had made up his mind that if his appearance in the army should be in any way resented, he would return immediately to France.[188] In Washington's orders of November 22, 1777, the final paragraph reads: "The brigades commanded by generals Paterson and Learned are to form one division under Major General the Baron de Kalb."[189] The Commander-in-Chief and his officers received the veteran officer quite cordially; therefore in the middle of November de Kalb assumed command of the division assigned him at headquarters, then located at White Marsh, Montgomery County, Pennsylvania.

While the experienced veteran of European wars was welcomed by the American officers, it was a foreign officer who caused de Kalb annoyance – namely, Thomas Conway, an Irishman from County Kerry who at the age of fourteen became a second lieutenant in the French army and rose to the grade of colonel. Catholics were excluded by law from commissions in the British army. Hence many Irish gentlemen served in foreign armies, particularly the French army. When the French government decided secretly to encourage certain officers to fight against the British in their war against the Americans, Conway went eagerly. Arriving early in May, 1777, he was given the rank of brigadier general on May 13. Washington, after observing Conway for several months, gave his opinion of him in a letter to Richard Henry Lee on October 17, 1777.[190] "General Conway's merit then, as an officer, and his importance in this army, exists more in his imagination than in reality; for it is a maxim with him to leave no service of his own untold, nor to want anything which is to be obtained by importunity."

Washington thus considered him not much of a soldier, but a very demanding boaster. Deane had recommended him as a very valuable man, one reason being that he spoke English. When de Kalb, on September 15, 1777, was appointed major general, Conway wrote an indignant letter to Congress. "It is with exquisite concern that I find myself slighted and forgot when you have offered rank to persons who cost you a great deal of money and have never rendered you the least service. Baron de Kalb, to whom you have offered the rank of major general, is my inferior in France."[191] The validity of this claim is doubtful – Lafayette says de Kalb and Conway held the same rank in France.[192] Both men were given the rank of brigadier general for the foreign service at the time they received leave to serve with the Americans; however, previously, according to a French historian, Conway had held the rank of colonel while de Kalb was a lieutenant colonel. At any rate, Conway demanded the rank of major general, i.e., at least equal to de Kalb.[193]

At first Congress took no notice, not even when Conway threatened to resign. He then sent Washington a letter of resignation, whereupon, to his great chagrin, he was taken at his word and hoist by his own petard. Washington, far from urging him to withdraw his resignation, wrote on November 16, 1777, a curt though courteous note:

> Sir: In answer to your favor of this day, it remains with Congress alone to accept your resignation. This being the case, I cannot permit you to leave the army till you have obtained their consent. When this is done, I do not object to your departure, since it is your inclination.[194]

Thereafter, Washington and de Kalb were the objects of this man's envious hatred. Conway then associated himself with others who likewise were eager to replace Washington, defeated at Brandywine and Germantown, by the victor of Saratoga, to whom Burgoyne with his entire army had surrendered – Horatio Gates.

It was to Gates that Conway addressed his notorious letter containing the supposedly witty aphorism, extremely offensive to the Commander-in-Chief: "Heaven has been determined to save your country, or a weak general and bad counsellors would have ruined it." General Stirling informed Washington of these disloyal agitations. By letting Conway and Gates know, in a letter dated January 4, 1778, at Valley Forge, in very firm words that he knew all about this letter, Washington crushed the so-called "Conway Cabal," speedily and finally.[195] But criticism of the Commander-in-Chief was widespread and continued for a considerable time.[196]

There is reported and widely quoted, a conversation between General Pickering and Nathanael Greene at a chance meeting shortly after the battle of Brandywine. Pickering himself was said to have related that he remarked to Greene, "General Greene, I once had conceived an exalted opinion of General Washington's military talents, but since I have been in the army, I have seen nothing to enhance that opinion. In fact it was lowered." And he added, "Greene must have understood me, for he answered promptly and precisely in these words, 'Nay, the General does want decision.' "[197]

Christopher Marshall, the Quaker turned patriot, knew how to evaluate anti-Washington feeling: He writes in his diary on January 17, 1778, in the darkest days of Valley Forge:

> Murmur of people against George Washington, his slackness and remissness in the army, are so conspicuous that a general languor must ensue, except that some heroic action takes place speedily, but it's thought by me that George Washington must be the man to put such a scheme into practice.
>
> Notwithstanding a cry begins to be raised for a Gates, a Conway, a de Kalb, a Lee;[198] but those men can't attain it. Such is the present concern of fluctuating minds.

Many fluctuating minds were agitating for Gates in those days of American defeats.

Regarding the recipient of Conway's letter, Professor Burnett writes:

> General Gates, after resorting to numerous subterfuges and much devious squirming to clear himself, demanded of General Washington to know who had been treacherously snooping among his private papers, professing to have found the obnoxious statement by General Conway, and was calmly informed by Washington that the revelation had come from none other than his own aide and intimate, General Wilkinson. Gates thereupon turned furiously on Wilkinson, who had meanwhile been made secretary of the Board of War, of which Gates was president, denouncing him with such blistering language that Wilkinson challenged the old general to meet him on the field of honor (or in the back alley.) Gates must have missed his calling in not becoming an actor, for there, with tears and the tenderness of a fond father for a wayward son, he disarmed his irate antagonist and sent him away completely reconciled. That is, until Washington subsequently took occasion to show Wilkinson the entire correspondence; whereupon Wilkinson could only exclaim upon such a "scene of perfidy and duplicity."
>
> The time was to come, however, when he would obtain to the full, so he afterwards professed, the satisfaction denied him on the field of honor. That was at Camden in 1780, when Heaven precipitated Gates "from the pinnacle of undeserved fame to the abyss of humiliation."[199]

It was at the very time of the anti-Washington agitation that de Kalb assumed command of his division. The first assignment for de Kalb in the army is found recorded in a letter from Washington to the President of Congress, November 17, 1777. It concerns Redbank, a fort on the Schuylkill, which it was feared would be attacked by General Howe, since nearby Fort Mifflin had been lost. Washington writes, "I have determined to send General St. Clair, General Knox and Baron de Kalb to take a view of the ground and to endeavor to form a judgment of the most probable means of securing it." Washington accepted the advice of the generals that Redbank could not be held. He therefore wrote General Varnum on November 19: "The Generals St. Clair, Knox and Kalb returned to camp this evening; they are all clear in their opinions that keeping possession of the Jersey Shore at or near Redbank is of the last importance.[200]

On November 24, 1777, de Kalb attended a council of war called to discuss the feasibility of an attack on Philadelphia, a return engagement, as it were, for the almost success of the battle of Germantown. He was one of eleven generals who voted against the plan, proposed vigorously by General Wayne. Since only four officers voted in favor of the plan, it was not adopted. "An open town like Germantown, with only a part of the enemy's force to defend it, was one thing; a fortified city, garrisoned by such troops as held Philadelphia, was quite another thing. Disaster would have certainly resulted from such an attempt."[201]

From the time de Kalb joined the American army in the middle of October, 1777, to his death on the battlefield of Camden, South Carolina, in August 1780, he continued to write frequent and lengthy letters to his friend and patron, the Comte de Broglie, and to Mme. de Kalb. These letters were personal, and definitely not intended for publication. They form the chief sources of the following chapters, telling of his impressions of the American way of life, of the army, of officers from Washington down, and of course, of the great events. They likewise tell a great deal about the writer himself.

If de Kalb appears to be sharply critical, it should be recalled that he did not have the benefit of hindsight regarding the men and events that brought about American independence. Far from being unique, his strictures were shared by many Americans. Frequently his letters were composed under extremely difficult conditions in the field, as for example in winter quarters in Morristown, where the ink in the inkwell froze as he sat before the fire. His favorite phrase in writing to his wife is that he will "have a chat with her," and thus to his sympathetic listener he communicates his difficulties, his ambitions, his restrained boasts, his opinions and his homesickness.

He is frank in acknowledging it when he finds that he has been mistaken. Very striking in this respect is the change in his estimate of Washington. On October 17, 1777, shortly after the battle of Brandywine, he writes to Broglie:

> I have not yet told you anything of the character of General Washington. He is the most amiable, kind-hearted and upright of men; but as a General he is too slow, too indolent, and far too weak; besides, he has a tinge of vanity in his composition, and overestimates himself. In my opinion whatever success he may have will be owing to good luck and to the blunders of his adversaries. I may even say that he does not know how to improve upon the great blunders of the enemy. He has not yet overcome his old prejudices against the French.[202]

On December 12, 1777, he writes, also to the Count, of an opportunity missed because of Washington's great caution:

> The English finally retired to Philadelphia, after ravaging the country and burning many houses. I had correctly divined their intention to retreat from the position assumed by them; knowing, also, that their provisions were exhausted, their supplies cut off, and the surrounding country laid waste, I calculated upon defeating their rear, being well acquainted with the ground, and knowing that the main body could not be brought into action against me. Besides, it was already three o'clock in the afternoon, and my retreat perfectly secure. I requested the commander-in-chief to allow me to make a sally with a part of my division. He thanked me very kindly, but only permitted me, if I thought proper, to detach a little corps of observation, and desired any attack to be avoided. I therefore sent a little detachment of infantry and cavalry after the English, directing Major Dubuysson to show them the way. They hung on the rear of the enemy for five miles, and by that gentleman's report to the commanding general it appeared that nothing could have been easier than, with four field pieces, to have utterly defeated and indeed cut off and captured a part of the rear guard, numbering some five hundred men, while passing a long defile.[203]

On Christmas day at Valley Forge he writes a bit more warmly about Washington:

> It is unfortunate that Washington is so easily led. He is the bravest and truest of men, has the best intentions, and a sound

judgment. I am convinced that he would accomplish substantial results if he would only act more upon his own responsibility; but it is a pity he is so weak, and has the worst of advisors in the men who enjoy his confidence. If they are not traitors, they are certainly gross ignoramuses.[204]

General Wayne casts an interesting side-light on Washington's Fabianism, as quoted by his biographer Stillé: Washington's indecision at times Wayne ascribed wholly to his own modesty and his readiness to yield to inferior men who had had more military experience than himself – notably Lee and Gates.[205]

On January 7, 1778, writing to Henry Laurens, de Kalb gives an estimate of Washington that shows an appreciation of the Commander's very difficult position:

> I cannot but observe, in justice to General Washington, that he must be a very modest man, and the greatest friend of the cause, for forbearing public complaints on that account, that the enemy may not be apprised of our situation and take advantage of it. He will rather suffer in the opinion of the world than to hurt his country, in making appear how far he is from having so considerable an army as all Europe and a great part of America believe he has. This would show, at the same time, he did and does more every day than could be expected from any general in the world, in the same circumstances, and that I think him the only proper person (nobody actually being or serving in America excepted) by his natural and acquired capacity, his bravery, good sense, uprightness and honesty, to keep up the spirits of the army and the people, and that I look upon him as the sole defender of his country's cause. Thus much I thought myself obliged to say on that head. I only could wish in my private opinion he would take more upon himself, and trust more to his own excellent judgment than to councils, but this leads me out of my way.[206]

By way of comparison, it may be interesting to cite an undoubted patriot and enthusiast for the American cause, Christopher Marshall, who, writing in his diary on December 28, 1777, must needs paraphrase David's famous lament on the defeat of King Saul, to express his feelings concerning the low state of the American cause in the winter of Valley Forge:

> 28th. Our affairs wear a very gloomy aspect. Great part of our army gone into winter quarters; those in camp wanting breeches, shoes, stockings and blankets, and by account

brought yesterday, were in want of flour, yet being in the land of plenty; our farmers having their barns and barracks full of grain; hundreds of barrels of flour lying on the banks of the Susquehannah perishing for want of care in securing it from the weather and from the danger of being carried away if a freshet should happen in the river; fifty wagon loads of cloth and readymade clothes for the soldiery in the Clothier General's store in Lancaster; (This I say from the demand made by John Mease to the President a few days past, when the enemy was expected to come this way, for the number of wagons to take away these stores); our enemies reveling in balls, attended with every degree of luxury and excess in the City; rioting and wantonly using our houses, utensils and furniture; all this (and) a numberless number of other abuses we endure from that handful of banditti, to the amount of six of seven thousand men, headed by that monster of rapine, General Howe. Add to this their frequent excursions round about and burning what they please, pillaging, plundering men and women, stealing boys above ten years old, deflowering virgins, driving into the City for their use droves of cattle, sheep (and) hogs; poultry, butter, meal, meat, cider, furniture and clothing of all kinds, loaded upon our own horses. All this is done in the view of our generals and our army, who are careless of us, but carefully consulting where they shall go to spend the winter in jollity, gaming and carousing. O tell this not in France or Spain! Publish it not in the streets of London, Liverpool or Bristol, lest the uncircumcised there should rejoice, and shouting for joy, say "America is ours, for the rebels are dismayed and afraid to fight us any longer! O Americans, where is now your virtue? O Washington, where is now your courage?"[207]

Washington's fatherly interest in young Lafayette and the latter's absolute loyalty to the Commander were well known. It was through an attempted disruption of this relationship that Washington's enemies tried to strike at him. The Board of War under the presidency of General Gates proposed the invasion of Canada without consulting the Commander-in-chief, naming as the leaders of the expedition the Generals Lafayette, Conway and Stark. The first thing Washington heard of the plan was through a letter from Gates asking him to transmit the enclosed orders to Lafayette. The instructions were that Lafayette was to proceed to Albany, take command of 2500 troops assembled there, invade Canada to stir up a revolt among the French Canadians, and if this proved impossible, to destroy forts and shipping before retiring to the Hudson country.

The expedition was to start in February – into the Canadian snows![208]

Washington swallowed his pride and acceded to the directions of the Board of War. Lafayette was astute enough to see in the flattering offer of a command only an attempt to alienate him from Washington. Therefore he declined the commission unless he were to serve under Washington and report directly to him. Furthermore, he objected to Conway as second in command, demanding either McDougall or de Kalb; when the former withdrew because of illness, de Kalb became second in command with Conway third. Lafayette, with characteristic self-assurance, confronted Congress with an ultimatum: unless his terms were granted, he would return to France, taking with him all the French officers, including some very much needed engineers – Congress yielded.[209]

On February 8, 1778, Lafayette started on his four-hundred mile ride to Albany, arriving February 17, while de Kalb followed a few days later. Conway, who had preceded Lafayette, broke the news that the irruption into Canada was impossible because neither necessary soldiers nor supplies were available. The whole thing was a fiasco, providing no glory for either Lafayette or de Kalb, but possibly ridicule and distress. When it became evident that the invasion was absolutely impossible, Congress on March 2nd called off the expedition, praising Lafayette for his zeal and prudence. On March 13, 1778, Washington was authorized to recall Lafayette and de Kalb; after their departure, Conway remained in command at Albany. One might well ask, with de Kalb, were the sponsors of this Canadian expedition traitors or ignoramuses?[210]

A characteristic little scene took place the day before de Kalb left. Conway had protested against de Kalb's appointment to a major generalship, spreading reports about his disloyalty to the American cause; hence there was no love lost between the two men. At one time Lafayette absented himself from Albany for a day, whereupon Conway issued some orders; Gates had sent via Conway the resolution of Congress recalling Lafayette and de Kalb, at the same time placing Conway in charge at Albany. As proof of his succession in command he quoted Gates' letter. De Kalb, who had not yet received orders from Washington, took the position that the letter from the president of the Board of War was not an order; he claimed firmly that his superior rank entitled him to the command in the absence of the Marquis. Whatever ranks they may have held in France, in the American army both were major generals, but de Kalb had definite seniority. The Baron, as he wrote later to de Broglie in quiet amusement, maintained his position "with more warmth and obstinacy than I should have done against any other on another occasion."[211]

In a letter to Washington, dated March 25, 1778, Lafayette speaks bitterly of the promoters of the Canadian expedition, and with irony about Conway:

> How happy I have been in receiving your Excellency's favor of the 10th present. I hope you will be convinced by the knowledge of my tender affection for you. I am very sensible of that goodness which tries to dissipate my fears about that ridiculous Conway expedition. At the present time we know which was the aim of the honorable Board, and for which project three or four men have rushed the country into a great expense, and risked the reputation of our army and the loss of many hundred men, had the general, your deceived friend, been as rash and foolish as they seem to have expected. O American freedom! What shall become of you if you are in such hands?
>
> I have received from the Board, a letter, and a resolve from Congress, by which you are directed to recall me and the Baron de Kalb, whose presence is deemed absolutely necessary to your army. I believe that of General Conway is *absolutely necessary* to Albany, and he has received orders to stay there, which I have no objection to, as nothing perhaps will be done in this quarter but some disputes of Indians and Tories. However, you know I have wrote to Congress, and as soon as this leave will come, I shall let Conway have the command of those few regiments, and I shall immediately rejoin my respectable friend; but till I have received instructions for leaving this place from yourself, I shall stay, as powerful commander-in-chief, as if Congress had never resolved my presence absolutely necessary for the great army.[212]

The outcome of the Canadian expedition was so severe a humiliation to General Conway that on April 22, 1778, he again sent a resignation to Congress which, this time, was accepted. But the recriminations resulting from the "cabal" were not yet at an end. For repeated insults to American officers on the part of Conway, he was challenged to a duel by General Cadwalader, an admirer of Washington. It took place on July 4, 1778, near Philadelphia, with the result that Conway was shot in the mouth. "I've stopped that damn' lying mouth for a while," Cadwalader explained. Expecting that his wound would prove fatal, Conway sent an apology to Washington, "but lacking a sense of the dramatic, he didn't die." He returned to France, where he rose to the rank of maréchal de camp and later became governor of the colony of Pondicheri, to rule over the Hindus.[213]

The day after his *brouhaha* with Conway, March 29, 1778, de Kalb left Albany to rejoin Washington's army. He rode down the Hudson to New Windsor, then turned westward through New York and Pennsylvania to Lancaster, where he rested a while, visiting his friends Dr. Phile and the Marshall family. He reached Valley Forge in time to take part in the celebration of the defensive and offensive alliance between France and the United States ordered by Washington on May 6, 1778.

Much later, in a letter to his wife dated July 18, 1779, de Kalb speaks of his American war record with some mild puzzlement:

> It is odd that in the two years I have been in service here, constantly with the army, the troops under my command (and I have always had very strong divisions) have not taken part in any battle or engagement, and that I myself, so to speak, have not seen a gun go off. Were I a braggart I might go on to say that since I have been with the army the enemy have had very little success, and that they are afraid to attack us because they know I am here; but the coincidence is really singular.[214]

There were of course some good reasons for de Kalb's failure to get under fire until his gallant death on the field at Camden August 16, 1780. The Revolutionary War was a war of movement and counter movement, rather than of great battles such as occurred in the Seven Years' War or our own Civil War. Also, because the British fleet was engaged by French fleets, there was much less fighting on land. De Kalb did not receive his commission in the American army until after the engagements at Brandywine and Germantown, and he was very seriously ill at the time of the battle of Monmouth June 28, 1778.

With his division, de Kalb spent most of the years 1778 and 1779 in New Jersey and the Hudson region. From December 15, 1777, to May 1778, he lay in winter headquarters at Valley Forge, with the exception of the weeks taken up by the futile Canadian expedition, February 16, 1778, to the end of April of that year. He was encamped at White Plains in July, 1778, and moved to Fishkill September 16, where he remained until November. On November 24 he moved to Newburg on the Hudson, then to Smith's Clove on the west bank of the river. Part of the winter he spent in Philadelphia, then on March 30, 1779, encamped at Middlebrook. From here he moved back to Smith's Clove, then to Buttermilk Falls near West Point in the Hudson region. On November 26, 1779, he marched to Morristown, New Jersey, where he experienced another bitter winter, worse even than Valley Forge. In the spring of that year he was placed in command of the southern army, which did not meet the enemy until August 16, 1780, at the battle of Camden, South Carolina, where de Kalb met heroically his chance to win glory.[215]

CHAPTER XII

VALLEY FORGE

Valley Forge, as every schoolboy knows, signifies the epitome of bitter suffering of Washington's army. The General himself summed it up in one vivid phrase: "You might have tracked the army from White Marsh to Valley Forge by the blood on their feet."[216] But it is also true that Valley Forge marked the turning point in the Revolutionary War. The hungry, frozen, tattered, barefoot men who arrived there dispirited in December, marched off disciplined and confident of victory the following June.

The selection of this inhospitable location for winter quarters was a compromise, and like most compromises, not a good solution. Added to other disadvantages was a raid by the British in September, 1777, in which the iron forge was utterly destroyed, houses burned, the magazine containing thousands of barrels of flour, huge supplies of axes, shovels and horseshoes looted. Hence this location seems not to have come into consideration in the earlier discussions of where the army was to pass the winter.

Washington's difficulties come into glaring light as one reads the letter of December 2, 1777, to his close friend and aide, Joseph Reed. It seems almost pitiful that Washington, after endless discussions with his generals, was searching for advice and support from a man whose judgment and opinion would, he hoped, sustain his own choice – which obviously was a Lancaster – Reading line:

> Dear Sir: If you can with any convenience let me see you today, I shall be thankful for it. I am about fixing the winter cantonments of this army and find so many and such capital objections to each mode proposed, that I am exceedingly embarrassed, not only by the advice given me, but in my own judgment, and should be very glad of your sentiments on the subject, without any loss of time. In hopes of seeing you, I shall only add from Reading to Lancaster inclusively is the general sentiment, whilst Wilmington and its vicinity has powerful advocates. This, however, is mentioned under the rose; for I am convinced in my own opinion, that if the enemy believed we had this place in contemplation, they would possess themselves of it immediately.[217]

There is a footnote to the letter listing three different opinions: First, a line from the Schuylkill River to Bethlehem; second, a line from Reading to Lancaster; third, Wilmington, Delaware. Six generals, Greene, Lafayette, Amstrong, Smallwood, Wayne and Scott in favor of Wilmington; nine, Sullivan, de Kalb, Maxwell, Knox, Poor, Muhlenberg, Varnum, Weedon and Woodford for the Lancaster-Reading line; Lord Stirling for the Great Valley; du Portail and Irvine for hutting in a strong position, and Pulaski for a winter campaign. Characteristically, de Kalb's opinion emphasized the welfare of the soldiers and sound strategy:

> At Camp, December 1, 1777
> Rest, recruiting and clothing being most necessary to the army, I am of the opinion that taking winter quarters at Wilmington almost behind the ennemy will not answer the purpose, because every movement the enemy will make up Schuylkill River we must follow their motions or be cut off from our stores of forces to fight, whether it suits us or not. I am apprehensive this position will of necessity bring a winter campaign.
>
> It appears to me, unless His Excellency has very strong reasons to maintain Delaware State and part of Chester County, that more tranquility and safety could be expected from Lancaster to Reading.[218]

But after all his balancing one place against another and listening to opinions in long drawn out staff meetings, it was not Washington who selected Valley Forge. The decision was taken out of his hands by the Pennsylvania Executive Council, which sent a letter to Congress demanding that the army should be kept within twenty or thirty miles of Philadelphia; in fact, it was laid down as an ultimatum that unless this were done, Pennsylvania would withdraw all aid, including men and supplies, from the army.[219] Wayne, a Pennsylvanian, then suggested Valley Forge "to cover this country against the horrid rapine and devastation of a wanton enemy."[220] But Chester County had already been stripped, hence, Rupert Hughes remarks cynically, "It is doubtful if any location could have been secured where supplies were more difficult to secure than at Valley Forge."[221]

Historians writing about de Kalb employ the epithets "crusty," "testy," "melancholy," "morose," "critical," "not completely in good humor," "the seasoned and critically sardonic French veteran," and more of the same, thus creating an image of him based largely on his remarks concerning Valley Forge. If his sharp words at the winter quarters are to stamp him a man of sour disposition, a great many other officers deserve the same epithets; for one might ask, Breathes there a man with soul so dead who would not explode at what he saw at Valley Forge? Particularly de Kalb, who had been assistant quartermaster general in the Seven Years' War!

Varnum expressed himself very bitterly on the chosen site: "I have from the beginning viewed this situation with horror! It is unparalleled in the history of mankind to establish winter quarters in a country wasted and without a single magazine."[222]

On December 19, 1777, the army had made its bitter march to the bleak and windswept hills eighteen miles north of Philadelphia. On Christmas Day de Kalb wrote to his friend, the Comte de Broglie, about the winter quarters in a region through which he had travelled repeatedly:

> On the 19th instant the army reached this wooded wilderness, certainly one of the poorest districts of Pennsylvania; the soil thin, uncultivated, and almost uninhabited, without forage and without provisions! Here we are to go into winter quarters, i.e., to lie in shanties, generals and privates, to recruit, to re-equip, and to prepare for the opening of the coming campaign, while protecting the country against hostile inroads. The matter has been the subject of long debates in the council of war. It was discussed in all its length and breadth – a bad practice to which they are addicted here – and good advice was not taken. The idea of wintering in this desert can only have been put into the head of the commanding general by an interested speculator or a disaffected man. Means were found of implicating Congress, which body has the foible of interfering with matters which it neither understands nor can understand, being entirely ignorant of the locality.[223]

The distinguished French engineer Duportail, one of the four engaged by Franklin, was shocked at conditions in the army. On his arrival on November 12, 1777, he wrote to the French Minister of War, Vergennes, "Such are the people that they move without spring or energy, without a passion for the cause in which they are engaged and in which they follow only as the hand which puts them in motion directs. There is a hundred times more enthusiasm in any coffee house in Paris than in the thirteen colonies united."[224]

The housing among the barren hills was a project of the first importance. In the general orders of December 18, 1777, Washington gives the details for the construction of the huts.

> The soldiers' huts are to be of the following dimensions, viz: fourteen by sixteen each, sides, ends and roofs made with logs, and the roof made tight with split slabs, or in some other way; the sides made tight with clay, fireplace made of wood and secured with clay on the inside eighteen inches thick, this fireplace to be in the rear of the hut; the door to be in the end nearest the street; the doors to be made of split oak slabs, unless boards can be procured. Side walls to be six and a half feet high. The officers' huts to form a line in the rear of the troops'; one hut to be allowed to each general officer, one to the staff of each brigade, one to the field officers of each regiment, one to the staff of each regiment, one to the commissioned officers of two companies, and one to every twelve non-commisioned officers and soldiers.
>
> As an encouragement to industry and art, the general promises to reward the party in each regiment who finishes the work in the quickest and most workmanlike manner with a bonus of ten dollars. And as there was reason to believe that boards for covering might be scarce and difficult to be got, he offers a hundred dollars to any officer or soldier who in the opinion of three gentlemen he shall appoint as judges, shall substitute some other covering that may be cheaper and quicker made and will in every respect answer the need. [225]

However, despite the monetary incentive, no such invention was made. The crude huts naturally were drafty, the floors generally only stamped clay, the fireplaces, lacking adequate chimneys, filled the hut full of smoke, so that the soldiers frequently preferred to spend even their sleeping time outside the huts around huge fires burning day and night. De Kalb's adjutant Dubuysson found a cave and lived in it. Anyway, there was plenty of wood, neither the quartermaster's department nor the commissary having anything to do with it! Miserable as these living quarters were, they took a long time in the building – it was only on February 8, 1778, about three weeks after the army's arrival, that Washington could report "most of the men were in tolerable good huts." Lafayette referred to them as "no more cheerful than dungeons." [226] De Kalb wrote to de Broglie:

> The miserable hovels we are constructing in these dreary mountains are therefore very far from deserving the honorable designation of winter quarters. Houses are not to be had, even for generals. I shall personally superintend the erection of my castle in order to have it as little badly built as possible. [227]

Later all generals were given better housing. Greene wrote in the same tone: "We are all going into log huts, a sweet life after a fatiguing campaign." [228]

Regarding the lack of clothing for the soldiers, Washington wrote bitterly to the president of Congress on December 23, 1777 (speaking of members of Congress who insisted on a winter campaign):

> I can assure these gentlemen that it is a much easier and less distressing thing to draw remonstrances in a comfortable room by a good fireside than to occupy a cold bleak hill and sleep under frost and snow without clothes or blankets; however, though they seem to have little feeling for the naked and distressed soldier, I feel superabundantly for them, and from my soul pity those miseries which it is neither in my power to relieve nor to prevent. [229]

Wayne said, "The army is worse off than Falstaff's recruits, with not a whole shirt to a brigade." [230]

Had even clothing and food been supplied, Valley Forge would not have been so notorious, and of course the quartermaster and commissary departments were to blame. On November 7, General Thomas Mifflin resigned his post as quartermaster at a very unfortunate moment, a fortnight before the march to Valley Forge. Unbelievable as it seems, he was not replaced until March. De Kalb expressed his disgust with this situation:

> I do not know what is done in the clothing department, but it is certain that half the army are naked and almost the whole army go barefoot. [231] While the army was suffering for want of shoes, etc., ... hogsheads of shoes, stockings, and clothing were at different places upon the road and in the woods, lying and perishing for want of teams and proper management. [232]

Lafayette, who usually saw things in a rosy light, wrote:

> The unfortunate soldiers were in want of everything; they had neither coats, hats, shirts nor shoes; their feet and legs froze until they became black and it was often necessary to amputate them. The army frequently remained whole days without provisions, and the patient endurance of soldiers and officers was a miracle which each moment seemed to renew. [233]

Sad as the condition of the hapless soldiers was, there were ever present greedy men eager to profit from their plight. A "salty

Major Samuel Hay" wrote his colonel: "The generality of people would much rather take a blanket from a soldier at half price than let him have one at double its value. The devil will get half of them yet."[234] De Kalb wrote: "I have no doubt that the contractors make fifty percent on every contract, not to speak of other defraudations, the mere enumeration of which would be endless."[235] Among the latter, of course, numerous farmers of the vicinity preferred to sell their products to the British in Philadelphia for gold than to accept the paper money of the army.

In a lengthy letter to the Committee on Conference Washington reported on January 29, 1778, among various other items:

> Among the complicated causes of complaint in this army, none seems to have taken deeper root, nor to have given more general dissatisfaction than the lavish distribution of rank. No error can be more pernicious than that of dealing out rank with too prodigal a hand. The inconveniences of it are manifest. It lessens the value and splendor of it, in some measure degrades it into contempt, breeds jealousies and animosities, and takes away one of the most powerful incitements to emulation.[236]

De Kalb is more specific in a letter written to de Broglie on Christmas day, 1777, from Valley Forge:

> In addition to this there is a series of officers very expensive and totally superfluous. Every brigade has its commissary of subsistence, its quartermaster, its wagonmaster, its commissary of forage, and each of these again has his deputies. Each general, again, is entitled to a special commissary of subsistence and three commissaries of forage. All these men rank as officers, and really have nothing to do. My blacksmith is a captain!... It is safe to accost every man as a colonel who talks to me with familiarity; the officers of a lower rank are invariably more modest. In a word, the army teems with colonels.[237]

Equally dismal was the matter of food supply. De Kalb gave free rein to his feelings regarding the commissary in his Christmas-day letter: "Now we have hardly been here six days, and are already suffering for want of everything. The men have neither had meat nor bread for four days, and our horses are often left for days without any fodder. What will be done when the roads grow worse and the season more severe?"[238]

General Varnum reported to Washington almost unbelievable conditions:

Valley Forge, Dec. 22, 1777. According to the saying of Solomon, hunger will break through a stone wall. It is therefore a very pleasing circumstance to the division under my command that there is a probability of their marching. Three days successively we have been destitute of bread. Two days we have been entirely without meat. It is not to be had of the commissaries. Whenever we procure beef it is of such vile quality as to render it a poor succedaneum for food. The men must be supplied or they cannot be commanded.[239]

Under such conditions it is not surprising that Washington reported to Congress that on December 22 lack of food had caused "a dangerous mutiny" which was repressed with difficulty; there was on hand in camp "not a single hoof of any kind for slaughter and not more than twenty-five barrels of flour."[240] "Firecake," that is, a flour paste baked on hot stones, was the common diet. Dr. Albigense Waldo wrote in his diary December 21, 1777:

> Heartily wish myself at home; my skin and eyes are almost spoiled with continued smoke. A general cry goes through the camp this evening among the soldiers, "No meat! No meat!" The distant vales echoed back the melancholy sound, "No meat! No meat!" imitating the noise of crows and owls also made part of the confused music. "What have you for your dinner, boys?" "Nothing but fire-cake and water, sir!" At night, "Gentlemen, the supper is ready." "What's your supper, lads?" "Fire-cake and water, sir."
>
> December 22. Lay excessive cold and uncomfortable last night – my eyes are started out from their orbits like rabbit's eyes, occasioned by great cold and smoke. "What have you for your breakfast, lads?" "Fire-cake and water, sir." The Lord send that our commissary of purchases may live on fire-cake and water till their glutted guts are turned to pasteboard."[241]

On February 16, 1778, Washington wrote to Governor Livingston of New Jersey:

> Sir: I had the honor of writing to you a day or two ago and transmitting a letter from the Committee of Congress now at camp, containing a representation of the present alarming distress of the army for want of provisions; they press us with most alarming violence, and threaten such fatal consequences unless the most vigorous measures be pursued

> to effect an immediate remedy, that I have thought proper to send Mr. Tilghman, in case any accident should have happened to those letters, to give you a just picture of our situation, and with your aid and concurrence to take the most effectual methods for procuring a speedy though temporary relief from the magazines that have been established in your state. I have the honor, etc.[242]

Earlier General Jedediah Huntington had written to General Pickering:

> I received an order to hold my brigade in readiness to march; fighting will be far preferable to starving; my brigade are out of provisions nor can the brigade commissary procure any meat. It has several times been the case before, though the failure has generally been in flour. I am exceedingly unhappy in being the bearer of complaints to headquarters. I have used every argument my imagination could invent to make the soldiers easy, but I despair of being able to do it much longer.[243]

Perhaps Gouverneur Morris, aghast at what he witnessed at Valley Forge, spoke out most sharply: "An army of skeletons appears before our eyes, naked, starved, sick, discouraged."[244]

It is noteworthy that the soldiers bore their lot bravely, despite the lack of food and clothing. Dr. Waldo remarked concerning their morale: "Were the soldiers to have plenty of food and rum I believe they would storm Tophet."[245] De Kalb wrote to de Broglie: "How sad that troops of such excellence and so much zeal should be so little spared and so badly led."[246]

General Greene wrote Washington October 3, 1776: "We want nothing but good officers to constitute as good an army as ever marched into the field. Our men are much better than their officers."[247]

From the enemy side came similar testimony in letters written by a Hessian major to his superior in Germany: "The Americans are bold, unyielding and fearless – and by no means conquered."[248]

De Kalb complained bitterly about the lack of consideration shown the men by their officers:

> The other day, when I was relieved from being officer of the day, my successor inquired whether I had held a parade. I answered that I should never unnecessarily increase the troubles of the soldiers, nor keep them under arms to no purpose. For it has been very cold for a month, and the

assembly as well as the mounting of the guard is done so slowly that it generally consumes two hours. My comrade replied that he had ordered up all the drummers and meant to have a grand parade.[249]

It is not surprising that from Valley Forge de Kalb should write to de Broglie, with whom he had served under very different conditions in European wars, and who was still his superior officer: "Everything here combines to inspire disgust. At the smallest sign from you I shall return home."[250] It was a very natural feeling, which affected even the sanguine young Lafayette: "The bearer of this letter," he wrote to Mme. de Lafayette on January 6, 1778, from Valley Forge, "will describe to you the pleasant residence which I chose in preference to the happiness of being with you, with all my friends, in the midst of all possible enjoyments; in truth, my Love, do you not believe that powerful reasons are requisite to induce a person to make such a sacrifice? Everything combines to induce me to depart – honor alone tells me to remain."[251]

In a letter of March 30, 1778, from Albany, where he and Lafayette had gone on their abortive expedition to win Canada for the cause – de Kalb tells his wife that he has been writing her regularly, but has not heard from her for more than a year. Were she and the children well? Did she undertake the trip to Germany (where their older son was attending a military school)? He asks many more questions about the management of the estate, etc., and closes the letter: "Goodbye, my dear, I cannot express to you the worry which your silence causes me, nor how much I desire to return to you. It requires all the reasons which caused me to undertake this voyage to resist the temptation of going home."[252] But he stayed.

Reporting on commissioned officers to Washington, Greene told his superior that it gave him the greatest pain to "hear the murmurs and complaints among the officers for want of spirits. They say they are exposed to the severity of the winter, subject to hard duty, and nothing but bread and beef to eat, morning, noon and night." If the officers complained more than the soldiers, it was that they felt their privations more. Their families, too, were generally used to a higher standard of living and found they could not live on the little money from the officers' pay. On December 27, fifty officers in Greene's division resigned for this reason. When shown the pleading letters from the wives of these men, what could Greene say? Inflation was sending prices skyward and driving the soldiers to desperation. Congress must do something to relieve the plight of the officers, declared Greene, or Washington would have a leaderless army.[253]

De Kalb gives a few details about living on an officer's pay:

> I have never mentioned the subject of my pay, because I know nothing about it. I cannot say whether it amounts to a hundred and fifty or to two hundred dollars a week, or more, but it ought to run from last July. The sum looks large, but horses are excessively dear at this place, and all necessaries so much above the ordinary price, that the best I can hope for will be to escape a loss. I am the only general who practises economy and restricts his table to what is most needed. Nethertheless, at the last camp I had to pay my purveyor of milk and butter two hundred and forty-two francs for the consumption of two weeks. Besides, the pay is made in paper money, on which there is a loss of four hundred percent in exchanging it for silver. No one, therefore, ought to serve from interested motives.[254]

While the American officers had their so-called "Conway Cabal," de Kalb could report similar bickerings and slanderings from the French officers at Valley Forge:

> On the whole, I have annoyances to bear of which you can hardly have a conception. One of them is the mutual jealousy of almost all the French officers, particularly against those of higher rank than the rest. The people think of nothing but their incessant intrigues and backbitings. They hate each other like the bitterest enemies, and endeavor to injure each other whenever the opportunity arises. I have given up their society and very seldom see them. Lafayette is the sole exception; I have always met him with the same cordiality and the same pleasure. He is an excellent young man, and we are good friends. It were to be wished that all the Frenchmen who serve here were as reasonable as he and I. Lafayette is much liked; he is on the best of terms with Washington; both of them have every reason to be satisfied with me also.[255]

A quaint volume called *The History of Valley Forge*, by Henry Woodman, written in 1850, first in the form of letters to local newspapers, sheds considerable light on de Kalb's personality, even though the statements of this amateur historian must be accepted with considerable reserve. The author was the grandson of Abijah Stephens, in whose home de Kalb had quarters during the later part of his stay at Valley Forge, after general officers were assigned to requisitioned homes of local residents. He succeeded General George Weedon when the latter left the army because of a disappointment regarding rank. Hence the author was in a position to write at some length about the two generals. Weedon, originally Gerhard von der Wieden, was born in Hanover, Germany. He served in the war of the Austrian Succession, distinguishing himself at Dettingen. In America he served in the French and Indian War, later settling in Virginia, where he conducted a tavern. An ardent patriot, he became a lieutenant colonel in the militia and later a brigadier general. He gained fame at the battles of Brandywine and Germantown. In the course of the winter at Valley Forge, he left the service, but returned in 1780 in time to command the militia at Yorktown.[256]

Following are some pages from Woodman, cited at length because Weedon serves as an excellent foil to de Kalb, and because this book is a fairly rare item.

> In one of my former letters some notice was given of General Wheedon (*sic*), and also of my intention of giving some further information concerning him. It has been observed that he remained at his quarters but a short time, but short as it was, it was long enough for the soldiers under his command to commit depredations to so great an extent, that it required years to overcome the effects, and to restore the waste places produced in consequence of their rapacity. Almost every tree on the place was cut down or destroyed; all the fences were either used for fuel, or carried off the premises, to be employed in constructing huts or forming picket guards. Their hay, grain, straw, fodder and vegetables were all taken, as the General said, for the use of the army, but the real object was believed to be for the sole purpose of serving his own private interests. He exercised no restraint over the soldiers in this particular; the consequence was that all their movable property, not secured or removed beyond their reach, was taken by the soldiers with impunity, and the family were left nearly destitute of even the common domestic utensils, such as buckets, pots, kettles, pans, plates, knives and forks, and such things as are indispensably necessary. During the time of his quarters there, these depredations were committed, and I have often heard it related by many of the family that the only thing not privately secured that escaped their rapacity was a grindstone, which the General had ordered not to be removed on account of the daily use they made of it to grind their knives and other edge tools. I have heretofore hinted at his severity to his soldiers; he always kept a strong guard at the house, and during the most inclement nights, exposed to all kinds of

weather, the poor soldiers thus employed walked to and fro through the yard, poorly fed and still more poorly clad. Often in the dead hours of the night, would some of the members of the family arise from their beds, and from the window of the second story of the house, which was the only part the family occupied, throw to the poor famished guards pieces of meat, crusts of bread, and any kind of provisions they had on hand, which, while shuddering with cold, they would seize with avidity and devour with the greediness of a ravenous animal.

His own aggrandizement and the acquisition of wealth seems to have been his leading motive in entering the service, and the accomplishment of these objects his governing principle. He had a number of private baggage wagons, conducted by his own slaves, and used for the purpose of conveying supplies for the use of the army, often at extravagant prices, which were extorted from the government on account of its necessitous situation, and at all times embracing every opportunity in his power to speculate on the public treasury, receiving his pay in continental money. But nearly enough has been said of him, unless it were better, and I shall soon take leave of him by just mentioning that having in various ways accumulated a large amount of continental money, and fearing it would die on his hands, he sold his teams, collected his slaves, resigned his commission and returned to his home, to invest his money in real estate, and this is the last account I ever heard of him.

Upon the resignation of Wheedon, the command of the Virginia line was given to Baron de Kalb, a German nobleman, whose character, life, services, and death at Camden, South Carolina, are too well known to need a description here. He also succeeded to the quarters of Wheedon, at my grandfather's, and soon a different state of things were produced, and while less servile homage was paid to his person by the soldiers, their affections were more firmly secured by his kind and affectionate treatment of them, at the same time his authority was more established, and his orders obeyed, and more restraint placed over the soldiers; order and regularity were restored, and the situation of the family much more pleasant than it had been previous to his arrival. The family having been supplied with things necessary for domestic purposes by some of their relatives and friends who lived beyond the scenes of devastation, the property was, through his authority, protected from much further depredation. His urbanity rendered him an agreeable companion, and laid the foundation of a lasting friendship between them. Much more might be related concerning the Baron during his residence at the house, for I call it his residence, as he was there more than four months and was always considered one of the family; and from the day of his arrival until he left the place, he was always viewed more as an old friend and acquaintance than a perfect stranger from a foreign land. After leaving the place, whenever opportunity offered, a correspondence was kept up between him and my grandfather, and his last letter was written a few days previous to the battle of Camden, where he fell, and not received until some weeks after his death. This letter I regret has been lost. Another letter that was written a few weeks previous is still in possession of the family, and was published in this and some other papers of this county about two years since.

I have often heard his person and habits described by my mother; he was tall of stature, and very erect for a person of his years, being more than sixty years of age, having been forty years in the Prussian service. He had a very open intelligent countenance, dark blue eyes, very expressive, and a good set of teeth, well formed head, his hair gray, and his complexion, from long exposure, rather swarthy: in his habits, temperate and abstemious; his conversation, bland and interesting, and manners polite and agreeable, given to sociability – a man of liberal education, speaking the English language well for a foreigner. I have heard her say he would sit for hours together with the family on long winter evenings, in relating incidents and many interesting accounts that had taken place under his immediate notice in Europe, one of which was a very lively account of a journey to his native place, a little before his embarking for this country, to visit his aged parents, whom he had not seen for more than twenty years. The distance was about two hundred miles. His father and mother were then about eighty-seven years of age, both of them enjoying good health and unimpaired faculties, and capable of performing bodily labor. They were not in affluent circumstances, and the Baron had risen to preferment, not through the influence of wealth or claims to nobility, but through his own merit, having in his early youth been accustomed to labor. He used to relate that when he arrived at his father's house, he found his aged mother busily engaged in her spinning, enjoying that satisfaction that can be felt only by those that can look in the evening of their day on the reward of a well-spent life. Upon inquiry for his father, he was informed that he was at work in a wood a short distance from the house; and shortly after he went out to seek him, and met him returning home in company with a grandson, each laden with billets of wood for fuel. The meeting was a joyful one to all parties.[257]

While he was a boy, Woodman informs us, his father frequently took him for a stroll about Valley Forge, pointing out various headquarters and telling him the story of the encampment. He heard a great deal also from his mother, who was nineteen in 1777. It is impossible to check everything he writes, but some lapses may be pointed out. De Kalb at the time was not over sixty years of age, but 56 – still an impressive age for a fighting general in those days. He served in the French – not the Prussian – army for about 35 years. There is no evidence showing that he visited his old parents in southern Germany, though it would have been in character for him to keep in touch with his family. According to his marriage certificate, his father was no longer living in 1764. However, as shown by a letter from Mme. de Kalb after his death to his brother in Huettendorf, there was a bond between the two families. If de Kalb had visited his parents, the distance covered would have been nearer 400 than 200 miles. The general tone of Mr. Woodman's description of de Kalb's stay in his grandfather's house is corroborated by a letter in the possession of the Stephens family dating from 1780 just before the General set out for the South on his last journey.

De Kalb, in the early part of 1778, was stricken by a severe fever that kept him in Valley Forge for weeks after the army left, depriving him of a chance to participate in the battle of Monmouth; he alludes to his very severe illness in a letter to his host in Valley Forge:

> Sir: Captain Du Ponceau, a particular friend of mine, is going to Valley Forge for change of air and the recovery of his Health, and being unacquainted with the Country, I shall take it a very particular favor, if you can and will do him Service, and introduce him into some neighboring houses. I shall be glad to hear from you and your family. I hope you are all well. Though I was very poorly yet when I left you in June 1778, I recovered so well during the Campaign that I have been hearty ever since. Col. Dubuysson whom I left in camp at Morristown is well, Major Rogers hath left the army in October 1778 and is since at home in Baltimore.
>
> I am to set out for S. Carolina in a short time; could have

wished to call on you before but do not think to have it in my power. I wish you all happiness, health and prosperity and am, Sir, your very humble servant,

The Baron de Kalb[258]

Mr. Stephens
Valley Forge

At Versailles on March 20, 1778, Franklin had his finest hour. This son of a Boston soapmaker, together with Silas Deane and Arthur Lee, was received formally by Louis XVI, the descendant of the Sun King, and member of the proudest royalty of Europe. A treaty of alliance was signed, which recognized the thirteen colonies as a nation, and assured American victory and independence. Conrad Gérard, the able diplomat, was named minister to the United States. News travelled slowly in those days – Congress learned of this diplomatic victory only on May 2nd of that year. At Valley Forge, Washington designated May 6, 1778, as a day of celebration, at which special honor was to be paid to the French officers. De Kalb described the great day in a letter to his wife, May 12, 1778:

> The alliance is, on the part of the King of France, so rational, and so generous beyond all expectation, that it has won him the hearts even of those who loved him but little before. At the same time, it may be said that this act of magnanimity is none the less a movement of the most subtle policy, which, quite apart from the glory reflected upon the king and his ministers, will prove of infinite commercial advantage to the French people. No means could have been adapted better to bruise the colossal power of England, and to snatch this great country forever from its allegiance. The treaty reflects the highest credit on M. Gérard, who was intrusted with its negotiation. His name will be inscribed upon the annals of this new empire by the side of Louis XVI, as the interpreter of the high-hearted sentiments of that noble monarch, to whom this immense continent owes its liberty and happiness.

> The solemnities were opened with divine worship at the head of each brigade. Then followed three volleys of artillery, each of thirteen guns, each succeeded by a round of cheers, of which the first was in honor of the King of France, the second in honor of European powers friendly to America, and the third in honor of the United States. The Commander-in-Chief gave a banquet in the camp. Fifteen hundred persons sat down to the tables, which were spread in the open air. All the

officers with their ladies, and the prominent people of the neighborhood, were invited. Wine, meats and liquors abounded, and happiness and contentment were impressed on every countenance. Numberless huzzahs were given for the King of France, and the French officers had no small share in the honors of the occasion. It was a fine day for us, and a great one for General Washington. Let me say that no one could be more worthy of this good fortune. His integrity, humanity and love for the just cause of his country, as well as his other virtues, receive and merit the veneration of all men. A French soldier had been condemned to death by a court-martial just before the festival. The Marquis and I sued for pardon for the guilty. The commanding general answered that on a day dedicated to the gratitude owing by America to the King of France, he could not refuse French officers a boon, and availed himself of the opportunity to pardon all other criminals at the same time.[259]

Central to the celebration was a feu-de-joie, that is, the firing of cannons and muskets for the joy the noise affords. Washington's orders, issued on May 5 at six o'clock in the evening, outlined the program of the festive day:

> It having pleased the Almighty Ruler of the Universe propitiously to defend the cause of the United American States, and finally, by raising us up a powerful friend among the Princes of the Earth, to establish our Liberty & Independence upon lasting foundations: – It becomes us to set apart a day for gratefully acknowledging the Divine Goodness, and celebrating the Important event which we owe to his Benign interposition –
>
> The Several Brigades are to be assembled for this purpose at 9 O'clock tomorrow morning, when their Chaplains will communicate the intelligence contain'd in the Postscript from the Pennsylvania Gazette of the 2nd Instant, & offer up a thanksgiving and deliver a discourse Suitable to the Occasion –
>
> At half after 10 O'clock a Cannon will be fir'd, which is to be a signal for the men to be under arms –
>
> The Brigade Inspectors will then Inspect their dress and arms... Form the Battalions according to the instructions given them, and announce to the Commanding Officers of the Brigades that the Battalions are form'd –

The Brigadiers or Commandants will then appoint the Field Officers to command the Battalions... after which each Battalion will be ordered to load & Ground their arms – At half after 11 a Cannon will be fired as a signal for the march, upon which the Several Brigades will begin their march – by wheeling to the right by platoons, & proceed by the Brigade Inspectors – a 3rd signal will be given, upon which there will be a discharge of 13 Cannon. When the 13th has been fir'd a Running fire of the Infantry will begin on the right of Woodford's, & Continue thro'out the whole front line – It will then be taken up on the left of the 2nd line & continue to the right – Upon a Signal given, the whole army will Huzza – long live the King of France – the artillery then begin again, and fire 13 Rounds: this will be Succeeded by a general discharge of the Musquetry in running fire – Huzza, and long live the Friendly European Powers. Then the last discharge of 13 pieces of Artillery will be given followed by a general running fire – and Huzza to the American states.

There will be no exercise in the morning, and the guards of the day will not parade till after the Feudejoy is finish'd; when the Brigadier Majors will march them out the grand Parade – the Adjutants then Tell off their Battalions into eight platoons, And the Commanding Officer will Reconduct them to their camp, marching by the left, Major Gen'l Sterling will command on the right and the Marques De. La. Fayette on the left, & the Baron De Kalb, the 2nd line – each Major General will conduct the 1st Brigade of his Division to its ground.

The other Brigades will be conducted by their Commanding officers in Separate columns – the posts of each Brigade will be pointed out by Baron Stubens Aide – Major Walker will attend Ld Stirling – Major De Poneza, the Marques D.L. Fayette & Capn Lendfant, the Baron De Kalb – the line to be form'd, with the Interval of 3 feet between each line – each man is to have a Gill of Rum – the Quarter Masters of the Several Brigades are to apply to the Adjutant Gen'l for an order on the Commissary of Military Stores for the number of Blank cartridges that may be wanted.[260]

An excerpt from a letter written by a soldier who participated in the celebration breathes the spirit of patriotism that by this time inflamed Washington's army:

What do you think, my dear friend, does the soldier feel, in reviewing danger he has passed – in planning or executing the overthrow of tyranny – or celebrating the exploits of heroes. And what spectacle can you imagine more splendid, than an order of freemen, drawn up within hearing of the enemy, to celebrate the acknowledgment of our Independence and alliance with the first monarch in the world; and whom can you conceive more happy than those who have borne no inconsiderable part in the struggles and adversities that served to produce an event so favourable to the interests of mankind. I wished for you more than once, during our *feu de joye*, to have shared with me in the festivity of the day. It would have given you new ideas of military pleasures, and helped the poem on our Independence which you have promised, to some elegant strokes of the epic. Heretofore we have celebrated the day on which a Prince was vested with the power to kill and enslave us; but this was a day of rejoicing at the interment of tyranny, and the coronation of American Independence. I have annexed to my letter the General Orders for conducting the *feu de joye* on so memorable an occasion.

After the Chaplains had finished their discourse, and the second cannon was fired, the troops began their march to the lines in the following order. Each Major-General conducted the first brigade of his company to the ground; the other brigades were conducted to their commanding officers in separate columns. Major General Lord Sterling commanded on the right; the Marquis de La Fayette on the left; and Baron DeKalb the second line. But this arrangement can convey no adequate idea of their movements to their several posts – of the appearance of His Excellency, during his circuit round the lines – of the air of our soldiers – the cleanliness of their dress – the brilliancy and good order of their arms, and the remarkable animation with which they performed the necessary salutes as the General passed along. Indeed during the whole of the review, the utmost military decorum was preserved while at the same time one might observe the hearts of the soldiery struggling to express their feelings in a way more agreeable to nature.

Some of the ancients were not more attached to their mistical figures than many of the moderns. We of America have our number THIRTEEN. The officers approached the place of entertainment in different columns, thirteen abreast, and closely lined together in each others arms. The appearance was pretty enough. The number of officers composing the line signified the Thirteen American States; and the interweaving arms, a compleat Union and most perfect Confederation.[261]

A letter from an officer who was present at the drill and the banquet testifies to the discipline instilled in the army by Baron von Steuben, as well as the popularity of General Washington:

> Dated Valley Forge, May 9, 1778
>
> Last Wednesday was set apart as a day of general rejoicing when we had a feu de joye, conducted with the greatest order and regularity. The army made a most brilliant appearance; after which his Excellency dined in public, with all the officers of his army, attended by a band of music. I never was present where there was such unfeigned and perfect joy as was discovered in every countenance. The entertainment was concluded with a number of patriotic toasts, attended with huzzas. When the General took his leave, there was a universal clap with loud huzzas, which continued till he had proceeded a quarter of a mile, during which time there was a thousand hats tossed into the air. His Excellency turned around with his retinue, and huzzaed several times.[262]

The Franco-American alliance brought about a change in de Kalb's status, as he explains in a letter to Mme. de Kalb of May 25, 1778. Characteristically, he realizes that he is not acting from one motive, but for several reasons.

> But for the late treaty, I should have returned to you ere this. Now I cannot and will not do it for various reasons, two of which I shall here specify. In the first place, war between England and France having become inevitable, should I fall into the hands of the English while at sea, my treatment would be that of a French prisoner of war, possibly without a claim to being exchanged, inasmuch as I should have left America without authority from my own government. In the second place, the alliance with the United States retransforms me from an officer on two years' furlough into a general of the French army with the same, if not a better title to promotion than if I had never quitted France. Henceforward, therefore, I shall only return by the express command of the minister.[263]

Shortly after the news of the treaty, de Kalb rendered his oath of allegiance to the cause of the United States before George Washington, renouncing all thought of a return to France before an American victory. He was thoroughly convinced of the inevitability of such an outcome.

Kalb's Oath of Allegiance

I, John Baron de Kalb, Major General, do acknowledge the United States of America to be Free, Independent and Sovereign States, and declare that the people thereof owe no allegiance or obedience to George the Third, King of Great Britain; and I renounce, refuse and abjure any allegiance or obedience to him, and I do swear that I will to the utmost of my power, support, maintain and defend the said United States against the said King George the Third, his heirs and successors and his or their abettors, assistants and adherents, and I will serve the said United States in the office of Major General, which I now hold, with fidelity, according to the best of my skill and understanding.[264]

John Baron de Kalb

Sworn before me, Camp at
Valley Forge, the 12th day of May, 1778
G. Washington

It should be remarked that the hardships borne by the American soldiers through the bitter winter at Valley Forge were not without advantage to the American cause. The hilly encampment protected by lines of fortifications gave the British, despite their superior numbers, no relish for a surprise attack to wipe out Washington's small force and thus bring the war to an early end. The failure of the commissary with the resultant lack of food and clothing should be set down as the chief cause of making Valley Forge the severe trial to men's souls which eventually hardened them into a finely disciplined army.

To end on a lighter note, a social item from de Kalb's stay at the Stephens household in Valley Forge is supplied by Mabel Lorenz Ives in her book, *Washington's Headquarters:*

> One day when the Baron had invited Washington to dine, the Commander, on dismounting and handing over his horse at the farm, noticed in the kitchen the roast goose sizzling on its platter, and no one for the moment in sight. Too good a chance to miss. They all needed a good laugh. Quickly

shutting the savory-smelling bird in a dresser, he went in by the main door and was duly welcomed and seated at table, when all at once – consternation in the kitchen! Where was the roast goose? What could have become of it?

"I saw him hide it in the cupboard," said little Betty Stevens. "I was playing in the corner and I saw him."

Sure enough – there it was – but who had done the hiding?

"Over there," said Betty, "the man with the big nose."

This goose story is no canard. In Doylestown, in the museum of the Bucks County Historical Society, any skeptic can see the very platter![265]

CHAPTER XIII

WORSE THAN VALLEY FORGE

A result of the alliance with France was that the British in Philadelphia, worried by reports of the French fleet heading for America, decided to evacuate the American capital. General Clinton set out across New Jersey toward New York on June 18, 1778, whereupon Washington broke camp at Valley Forge on June 19, and started in pursuit. His excellent plan to divide and destroy the British army failed because of General Charles Lee's bungling at the battle of Monmouth, which permitted the British to retreat to New York. The American forces were not strong enough to attack the well fortified British position; therefore their strategy was to prevent, or at least impede, sorties into the American countryside. Such constant alertness against enemy surprises was de Kalb's task when, after his recovery, he assumed command of his division. Monmouth, it turned out, was the last battle of any great importance in the North.

The naval war between Great Britain and France had begun. Clinton decided it would be best to remain generally quiet in New York. During the summer and autumn of 1778, Washington established camps in a large semi-circle around New York from New Jersey to Connecticut. Not long before he had been driven out of New York; now he was besieging the British army there!

As the cold season approached, the army once more went into winter quarters, and once more they built themselves huts, as they had done at Valley Forge. This time at least the soldiers had canvas tents to protect them until they had "hutted." In fact, Washington was in position to give Congress a much more favorable report than in 1777.

> To the President of Congress
> Headquarters, Fredericksburg (Now Patterson) N.J.
>
> November 27, 1778
>
> ... It is unnecessary to add that the troops must again have recourse to the expedient of hutting as they did last year, but

as they are now well clad, and we have had more leisure to make some little preparation for winter quarters, I hope they will be in a more comfortable situation than they were in the preceding winter.[266]

For more than a year de Kalb's division was stationed north of New York, near the Hudson, frequently moving between Fishkill, Newburg, West Point, Middlebrook, and other locations. Typical of the orders he received are the following, of December 4, 1778, which directed him to be prepared against an attack on West Point; Washington continues:

> I do not mean, however, that the directions here given should be so absolute as to preclude your deviation from them if your intelligence should make compliance unnecessary or improper. In this case you will act according to your own discretion in which I am persuaded you will act with the greatest circumspection.[267]

The American officers needed to be very circumspect indeed, as they had to be on the alert at all times against excursions on the part of General Clinton; for example, early in June, 1779, the British General took Stony Point, a very important fortress on the Hudson below West Point, and made it a strongly fortified bastion. In view of the incessant danger, de Kalb with his usual watchfulness did the checking of the outposts himself, not entrusting it to his aides. In a letter to Mme. de Kalb of July 14, 1779, he tells her of the monotonous routine which was forced on the American army, and of one inspection trip that he had undertaken from his headquarters at Smith Cove:

> What I am doing here is extremely disagreeable. Without my excellent constitution it would be impossible to bear up under this service. Yesterday I made the most wearisome trip of my life, visiting the posts and pickets of the army in the solitudes, woods and mountains, clambering over the rocks, and picking my way in the most abominable roads. My horse having fallen lame, I had to make the whole distance on foot. I never suffered more from heat. On my return I had not a dry rag on me, and was so tired that I could not sleep.[268]

He continues, explaining to her that his health is good because he has a regime that keeps him well. His breakfast consists of dry bread and water. At dinner he eats meat, while supper is a repetition of breakfast. He never indulges in alcoholic beverages, and does not even drink coffee. He concludes the paragraph by the earnest wish that he may soon again rejoin his wife and children. Undoubtedly such a stern regime could increase nostalgia!

In the autumn of 1778 Lafayette asked Congress for leave to return to Paris, which was readily granted. Expecting to sail from Boston, he set out from Philadelphia on horseback, despite a high fever and chilling rain. He was fêted at various places along the road, and the eager young man attempted to "strengthen himself with wine, tea and rum." But at Fishkill the violence of his fever compelled him to give up. He was hospitably received at the mansion of Colonel Brinckerhof, where Washington had stayed at times. De Kalb watched over his friend solicitiously, reporting on his gradual convalescence to their mutual friend, the Comte de Broglie, from Fishkill, November 7, 1778:

> He has just recrossed Hudson River and has fallen ill in my vicinity. The doctors affirm that his continued fever will have no other troublesome consequences than to keep him for some time in bed. I sincerely trust that he will recover promptly. The doctors were not frightened at this, but I fear it may cause him uneasiness and that his impatience to depart may increase his illness[269]

On November 11 de Kalb reported:

> M. de Lafayette is better and out of danger, but very weak. Some time will elapse before he is fit to start. M. Gimat returns with him to France.[270]

Lafayette had indeed been seriously ill and had expected to die. De Kalb calmed his worst fears and warned the impatient young traveler that thorough convalescence was required. Washington was very much concerned about his condition, and commended him to the special care of Dr. John Cochran, Surgeon General of the United States Army. The patient arrived at Fishkill November 1 and left for Boston December 2, 1778.[271]

De Kalb wrote to his wife on October 7, 1778:

> I am very tired of the war here and would have been but too glad to go to Paris with Lafayette. Receive him kindly.[272]

The two friends were never to meet again.

Just as de Kalb had employed his leisure time while waiting in the Spanish port by climbing a nearby mountain, so while stationed in

Newburg, New York, he did not miss the opportunity of seeing West Point with its magnificent view over the Hudson. He tells his wife about this expedition with almost boyish enthusiasm in a letter dated November 29, 1778:

> Yesterday I went to West Point on foot, being anxious to see it before quitting the Hudson forever. The weather was splendid, but the road contemptible. I had to choose between clambering over the rocks and wading in the morass, or going up to my knees in water. I returned the same evening, having made twenty-eight English miles in all, and was obliged to change my guides, as those who set out with me were too fatigued to go back. Never in my life have I made so fatiguing a jaunt; I hardly felt my feet at the last; but, while I certainly would not repeat the excursion, I am very glad to have seen the beautiful West Point.[273]

The type of warfare, which consisted of defense against marauding parties – guerilla warfare we should call it – allowing for no strategy on a larger plane, was extremely wearing. In his New Year's greetings of January 1, 1779, to his family, de Kalb mentions some of his trials, but adds with self-irony that after all, he is getting only what he deserves:

> The privations to which I am subjected, the extraordinary exertions incident to the mode of warfare and the variable climate of this country, the frequent movements from camp to camp, which makes rest and comfort unattainable even in winter, all these hardships are onerous to a man at my time of life, and make me extremely anxious to return. I have no just cause of complaint, however, because I have come of my own free will.[274]

About this time de Kalb received a letter from the Comte de Broglie, the only reply to the numerous letters written to him by de Kalb. There is no allusion to any creation of a generalissimo appointment – that subject has evidently been forgotten. But the tone of the French General's suggestions seems to imply that the Americans are really in need of good advice which a veteran of the French service is in position to offer:

> Mme. de Kalb has forwarded me the letters with which you have honored me from time to time. The time for your operations in the field has arrived. We are in hopes, here, that the weakness of the English at the isolated points of the coast in their occupation, which they are compelled to

> expose on all sides will justify the American troops in an effort to expell the enemy. It would seem, at all events, that they have it in their power to harass and enclose him, and to cut off or at least greatly impede his supplies and forage. I have not a moment's doubt that you will omit no opportunity of explaining to the leading men of the army and of Congress the views of what is judicious and practicable which you are so well qualified to impart. Too much cannot be done to make them understand the advantage offered by their position, if they will make the efforts fairly to be expected from them.[275]

The remainder of the letter gives de Kalb hopes that his name will be placed on the next list of officers to be created brigadier generals in the French army.

Washington considered Stony Point an enemy stronghold that should by all means be retaken. He ordered that a spy be sent into the woods at Stony Point "to obtain the best available knowledge of them so as to describe the particular sort of works, the precise spots on which they stand, and the strength of the garrison." Wayne secured the services of Captain Allen McLane, an astute and experienced scout. On July 2, 1778, in company with a Mrs. Smith who wished to see her sons, members of the garrison, he approached the fort with a flag of truce and was admitted. He was dressed like a farmer and acted like a simple countryman. Consequently, he was permitted an opportunity to obtain the desired information. On the strength of this report, Washington made a detailed plan of attack for General Wayne.[276]

> My ideas of the enterprise in contemplation are these. That it should be attempted by the light infantry only, which should march under cover of night and with utmost secrecy to the enemy lines, securing every person they find to prevent discovery. Between one and two hundred chosen men and officers I conceive fully sufficient for the surprise, and apprehend the approach should be along the water on the south side crossing the beach and entering the abbatis. This party is to be preceded by a vanguard of prudent and determined men, well commanded, who are to remove obstructions, secure the sentinels, and drive in the guards. They are to advance (the whole of them) with fixed bayonets and muskets unloaded. The officers commanding them are to know precisely what batteries or particular parts of the line they are respectively to possess, that confusion and the consequences of indecision may be avoided.[277]

More directions for further steps follow, all of which General Wayne carried out in bold fashion when he took the fort on July 16, 1778. It was the first time that American troops made a successful attack on British regulars in a fortified position with the bayonet alone.[278]

Congress, elated by the news, unanimously voted to award Wayne a gold medal for his "brave, prudent and soldierly conduct." It commended Colonel Fleury and Major Stewart for their "personal achievements" and promoted two sergeants to captaincies for their "cool, determined spirit." In further generosity, even the lowliest private was rewarded, because Congress ordered that the captured stores be evaluated and an equivalent sum divided among the troops. Washington wrote congratulatory letters to the most deserving officers.

In a letter to Mme. de Kalb of July 18, 1778, written in a happy mood inspired by the taking of Stony Point, de Kalb tells of his entertainment of the staff officers of his division at dinner:

> The staff officers of my division were my guests. We were all very hungry and did full justice to the mutton and beef which constituted the repast; large round crackers served as plates, in the absence of any kind of crockery. The scene forcibly reminded me of the conquest of Italy by Aeneas, and of the words of Ascanius, when they had reached the future site of Rome. There too, hunger impelled them to devour the cakes upon which their food had been set before them, and recalled the oracle of the harpies that they would not reach the end of their wanderings and toils nor call Italy theirs, until they would have eaten their tables with their meals. I have, unfortunately, no Ascanius with me, but I desire most ardently that my fate may be decided as was that of Aeneas, that the independence of America, like the conquest of Italy, may now be realized, and that, after we too have eaten our tables, the close of our warfare and our toils may likewise be approaching.[279]

Of course, de Kalb could have made this truly beautiful poetic allusion on the basis of a translation from Virgil, but since he was throughout his life working hard to improve himself, it seems not unlikely that lacking formal schooling he had studied diligently to acquire the fundaments of a gentleman's education, Latin in addition to his French and English. It may be interesting to quote here, in Dryden's translation, the charming scene in which Ascanius, Aeneas' young son, recognizes the harmless fulfillment of the oracle that so ominously hung over the heads of the daring band of Trojans:

> Beneath a shady tree the hero spread
> His table on the turf, with cakes of bread;
> They sat, and not without the God's command,
> Their homely fare despatched; the hungry band
> Invade their trenchers next, and soon devour,
> To mend the scandy meal, their cakes of flour.
> Ascanius this observed, and smiling said:
> "See, we devour the plates on which we fed."

His letter continues, exuberant because of the American victory:

> While we were still at table, a letter came from General Washington, dated the 16th of July from his headquarters in New Windsor, in which I receive my share of compliments for the valor and good conduct of our troops, for my division was also represented at the assault on Stony Point of the previous evening. The letter put our whole company into excellent humor, though of course we have been longer and better acquainted with all the details of the successful *coup de main* than the general himself. I drank no rum as the others did, yet I was carried away by the same enthusiasm. I called Mr. Jacob and told him to bring me a bottle of champagne. He stared at me in astonishment, saying he had none. Then there must be some wine at least? "That is on the baggage wagons," answered Jacob. I apologized for my defective memory, and was sorry to have tantalized the company with delusive hopes; but they were satisfied to take my good will for the deed. I promised all my guests to give them the best of champagne in Paris, and shall be delighted to keep my word.[280]

In evaluating the battle of Stony Point, de Kalb's judgment coincides with that of current historians, that the capture of the fort was not important in itself, but that it had a fine effect on the morale of the American troops. It is characteristic of de Kalb, a commander always very solicitous of the welfare of the soldiers under his orders, that he was not sentimentally squeamish about sending men into battle if the occasion required it, or of himself fighting in the first line:

> The taking of Stony Point forms an epoch in the history of the war of American Independence, because it was on this occasion that our troops first ventured to attack the intrenchments of the enemy, and because they displayed great bravery in doing so. The action lasted only about twenty-five

minutes. A hundred or a hundred and twenty of the British were killed or wounded, while we had thirty killed and sixty wounded. I mean to tell the truth, in spite of what the newspapers will say about our losses, greatly exaggerating, of course, the number of fallen foe, and cutting down our own casualties. But I am unable to appreciate the subtlety of this system of lies told by everybody and believed by nobody, and prefer to comfort myself with the well-tried proverb, "On ne fait point d'omelette sans casser des oeufs." Every cook knows that, and every officer knows that in assailing a post when the garrison have not fallen asleep, lives must be lost.[281]

But plundering and brutalizing the civil population was quite a different matter. On the subject of the brutality of the British army, de Kalb waxes quite indignant. "In Fairfield, Bedford, Norwalk, New Haven, and West Haven, the British have followed the principle that whatever they cannot carry off is to be destroyed or burned. They cannot possibly triumph in the end. Their cruelty and inhumanity must sooner or later draw down upon their heads the vengeance of Heaven and blast a government which authorizes these outrages." Friedrich Kapp, de Kalb's biographer, remarks that such indignation on the part of an officer who had been present at the invasion of Germany under Soubise and Richelieu in the Seven Years' War is surprising, because one would scarcely expect him to be shocked at ordinary plundering and destruction which could be passed off with a "c'est la guerre." The British must indeed have behaved brutally if a life-long soldier could grow sentimental about their ravaging and invoke the wrath of heaven on their heads.[282]

By way of contrast, clemency shown by the American troops toward their foes is striking; British officers reported no single instance of inhumanity to any of the unhappy captives. No one was unnecessarily put to the sword or wantonly wounded. The laws of war gave a right to the assailants to put to death all found in arms. The rebels had made the attack with a bravery never before exhibited, and showed at this moment a generosity and clemency which during the course of the Revolution had no parallel. The surprise of the British officers tends to confirm de Kalb's observations on brutality in the War of the Rebellion.

De Kalb spent the summer and autumn of 1779 at Buttermilk Falls near West Point. His division consisted of one regiment from Delaware and seven from Maryland. It was divided into two brigades; the first under General William Smallwood, comprised the first, third, fifth and seventh Maryland Regiments, while the second under Colonel Mordecai Gist was formed of the second, fourth and sixth Maryland and a Delaware Regiment. All troops under de Kalb's orders then numbered 2030. There was no engagement, the troops being occupied in constant reconnaissance and frequent movements requiring them to camp in the open or in the woods without their luggage. De Kalb for a whole month slept on the bare ground or in his camp chair.[283]

As winter arrived, a worse experience than Valley Forge was in store for the army. Washington decided that the main force, comprising about 10,000 men, was to pass the winter at Morristown, New Jersey. Accordingly, de Kalb led his division from Buttermilk Falls, starting November 26, 1779, on a six-day march in the course of which quite a number of his men died because of the fearful cold.[284] On arrival at winter quarters the soldiers had to build their own huts with lumber from trees which first had to be felled. Though Valley Forge is fixed forever in the popular imagination, it deserves forgetfulness in comparison with the stay at Morristown. Very early that winter the cold came. And such cold! There had been nothing like it in the memory of the oldest inhabitants. Roads disappeared under snow four feet deep. New York Harbor was frozen over.

His letter continues:

> The roads are piled with snow until, in some places, they are elevated twelve feet above their ordinary level. The present winter is especially remarkable for its uninterrupted and unvarying cold. The ice in the rivers is six feet thick. Since this part of America has been settled by Europeans, the North River at New York, where it is a mile and a half wide near its mouth, and subject to the ebb and flow of a strong tide, has not been frozen over so fast as to be passable by wagons. Unfortunately our camp will suffer even more from the thaw than from the frost, for it is but too much exposed to inundation. Those who have only been in Valley Forge and Middlebrook during the last two winters, but have not tasted the cruelties of this one, know not what it is to suffer.

An additional extremely trying evil was the terrible inflation that made money almost worthless and of course made even necessities hard to come by.

> The times are growing worse from hour to hour. The dearth of the necessaries of life is almost incredible, and increases from day to day. A hat costs four hundred dollars, a pair of

boots the same, and everything else in proportion. The other day I was disposed to buy a pretty good horse. A price was asked which my pay for ten years would not have covered. Of course I did not take it, and shall try to get along with my other horses. Money scatters like chaff before the wind, and expenses almost double from one day to the next, while income, of course, remains stationary. I have reduced my servants to the smallest number possible, which involves no great self-denial, as almost all servants are lazy, addicted to drink, and unreliable. The barber's compensation would at present consume all my pay; I have, therefore, made up my mind to shave myself. Being entirely in rags, I shall go to Philadelphia as soon as I can, to purchase new clothes, especially linen.[285]

Naturally enough, de Kalb asks himself why he is undergoing all this misery. His answer makes clear the motives that impel his actions: 1) his sympathy with the American cause; 2) his desire for glory; 3) his ambition to rise in his profession through his own zeal.[286]

On the night of January 25, 1780, a British force made a surprise attack on Elizabeth, New Jersey, and burned many houses. In order to prevent similar disasters, Washington appointed General Arthur St. Clair to be stationed there with a corps of two thousand men, to repel similar attacks. The General was expected not only to defend the camp and headquarters at Morristown against attacks, but to cover the country bordering the enemy lines, to suppress all traffic with the city of New York, to ascertain the positions of the British along the coast of New Jersey and Staten Island, and to report his findings to Washington. It was also his task to protect the army against disasters such as "the late misfortune and disgrace at Elizabeth." General St. Clair performed this difficult task efficiently until it became necessary for him to ask for some leave. Washington wrote to de Kalb on February 29, 1780:

> A particular piece of business has occurred which will require Major General St. Clair to leave for the present the command of the troops advanced below and which will probably occasion him to be absent from it till the middle or the latter end of the week after next; it is therefore my wish that you should supply his place and that you will proceed as soon as you conveniently can and take the command. If you can do it today it will be so much the better...[287]

On the first of March de Kalb repaired to the lines. During the entire month, amid cold, snow and thaw, he had the hardest duty to perform, in visiting an extended line of posts, reconnoitring his position, supervising the troops, and inspecting by turns every important point of the line. He was all day in the saddle, and moved his quarters back and forth between Amboy, Elizabethtown, Newark, Springfield, Westfield and Scotch Plains, and every other point possibly threatened by the English forces.[288]

Since British forces were moving from New York to attack Charleston, South Carolina, it was obvious that the theatre of war was moving to the South. Washington desired that a strong force should march south to come to the aid of General Benjamin Lincoln, who was in command at Charleston. This critical post was under siege by a strong British army at the time. For this task Washington selected de Kalb, ordering him to march on March 3, 1780, to Philadelphia, to make preparations for his southern expedition.[289]

On September 15, 1779, there had come to de Kalb a very pleasant interlude in the irksome bivouacking in the woods without the most necessary supplies. The new French minister plenipotentiary, the Marquis de la Luzerne, had arrived to replace Gérard, and was going to pay a visit to de Kalb as an old friend and comrade in arms of the Baron from the days of the Seven Years' War. Wharton, in speaking of this excellent diplomat, says... "He applied himself sedulously to the duties of his station, and by the suavity of his manners, as well as by the uniform discretion of his official conduct, he won the esteem and the confidence of the American people. His efforts were all directed to the support of the alliance, on the principles of equity and the broad basis of reciprocal interests established in the treaties."[290] De Kalb rode eighteen miles to meet his old friend, invited him to dine with all the officers at his headquarters on the best their frugal supplies could furnish, and afterward accompanied him for twenty-eight miles on his way toward Philadelphia.[291]

Interesting light on de Kalb's character is revealed by his friendships; he had not many, but of the best. His relationship with Lafayette is marked by one touch of nobility after the other. De Kalb advised, against his own interests, when he learned that Lafayette's father-in-law was going to take steps against the lad's decision to sail for America; he urged him not to break with his family.[292] Again, when Lafayette vowed to return to France unless de Kalb were granted the major generalship that Congress had awarded to the Marquis, de Kalb advised him to abide by his original plan lest he be ridiculed in France. When Congress later decided to bestow this grade also on de Kalb, dating the seniority back to November 7, 1776, a month before Lafayette's contract with Deane, de Kalb requested that his and Lafayette's commissions be of the same date; in writing about this to his wife, de Kalb said that he had given the ambitious young man "a little present."[293]

The historian Jared Sparks, writing about the Canadian expedition under Lafayette's command in the winter of 1777 to 1778, says that Lafayette "succeeded in having the Baron de Kalb appointed to the expedition, who, being older in rank than Conway, would of course be second in command. This request was not readily granted, but he insisted on it so strenuously that it was finally conceded."[294] During the following winter, de Kalb watched over Lafayette during the latter's serious illness at Fishkill near de Kalb's camp. He regretted very much that he could not accompany his protégé to Paris, but asked Mme. de Kalb to "receive him kindly and courteously and thank him for the numerous proofs of regard he has extended to me since the beginning of our friendship. I shall thank him as long as I live, and value and esteem him most highly."[295]

In the previous chapter there is quoted the letter of introduction de Kalb wrote for his friend Duponceau, one of the most interesting Frenchmen to come to the United States. In his youth this idealist had received thorough education as a preparation for the priesthood, but his love for the American cause induced him to join von Steuben in coming to America. He served as the General's aide in various campaigns, and decided at the end of the war to remain in this country. As a linguist he showed rare mastery of not only European languages but also those of the Far East and of the American Indians. Likewise as an expert on international law he was of great service to the young republic. De Kalb, himself something of a linguist, and this "guileless and pure" scholar found each other quite congenial.[296]

De Kalb's self-discipline was always remarkable. For example, the news of his appointment by Congress to a major-generalship reached him on his way home to France with three fellow officers, a day's journey from Philadelphia, confronting him with a difficult dilemma. On the one hand, here was the fulfillment of a long cherished hope; but on the other hand, could he now desert his colleagues who had been rejected by Congress? He decided it was his duty to refuse. Lest his refusal seem ungracious, he wrote what he considered a farewell note to his friend, Charles Henry Lee, telling him he would never forget his kindness.

Later, when he had been placed by Washington in command of the Army of the South, offering him an opportunity for glory which he had long awaited, Congress abruptly appointed over his head the egregiously incompetent Gates, whose disastrous management of the campaign he consistently obeyed, though he well knew he was more versed in warfare than any of the Generals in the American army, and that his competence was acknowledged by all, even the British officers. It is striking to note how many contemporaries bear witness to this nobility of character.[297]

Fortunately, Mr. Thomson's persuasion and concessions by Congress induced de Kalb to remain. Many years later Lee wrote in his *Memoirs:*

> No man surpassed this gentleman in simplicity and condescension* which gave to his comportment a cast of amiability, extremely ingratiating, exciting confidence and esteem. Although nearer seventy than sixty years of age, such had been the temperance of his life that he not only enjoyed to the last day the finest health, but his countenance still retained the bloom of youth, which circumstances very probably led to the error committed by those who drew up the inscription on the monument erected by order of Congress. This distinguished mark of respect was well deserved. (The inscription on the monument in Annapolis says that he died in "the forty-eighth year of his age" – it should read "the fifty-ninth."[298] *Samuel Johnson defined "condescend" as "To depart from the privileges of superiority by a voluntary submission, to sink willingly to equal terms with inferiors." In current usage "condescend" has, of course, definitely patronizing overtones.)

De Kalb chose his faithful aide Dubuysson as his messenger to Congress to submit the conditions under which he could accept the belated appointment. This young nobleman later gave the full measure of devotion to his commander and friend when in the Battle of Camden he threw himself on the mortally wounded, prostrate General to protect him with his own body from British bayonets. Dubuysson was severely wounded and taken prisoner. When, after de Kalb's death, an offer was made to exchange him for a British officer who had influence among certain Indian tribes such that he might incite them to fight against the Americans, Dubuysson declared that he would rather remain a prisoner than cause such a dangerous man to be set free.[299]

When General Richard Henry Lee in 1810 was writing his memoirs, he asked Colonel Nicholas Rogers of Baltimore for his recollections of de Kalb. He was well qualified, for he had been de Kalb's aide-de camp at Valley Forge and later:

> In Europe, I believe, he was engaged chiefly in the *Quartermaster* Department where, from his great aptitude for detail and minutiae, he must have been valuable. Had we employed him in that line, he might have been of great service, for we frequently felt many inconveniences and suffered much from our ill-judged arrangements and want of foresight.

Besides his extreme temperance, sobriety and prudence, with his great simplicity of manners which highly fitted him for his undertaking, he also had many of the other qualifications for a soldier, such as patience, long-suffering, strength of constitution, endurance of hunger and thirst, and a cheerful submission to every inconvenience in lodging, for I have known him repeatedly to arrange his portmanteau as a pillow, and wrapping his great horseman's coat around him, stretch himself before the fire and take as comfortable a nap as if he were in a bed of eiderdown. He would rise before day, light his candle and work till nine, then take a slice of dry bread with a glass of water, and go to work again until about twelve or one, when he would ride to headquarters, pick up the news of the day, and return to dinner. This meal consisted of a little soup and a shin of beef, or of a dry tasteless round, with his favorite beverage, water. After this he would go to work again, and so continue until dark, when, without using his candle, he would get to bed, that he might rise at the earliest hour in the morning.

This was his mode of life generally, while we were at the Valley Forge, where we all suffered not a little.

In size, he was a perfect Ariovistus, being upwards of six feet, and fully equal to the fatigues of a soldier. He would often walk twenty or thirty miles a day without sigh or complaint, and indeed, often preferred that exercise to riding. His complexion and skin were remarkable, being as fair and fresh as those of a youth.[300]

Another aide-de-camp of de Kalb's was that gallant Marylander Colonel Otho Holland Williams, who as ensign had fought under Washington before Boston, rising to a colonelcy in the Maryland troops which became a part of de Kalb's division. He is described as "well educated, tall and elegantly formed, his manner such as made friends of all who knew him." He and de Kalb worked together to induce Gates to adopt a more reasonable plan of action, but could not prevail against his obstinacy and rashness. Williams' account of de Kalb's conduct at Camden is a fine monument to this brave soldier.[301] The same is true of Dubuysson's letters.

De Kalb's friendship with Dr. Phile and Christopher Marshall has been discussed; of decidedly less importance, but possibly significant in this connection, is a letter of the Baron to be found in the de Kalb material of the Pennsylvania Historical Society. It was written on November 1, 1779, from de Kalb's camp at Buttermilk Falls to Colonel Wadsworth, Commissary General:

Sir:
Having General Washington and other gentlemen to dine with me the day after tomorrow, I shall be much obliged to you to procure me a ham and a couple of neat's tongues if possible, or some other provisions. Nothing is to be had at Commissioner Kean's, nor any of the commissaries of brigades, not even a leg of mutton.

The Commissary General wrote his reply on the bottom of the sheet: "The Baron has a blank receipt from me – please to fill it up."

CHAPTER XIV

WASHINGTON SENDS DE KALB TO RESCUE CHARLESTON; CONGRESS SUBSTITUTES GATES

The troops ordered to march south under the command of General de Kalb were despatched to relieve Charleston, at the time besieged by a strong British force and in danger of having to capitulate. But whether or not Charleston fell, Washington wished to send troops into the South because the British movements in that direction were making it the vital theatre of war. The troops selected for this campaign were from Maryland and Delaware – states represented in practically all engagements from the siege of Boston in 1776 to the end of the war. The contingents were few in number but distinguished for their courage.

In a letter from his headquarters at Morristown, dated April 2, 1780, Washington placed in the hands of Congress the decision as to whether or not the expedition should be undertaken.

> In case the detachment is to march, its ulterior proceedings and route from Philadelphia will depend upon the orders which Congress or the honorable Board of War by their direction shall give; for it is impossible for me, under my circumstances, to give directions upon the occasion. The Quartermaster and Commissary General are both at Philadelphia, and will exert themselves, I am persuaded, to carry into execution any plan for the transportation and accommodation of the troops that may be judged eligible as far as it may be in their power. Baron de Kalb, who is now at the head of the Maryland division, will command the detachment in case it proceeds and will set out tomorrow or next day to assist and expedite the arrangement for its future movements.[302]

Washington suggested that the troops might embark at Head of Elk (present Elkton) and sail down Chesapeake Bay, entering the James River en route to Petersburg. This procedure would not only make the trip easier for the soldiers, but would also serve to prevent desertions as the men moved through their home states. Washington was well aware of the risks involved from a possible attack on the troop transports by a British fleet, but he decided "something should be hazarded here."[303]

On April 4, 1780, Washington sent de Kalb the following orders:

> I have, in consequence of the opinion of the last council of war, left it with Congress finally to determine upon the march of the Maryland division to the southward. That no time may be lost in the transportation of troops, should Congress agree in sentiment with the Council, I am to desire you to proceed immediately to Philadelphia; and if you find, upon your arrival there, that the troops are to move, concert with the Board of War and the commissary and quartermaster general the necessary arrangements for their provision and accommodation. But if it should be determined that the march of the body of men alluded to is at this time inexpedient or unnecessary, you will be pleased, after completing your private business, to return to your command in the army. If you proceed to the southward, I wish you a safe and expeditious march, and every success you can possibly desire.[304]

De Kalb accordingly arrived in Philadelphia on April 8, and was pleased to find that Congress had already decided to accept Washington's suggestion. At last he would go into battle and win glory! But from this point on, one disappointment followed upon the other in his efforts to secure the necessary items for the equipment of his troops.

Washington was well aware of de Kalb's desperate situation. In a letter of April 13, 1780, to Major General Robert Howe, he expressed his disgust in, for Washington, very strong terms:

> About the time that your letter came to hand, directions from Congress respecting the march of these troops arrived. Accordingly, this division as it is, is preparing to march, but how they will get on for want of provisions, transportation, etc. Heaven alone can tell. I cannot.[305]

As soon as it was ascertained that the enemy forces had left New York, the Maryland Division broke camp at Morristown and on April 16, 1780, started the march to Philadelphia. Here de Kalb superintended their equipment. He then sent the infantry, numbering 1400 men, to Elkton, the northernmost point of Chesapeake Bay, where they embarked on May 3 for Petersburg, Virginia, while the artillery with the baggage and ammunition, proceeded south by land.

At the very time Washington wrote the letter quoted above, de Kalb reported to the Commander-in-Chief in a similarly pessimistic vein:

> The providing the troops under my command with every necessary for their march has been attended with many difficulties and delays which it was not in my power to remove as soon as I could have wished; and therefore I was not able to give a satisfactory account to Your Excellency before now.
>
> The Board of War have fixed upon Richmond as the place of rendezvous for the whole. The two brigades embarked at the Head of Elk, the artillery, ammunition and baggage proceeded by land. I shall set out tomorrow morning. I should have done it many days ago had I not been detained by the Board of War and the Treasury. I should have been happy to see the Marquis de Lafayette but would not lose a moment in going on.
>
> From Richmond I will write to your Excellency the situation of the troops, the number of recruits joined on the march, and the measures I shall take to march with most expedition.[306]

On May 13, 1780, de Kalb left Philadelphia, was detained two days at Annapolis, waiting for money to be paid by the treasurer of the State of Maryland, and arrived at Richmond May 22. Governor Thomas Jefferson having removed the rendezvous of the troops twenty-three miles southward, to Petersburg, de Kalb rode there on the next day. He found that the last of the troop transports had just arrived, which kept him busy day and night putting his forces into marching order. Nevertheless, on May 23, from the same place he wrote a tender letter to his wife. He regretted that he could not meet with Lafayette, because his troops were already under way to march 500 miles through a hot, disagreeable plundered region. "I think my troops will have much to suffer," he closed. "I shall write as often as possible; keep well, chère bonne amie! Je suis tout à toy, pour la vie."[307]

After another week of unceasing struggle with the problem of making bricks without straw, as it were, he found time to write his wife again on May 29, 1780 still from Petersburg. The lost opportunity of a meeting with Lafayette was still preying on his mind:

> How gladly would I have tarried a few days in Philadelphia

to await the arrival of the Marquis de Lafayette, announced in your last letters. I had hundreds and hundreds of questions to ask him, and would have been glad to have chatted with him for some hours; but it was impossible to postpone my departure even a single day, as my troops were already on the march for this place, and as the fate of Charleston evidently depends upon the succor to be brought by me, it is to be hoped that I shall come in time. But I cannot be there before the end of June. Everything seems to have conspired against me and the interests of the service. Come what may, however, I will not have the blame of any delay laid at my door. I have under my orders the troops of Maryland and Delaware, Lee's corps, and a regiment of artillery with twelve pieces. I have been promised further reenforcements of militia from Virginia and North Carolina; but such is the dilatory manner in which all things are done here, that I cannot depend upon them, much less wait for them. Tomorrow and next day my troops, divided into three brigades, will take up their line of march, provided always the long promised wagons are forthcoming. In spite of the haste with which I shall move, it is very possible that the fate of Charleston will have been decided before my arrival. For, although the city has long been threatened with a siege, and the enemy was in close proximity for a long time before he could complete the investment, although, therefore, there was the largest abundance of time to stock it with supplies, yet I fear this essential matter has been entirely overlooked, or has received the necessary attention only when it was too late.[308]

Wagons, absolutely essential to an army on the march, had been promised to de Kalb, but they arrived only in negligible quantity. This caused irritating delays, but in his determination to proceed toward the enemy, on June 1, 1780, he ordered his first brigade to advance; the few wagons on hand had to be used to transport the tents, while the soldiers, despite the terrific heat of the Virginia summer, were required to carry their own baggage. The second brigade started on June 6, while de Kalb brought up the rear on June 8. The direction of his march from Petersburg, Virginia, was toward Hillsboro and Salisbury, towns in central North Carolina. But due to lack of even the most essential supplies, it was only on June 20 that he reached the border of North Carolina.

The bitterness of his disappointment is expressed in a letter to Dr. Phile: "I meet with no support, no integrity, and no virtue in the State of Virginia... For my part I expect a most toilsome campaign, having been detained much too long by the non-arrival of my wagons."[309]

While still in Petersburg, de Kalb received news of a major disaster, causing him to write the Board of War for further orders:

> I am this moment informed by Major Jamison, who arrived from Georgetown, South Carolina, that Charleston capitulated on the 12th of May, our garrison prisoners of war, the enemy advancing this side Georgetown, their forces in that quarter unknown, but that their army under General Clinton was with a late reenforcement he received, about 12,000. No certainty where Governor Rutledge is with the troops under his command, and have sent orders to the first brigade and artillery to halt where they are until I shall join with the second brigade. I suppose my orders will find them not far from Salisbury. There I will consider what steps to take, if a junction with Governor Rutledge may be expected, and whether there will be any prospect of obtaining militia from Virginia and North Carolina; but even then the enemy will be vastly superior in number. I am determined to be on the defensive until reenforcement, and further orders and directions either from your Board, Congress, or the Commander-in-Chief. By Major Jamison I also understand that Colonel Armand's corps is in Wilmington. The State artillery of Virginia moved from this place twenty-eight days ago by the same road I am marching; they are supposed to be actually about Camden or with Governor Rutledge.[310]

Washington, foreseeing the continuance of the war in the South, wrote on April 15, a month before Charleston fell, to Thomas Jefferson, the Governor of Virginia: "There never was greater occasion for the states to exert themselves" and "I thought it expedient to communicate our situation to your Excellency that you might perceive the necessity the State of Virginia will be under..." Virginia, hitherto untouched by the war, was now made painfully aware of the danger of invasion from the Carolinas. The state was unprepared.[311]

On June 11 Jefferson wrote Washington:

> There is really nothing to oppose the progress of the enemy northward but the cautious principles of the military art. North Carolina is without arms. We do not abound. Those we have are freely imparted to them, but such is the state of the resources that they have not yet been able to move a single musket from this state to theirs. All the wagons we

> can collect here have been furnished to the Marquis (sic) de Kalb, and are assembling for the march of 2500 militia under General Stevens of Culpeper, who will move on the 19th instant.[312]

Jefferson does not tell how many wagons were furnished to de Kalb, but they were by far not enough to spare the troops the extra burden of marching loaded down by their personal baggage.

On June 25, Abner Nash, Governor of South Carolina, wrote Thomas Jefferson about de Kalb's "little army" stationed at Hillsboro and "exceedingly distressed for provisions and forage." The Governor then outlined a plan of action for de Kalb:

> An express went off to him four days ago, advising that it would be our opinion that it is best for him to direct his course southwestwardly toward Charlotte in order to support General Rutherford and to prevent the army of the British by all possible means from turning the right of our armies, thereby cutting off from us the fertile hilly and thick settled back country whose inhabitants at present are well attached to us but who under circumstances so unfavorable, it is to be feared, would fall off.[313]

This sensible route was also de Kalb's plan, but, as we shall see, it was not followed.

James Monroe wrote Jefferson on June 26 about the universal scarcity in de Kalb's army "of all kinds of provisions except meat which prevails in this country. Upon this account the army under General de Kalb at Hillsboro and that under General Caswell here (at Cross Creek) are no longer able to hold these stations, and are in that dilemma, that they have only the alternative of advancing shortly upon the enemy or retiring to Virginia."[314]

The fall of Charleston frustrated the first objective of de Kalb's march south, but made his action there all the more necessary, yes, even possibly decisive. He was planning to follow principles laid down by his erstwhile commander, the renowned Maréchal de Saxe: "The wise general avoids pitched battles, especially at the beginning of a campaign. This is not defensive or waiting policy. It is necessary to engage in frequent combats followed by retreats and hiding, to demoralize the enemy. Then can come the great battle to crush him."[315]

Had such a policy been followed it would have put the British at a great disadvantage, for the possession of Charleston gave them no real foothold in the south. The Whigs in the westerly regions could have been organized into militia groups eager to suppress the Tories.

If the British moved toward the interior they could be harassed in many ways, and their line of supplies cut off, leaving them in barren, inhospitable territory while more and more patriots would rise against the enemy invader.

Meanwhile, however, de Kalb's army advanced under greater and minor hardships, as he describes them in a letter to his wife of June 21, the day after he reached the boundary of North Carolina:

> Here I am at last, considerably south, suffering from the intolerable heat, the worst of quarters, and the most voracious of insects of every hue and form. The most disagreeable of the latter is what is commonly called a tick, a kind of strong black flea which makes its way under the skin, and by its bite produces the most painful irritation and inflammation, which lasts a number of days. My whole body is covered with these stings. I do not yet know whether the strength and movements of the enemy, and the difficulty of feeding my little army will permit me to advance two hundred miles further to the borders of this state. I have ordered several detachments to rendezvous tomorrow thirty-three miles from here, if a violent storm does not prevent us from effecting a junction. Of the violence of thunderstorms in this part of the world Europeans cannot form any idea.[316]

Difficulties increased the further southward the army penetrated. At Hillsboro de Kalb had to stop for some days to permit the exhausted soldiers to rest. Not only did supplies for the sustenance of his men fail to arrive, but the likewise promised Virginia and North Carolina militia regiments. He resumed his march in a southwesterly direction toward Greensborough, but on reaching Wilcox's Iron Works on Deep River he had to halt once more because of want of provisions. From his camp he wrote to his wife on July 7:

> Since last giving you some account of myself at Goshen, I have had to make most fatiguing marches, endure much heat, and overcome great difficulties, but am still far from the end. It is even possible that after having reached the goal assigned myself, I shall be compelled to retreat without striking a blow, for want of provisions. What a difference from warfare in this country and in Europe! They who do not know the former, know not what it is to contend against obstacles. I would fain be rid of my command, than which there can be nothing more annoying or difficult. My present

position makes me doubly anxious to return to you as soon as possible.[317]

The State of North Carolina made no arrangements for the subsistence of the Union troops, but devoted all its efforts to building up its own militia. This left de Kalb no alternative but to send out foraging parties. Though these were ordered by no means to deprive any farmer of his total supplies, they, as well as the army as a whole, acted as starving men would act under such circumstances.

Some local color of de Kalb and his army in the South is given in the *Life of Francis Marion, a Celebrated Partisan Officer in the Revolutionary War against British and Tories in South Carolina and Georgia*, by Brigadier General P. Horry of Marion's Brigade and L. M. Weems, Formerly Rector of Mount Vernon Parish, Philadelphia, (Lippincott, 1860).

General Horry tells the reader in the introduction that as an old man he had been incessantly urged by admirers of Marion to write a biography of the "Swamp Fox," one of the great heroes of the Revolutionary War, under whom Horry served. "With one foot in the grave and the other hard by," he was finally persuaded "to quit my prayer book and crutches (an old man's best companions), and drawing my sword, flourish and fight over again the battles of my youth," protesting that he was no scholar, no historian. According to the Dictionary of American Biography, in the article on Francis Marion, Horry turned his manuscript, full of anecdotes and interspersed letters, over to Parson Weems. This "historian and scholar" omitted the letters, garbled a number of statements of fact, introduced imaginary speeches, dressed up Horry's style, but left the authorship distinctly Horry's.

With this caution, one may well listen to Horry, embellished by Weems. After all, the author of the Cherry Tree Story also wrote a life of Franklin, but he attributed no little hatchet to the author of the hoax, *An Edict of the King of Prussia* and the *Speech of Polly Baker;* the story of the little boy's honesty and bravery in the face of possible severe punishment sits better on the meticulously honest and stern Father of his Country than it would have on Franklin, Hamilton, Burr, Patrick Henry, or any other great man of that day. Thus, while Weems may invent conversations, they are quite likely well fitted to the character of the speaker, and events are generally described as Horry remembered them. To cite a description of foraging:

> We did indeed sometimes fall in with a little corn; but then the poor, skinny sunburnt women with long uncombed tresses and shrivelled breasts hanging down would run screaming to

us, with tears in their eyes, declaring that if we took away their corn, they and their children would perish.

> Horry goes on to tell of the case of a well-to-do farmer who met the soldiers and begged that for God's sake they would not ruin him, for he had a large family of children to maintain. The soldiers replied that it would never do for them, as fighters for their country, to starve. The man heaved a deep sigh, without saying a word. His young corn, which seemed to cover about fifty acres, was just in the prime roasting ear stage and he had also a couple of beautiful orchards of peach and apple trees, loaded with young fruit. Scarcely were our tents pitched, before the whole army, foot and horse, turned in to destroy. The trees were all threshed in a trice; after which the soldiers fell, like a herd of wild boars, upon the roasting ears, and the horses upon the blades and stalks. So that by morning light there was no sign or symptom left that corn had ever grown there since the creation of the world. What became of the poor man and his children God only knows, for by sunrise we were all under marching orders again, heading for the South. I say all; but I only meant all that were able. For numbers were knocked up every night by agues, fluxes, and other maladies, brought on by excessive fatigue and lack of food.[318]

Marion and Horry had been in besieged Charleston, but escaped being taken prisoners by the British. They came north to join the Union forces, where they were introduced to de Kalb by a mutual friend.

Horry describes his feeling when he and Marion met de Kalb:

> I shall never forget what I felt when introduced to this gentleman. He appeared to be rather elderly, but though the snow of winter was upon his locks, his cheeks were still reddened over with the bloom of spring. His person was large and manly, above the common size, with great nerve and activity; while his fine blue eyes expressed the mild radiance of intelligence and goodness.

> De Kalb remarked in the course of conversation: "I thought the British tyranny would have sent great numbers of the South Carolinians to join our arms. But so far from it, they are all, as we have been told, running to take British protection. Surely they are not tired already of fighting for liberty."

De Kalb had a simple non-dogmatic Christian belief which he did not wear on his sleeve, but which he nevertheless cherished sincerely. This is manifest, for example, in his description of the visit he made to the Moravian settlement in Bethlehem when in September, 1777, he set out to return to France. He could never have written about the Quakers as Lafayette did in a letter to his wife of September 26, 1777:

> It (i.e. Philadelphia) is full of a scurvy kind of persons, doltish Quakers, who are good for nothing but to go into a room with great hats on their heads, no matter what the weather, and to wait there in silence for the Holy Spirit to descend, until one of them, grown tired of waiting, gets to his feet and talks a deal of nonsense, with tears pouring from his eyes.[319]

De Kalb's fellow-passenger on the "Victoire," the Vicomte de Mauroy, in a letter to de Broglie of August 28, 1778, after some sarcastic jibes about de Kalb, remarks on this same trait of the Baron: "His health up till now has forced him to fight his campaigns at Bethlehem, a charming abode of peace and happiness. He can stay there as often as he pleases, clasp the good Jesus in his arms and leave everything to him."[320] (The last sentence is omitted in Stevens.)

De Kalb's profession as a soldier did not in the least interfere with his religious belief, just as little as it did in the case of, say, Robert E. Lee or "Stonewall" Jackson, both of them devout Christians. Except, one might add, it was at the bottom of De Kalb's humane attitude toward soldiers and civilians, manifested on numerous occasions.

On learning of the surrender of Charleston, Congress in unbecoming haste and without consulting Washington, unanimously, on June 13 appointed as commander of the Southern army Horatio Gates, in the full knowledge that he was Washington's enemy. But Gates was the conqueror of Burgoyne, and had many friends in Congress. "Gates was the military idol of the day. He had actually compelled the surrender of an entire British army, and that was a pedestal large enough to sustain a popular hero. The fact that Gates had twice as many men as Burgoyne was not taken into account; nor was the fact the British at Saratoga were out of food and hopelessly lost in the woods. They would have surrendered if Gates had been in China."[321]

Gates set out to assume the command of the Southern Department with great self-confidence, despite the warning of his friend Charles Lee, "Take care lest your northern laurels turn to southern willows."

He gave no consideration to these ominous words, though he knew full well what was facing him: "The command of an army without strength, a military chest without money, a department apparently deficient in public spirit, and a climate that increases despondency instead of animating the soldier's arm.[322]

In a letter to Governor Jefferson from Hillsboro on July 19, 1780, Gates employs superlatives to describe the utter want of food, arms and ammunition for his army:

> When I had the honor of seeing your Excellency at Richmond, I was taught to look forward to much difficulty and a perplexed department, yet I cannot but profess that in the course of a long and often critical service, it has hitherto never fallen to my lot to witness a scene of such multiplied and increasing wants as my present command exhibits... An officer just from the Baron's headquarters has assured me that there are often intervals of twenty-four hours in which the army without distinction are obliged to feed upon such green vegetables as they can find, having neither animal food or corn. So frequent and total a want must eventually break up our camp, should not the evil be hastily remedied ..."[323]

Of course de Kalb had pleaded with Congress and with the Governor of North Carolina for aid for his distressed army. The Governor promised a plentiful supply of provisions and a strong reenforcement of North Carolina militia, which had then taken the field under Major General Caswell. But the supplies never arrived, while the commander of the militia, ambitious to gain glory for himself, refused to cooperate with the Union army. He employed his men in detachments against small parties of seditious or Tory inhabitants who, to avoid being drafted into the service of their country, retired into the swamps or woods. With the army in this inauspicious situation, the arrival of the new commander was announced for July 25.

The action of Congress in suddenly relieving him of his command might have induced de Kalb to resign from the army and return to his family and his estate. But he had rendered his oath to fight for American freedom, and he stayed, stoically returning to the command of his division of Maryland and Delaware troops. It was with some relief that he turned over the arduous responsibilities to a general who supposedly had the unanimous support of Congress. De Kalb had never cultivated his few influential friends in Congress; opportunities for showing his mettle against the enemy on the battlefield had constantly eluded him, and besides he was a foreigner – all of which makes the action of Congress understandable.

With some relief, but no rosy forecasts, de Kalb on July 16, 1780, wrote General Gates from his camp on the Deep River.

> I am happy by your arrival, for I have struggled with a good many difficulties for provisions ever since I arrived in this State; and altho' I have put the troops on short allowance for bread, we cannot get even that; no flour laid in, and no disposition made for any but what I have done by military authority; no assistance from the legislative or executive power; and the greatest unwillingness in the people to part with anything. Of all this I will give you a more particular account on your arrival. The design I had to move nearer the enemy to drive them from the Peedee River, a plentiful country, has been defeated by the impossibility of subsisting on the road, and no immediate supplies to be depended on in the first instance after a difficult march.
>
> I will prepare exact returns toward the time I shall have the pleasure of seeing you, of the regular troops of the department, but I could hardly depend on any but the Maryland and Delaware regiments of my division, with a small number of artillerymen and Colonel Armand's legion, and all those very much reduced by sickness, discharges and desertion. This induced me to leave three pieces of artillery at Roanoke River and to send some six to Hillsborough, having kept eight, which I thought sufficient for so small an army.
>
> I am to move towards Coxe's Mill, high up on Deep River, where I am to be joined by the North Carolina militia under Major General Caswell, of about 1200. The Virginia militia are still at Hillsborough, as you will be informed there. You may also have met with a small party of Colonel Buford's remains; I wanted to keep them in the army, but wanting arms and clothing he insisted on marching them to Virginia, and promised me he would join in the beginning of July. I have not heard from him since. Col. Washington's and Col. White's regiments of horse are at Halifax, it is said, unfit for service. I have wrote to them both several times to know their situations, but could not obtain an answer as yet; there were two troops of Virginia State light-horse under Major Nelson, in so bad order in respect to horses, wanting saddles and every article of accoutrement, that I have sent them to Halifax to refit and recruit.
>
> Col. White has left 25 of his light horse at Hillsborough; they

might serve you for an escort; if you order one from camp to meet you, let me be informed thereof in time. You will find the army in a few days at or near Coxe's Mill; your wagons, if you have any, would go better by Chatham Court House; your quarters will be marked near camp.[324]

Gates replied from Hillsborough on July 20, expressing his astonishment at de Kalb's difficulties and accepting the offer of a military escort.

Yesterday I had the honor to receive your obliging letter of the 16th instant, dated from your camp on Deep River. I am astonished at your distress and difficulties, and have ever since my arrival here upon last Tuesday been endeavoring to alleviate them. I have sent despatches to the Governor and Executive Council of this State, to Governor Jefferson of Virginia, and to Congress; in all these you may be satisfied I have endeavored to describe our real situation, so that no mistake may be entertained upon that head. Enough has already been lost in a vain defense of Charleston; if more is sacrificed, I think the Southern States are undone, and this may go nearly to undo the rest. I think all my writing business will be finished today; if so, I shall set out tomorrow for camp, and hope to be with you on Saturday. The troops as you mention for my escort are here without horses, and many of them sent by Capt. Gun to Halifax. I will acquaint you tomorrow the route I intend to come, and request an escort to meet me at a certain spot I will name.[325]

De Kalb arranged that the ceremony be performed in a most respectful manner, with a salute of thirteen guns. Gates made his acknowledgments to the Baron for his great politeness, and following the usual courtesy, confirmed all standing orders of his predecessor. But then came a great surprise. At the first review he ordered the troops in readiness to march at a moment's "warning."

Headquarters, Buffalo Ford, July 26, 1780
Officer of the Day tomorrow: Col. Hall

The standing orders of Major General de Kalb to be obeyed. The troops will hold themselves in readiness to march at a moment's warning – the army may be satisfied that such measures are taken and have for some time past been taken by Congress and the executive authority of all Southern States from Delaware inclusive that plenty will soon succeed the unavoidable scarcity; provisions, rum, salt and every requisite will flow into camp which shall then with a liberal hand be distributed to the army. The General thanks the troops for the patience and perseverance with which they have endured the wants and hardships of the preceding part of the campaign, and is satisfied that the future will add still more luster to the renown they have acquired, and give glory and triumph to the American arms.[326]

The latter order was a matter of great astonishment to those who knew the real situation of the troops. But all difficulties were removed by the General's assurances that plentiful supplies of rum and rations were en route and would overtake them in a day or two – assurances that were certainly fallacious and that were never verified.

On the day after Gates' General Order, on July 27, 1780, the Maryland Council in Annapolis acted on de Kalb's request for provisions for the Maryland troops under his command. The Council refused, on the ground that the distance was too great, and that North Carolina and Virginia should take care of these troops, since Maryland had often enough provided for the troops from distant places just because they happened to be in Maryland. Therefore, no provisions from Maryland "flowed to the Southern army to be distributed with a liberal hand."[327]

Gates' order of July 26 stood. The army got under way on July 27. De Kalb and the other officers all agreed that the Commander's plan was the result of his utter ignorance of the territory, of sources of supply, and of the condition of the half-starved soldiers. They induced Colonel Williams,[328] an old friend of Gates, to remonstrate with the Commander about his hazardous course. Williams made the following points:

1. The Country between Hillsborough and Camden was desolate, full of sandy plains alternating with swamps, and very thinly settled.
2. Whatever provisions and forage had been collected along the streams had been plundered in turn by the Whigs and Tories; hence the army would face starvation there. The only advantage of this road was that it was fifty miles shorter.
3. On the other hand, the nortwesterly route would lead to Salisbury in the midst of fertile country and a patriotic population. This route had been the choice of the most circumspect and efficient officers with de Kalb at their head, because it provided provisions, so badly needed by the starving soldiers.
4. In case of a reverse, it offered an asylum for the sick and wounded at Salisbury and Charlotte, towns where the militia were devoted to the cause of American independence.

5. This location was most favorable for the erection of a repair shop for arms.
6. Supplies coming from the North would find this route safest to the army's destination.
7. This circuitous route would make possible an outflanking of the enemy outposts, permitting later an advance on Camden with the Wateree River on its right flank and its friends in the rear.

To give more weight to these considerations, Colonel Williams had them drawn up in writing and signed by the leading officers. Gates refused to be swayed by reason, even when de Kalb pointed out the weakness of Gates' own plan. His one concession was a promise to convene with all the general officers (Williams was a colonel, and was thus put in his place!) for consultation, at noon of the first day of march – but he never invited them to such a conference.

One of the many mistakes Gates made was to refuse the offer of Francis Marion, the famous "Swamp Fox," of the services of his bold band of partisans; instead he ordered him to the Santee River to destroy all boats there in order to hamper the retreat of the British to Charleston – after their defeat!

Horry tells that on parting, the Baron gave them his judgment of the situation. Probably Parson Weems has embellished this passage, but it undoubtedly contains the sentiments of the experienced soldier:

> Here we are hurrying to attack an enemy who, if they but knew our condition, would long for nothing so much as our arrival. *We,* two thirds at least, raw militia; *they,* all regulars. *We,* fatigued, *they,* fresh. *We,* feeble and faint through long fasting; *they;* from high keeping, as strong and fierce as gamecocks or butcher's bull dogs. It does not signify, gentlemen; it is all over with us; our army is lost as sure as ever it comes into contact with the British. I have hinted these things more than once to General Gates, but he is an officer who will take no council but his own.[329]

De Kalb's understanding of and sympathy with the simple Christian groups led to some benefit to the men in the Southern army under the command of Horatio Gates. In a letter of July, 1780, to General Caswell of the North Carolina militia, Gates writes:

> General de Kalb has been the means of in some degree relieving, by a supply he had taken measures to procure from the Moravians, the distress here. This supply is also extended to the troops here, or I know not how we should have been able

to march forward – so clean General Rutherford's troops and yours have swept this part of the country.[330]

Evidently de Kalb paid a call on the Moravian colony in North Carolina and persuaded these German pacifists to extend aid to the starving soldiers.

CHAPTER XV

THE LAST FULL MEASURE OF DEVOTION

For lack of horses, two field pieces had to be left behind as the army, on orders of General Gates, began its inauspicious march southward from Wilcox's Mill on July 27, 1780. A week later, on August 3, the troops crossed the Peedee River in boats at Mask's Ferry. Here Lieutenant Colonel Charles Porterfield joined Gates with a hundred Virginia State troops, a most welcome reenforcement. Though the troops were half starved and almost exhausted, they were forced to march on, doing seventeen or eighteen miles a day. Being human, they showed their resentment at the General's unfulfilled promises. They began to straggle, to steal, and to plunder. Even those who remained in the ranks looked dark and scowling, and a mutiny, which would have produced the most deplorable circumstances, was on the point of breaking out when the officers, mingling with the men, and reasoning with them, succeeded in silencing the murmurs for which there was, unfortunately, only too much justification. They showed their own empty canteens and haversacks, and convinced the privates that the sufferings of all were equal, exhorted them to bear up under the hardships of the hour, and promised that if the expected supplies did not very soon arrive, foraging parties would be sent out by every corps in all directions to collect what little corn might still be stored in the country, and bring it to the mill.[331]

The desperate tone of Gates' letter to Governor Thomas Jefferson at this point shows that he had come to realize the dangerous impasse into which his folly had plunged the army:

> Sir: Since I joined the army upon Deep River, my distress has been inconceivable, of which the enclosed copy of a letter of this day's date to Governor Nash will convince your Excellency. I wish I could say the supplies of Virginia had been a reproval to North Carolina. I am ashamed to say, their backwardness rather countenances than disgraces their sister state. What can the Executive Councils of both states believe will be the consequences of such unpardonable neglect? I will yet hope your Excellency is doing all in your

power to supply your half-starved fellow citizens. Flour, rum, and droves of bullocks should without delay be forwarded to this army or the Southern Department will soon want one to defend it; it has rained furiously for several days, and your militia are still without tents. Therefore I expect desertion and the hospital will speedily leave General Stevens without any command. I wish I could present your Excellency with a more pleasing account of the public affairs this way, but the duty I owe the U.S. obliges me to represent things truly as they are.[332]

Gates' letter to Governor Nash of North Carolina makes an even more desperate appeal for supplies "for your almost famished troops."[333]

Shortly after the incident of the threatened mutiny, it happened that a little stock of corn was brought into camp. The mill began to grind, and in a few hours the soldiers were served with a meal such as they had long foregone. This sudden turn of affairs restored the composure of the men, and they conceived of fresh hopes for the future. Not so the officers, who at their own request, had been served last with rations. However, it was useless to complain to the commanding general, as no one could advise him how to extricate himself quickly at this stage of his dilemma. Nevertheless he was informed of what took place in the camp and was aware of the critical stage of feeling among the troops.

He now began to appreciate the difficulties pressing upon him, and sensible of the responsibilities incurred, he declared to Colonel Williams, (who since the 6th of August had acted as adjutant-general in place of Major Armstrong, who was ill), that he had in a measure been compelled to take the route he had adopted. General Caswell, he proceeded to explain, had evaded every order, both of de Kalb and Gates, to unite his militia with the regular army, being evidently vain of his independent command, and bent upon some enterprise flattering to his personal ambition. In his exasperation, Gates wished that Caswell be soundly rapped over the knuckles, but, unfortunately, such a defeat would lose the army badly needed reenforcements. He considered it absolutely essential that he unite the North Carolina militia to his army. Furthermore, such a junction would permit his troops to share the supplies the State had sent to its militia. He further justified his advance by saying that after he had gone so far to meet the army, a backward movement would discourage the troops and bitterly disappoint the inhabitants to whom protection from the British had been promised. De Kalb and Williams vainly argued that the road on the right, leading through fertile settlements, should be followed, in view of the half-starved condition of the troops.[334]

On August 6 Gates rode over to Caswell's camp, where he was entertained with a sumptuous meal and wine, showing that North Carolina took care of its own. In the best of spirits, arrangements were made for uniting the forces. General Richard Caswell appeared entirely satisfied with the position assigned him as third in command. He was in command of the left wing, while de Kalb was in charge of the right, composed of regulars. At noon on August 7 the forces joined, marched a few miles in the direction of the hostile post on Lynch Creek, and then encamped.

Colonel Williams reports in the third person an incident that seems like an ominous presage of the disastrous outcome of the Battle of Camden:

> The deputy adjutant general, who was as solicitous of the welfare of the army as if he had been personally responsible for it, requested Lieutenant Colonel Ford, the officer of the day, to visit the guard with him at an unusual hour in order to satisfy himself of the safety of the left wing. The guards and sentinels on the right wing were as vigilant as usual and saluted the round with that readiness which inspires a sense of security; but on the left wing all was silent. The patrolling officers were not once challenged, rode by the guards without being stopped and found their way unobstructed even to the tents of the generals and staff officers, some of whom complained of their unnecessary disturbance at an hour so unusual among gentlemen. The officers of the preceding day were called, and guards and patrols arranged, to secure the camp against surprise.[335]

On the morning of the 8th of August the enemy had disappeared. Under the guise of offensive movements, the officer commanding at Lynch's Creek had quitted this post, and skilfully withdrawn all his force unmolested to a much stronger position on Little Lynch's Creek. The latter was but a day's march from Camden, which, being the depot of provisions for the British troops scattered through the country, was strongly fortified and well garrisoned under Lord Rawdon. That general had been, since the beginning of June, in command of the advanced posts of the army, which were destined to invade North Carolina, and only kept back until the autumn by the heat and the want of provisions, while Lord Cornwallis, who, since the return of Sir Henry Clinton, had the command-in-chief of the four thousand English troops scattered over the Southern provinces, had his headquarters at Charleston. On receiving the news of the approach of the Americans under Gates, Lord Rawdon marched from Camden to meet them, took up a well-fortified position at the distance of about fourteen miles from that place, and called in the detachments which were scattered over the country to support the foraging parties sent to scour the land in all directions.[336]

In order to keep his army as mobile as possible, Gates on August 15 ordered women, children and wounded, as well as all heavy baggage to be sent back to Charlotte under the command of Major Dean. Of the "multitudes of women," not all left, many preferring to share every toil and danger with the soldiers to the security and the provisions promised them in the region further north.

Anent camp followers Ward remarks, "One finds it difficult to realize that in the eighteenth century all armies had their trains of camp followers, even of women and children. Many of the women were wives of the men in the ranks; others had more temporary or promiscuous attachments. They played their part in the camps, washing the soldiers' clothes, cooking their food, and so on. They were so customary and usual that the historians take them for granted and seldom mention them except on occasions such as this, when they were sent away."[337]

Washington was opposed to camp followers and frequently forbade their presence near the armies, especially that of "lewd women." The following order is typical of many to be found in his *Writings:* "The troops are in future to be exempted from exercise every Friday afternoon. This time is allowed them for washing their linen and for bathing." As on other occasions, Washington was solicitous of the soldiers' health, as shown by his order that no man should be in the water longer than ten minutes.[338]

With Lord Rawdon in command of his comparatively small force blocking the road to Camden, Gates had two choices. He had insisted on the short but barren road to the South with the idea of smashing the British force with his numerically superior army. He might have succeeded had he followed de Kalb's plan of a quick attack on Lord Rawdon before Lord Cornwallis arrived with reenforcements. Lord Rawdon's position was a strong one, and Gates acted cautiously in rejecting the Baron's plan.

De Kalb, usually conservative, with careful consideration of the possibilities of success as well as with a suitable retreat in case of failure, here advocated an attack on Lord Rawdon's forces encamped in a favorable position on the opposite shore of Lynch's Creek. In European wars he had learned from Maréchal de Saxe, who had gained great fame for his bold capture of Prague, and he had been present at Maréchal Lowendal's carefully planned night attack on the "invincible" Bergen op Zoom; he had also observed how Wayne's well planned action recently at Stony Point had led to a glorious success. In consideration of the determined bravery with which de Kalb and his well-trained regulars a few days later, fought against superior forces in the battle of Camden, it is conceivable that such a night attack might well have proved successful, thus changing radically the outcome of the Southern campaign. That it was a distinct possibility is shown by a letter written a fortnight later by Lord Rawdon to his mother:

> De Kalb, who was a good officer, saw so clearly the consequences of reducing their attack to one point, and thereby enabling me to unite my detachments, that he strongly advised Gates to pass Lynch's Creek and fight me; at all events this was related to me by de Kalb's aide-de-camp (a relation of M. de la Fayette) Colonel de Buysson, who was made prisoner. Gates rejected the advice, threw himself across the country into the other road above Hanging Rock Creek, and gave us three days to prepare to meet him in a country likewise very favorable to us.

Gates rejected the plan which Rawdon implicitly admits to have been excellent advice. The point with de Kalb evidently was, "Push the enemy and prevent the concentration of his forces."[339]

The precarious position of the British forces near Camden and the imminent possibility of their being cut off from their base in Charleston is described by Charles Stedman, the English historian who fought under Howe, Clinton and Cornwallis:

> The communication between Camden and Charleston appeared in danger of being cut off by the enterprising movements of Sumter, whose numbers were daily increasing by the junction of disaffected inhabitants. The safety of the army depended on preserving a communication with the seacoast; and something was necessary to be done immediately for extricating it from its perilous situation. At this juncture a retreat to Charleston might have been effected without much difficulty; but the sick must have been left behind (Stedman lists their number as nearly eight hundred), the magazines of stores either abandoned or destroyed, and the loss of the whole country would have necessarily followed, except indeed Charleston, in which there was already a sufficient garrison for its defense.[340]

The alternative plan which Gates might have followed with success was to march ten miles to the right, turn Rawdon's flank, and gain Camden before him. But Gates hesitated and thus let both opportunities slip. He waited for two days where he was, and only on the 13th of August marched to the right to take up his position at Clermont (or Rugely Mills – Clermont was the name of the owner's residence) on the westerly road. He thus abandoned the whole purpose for the sake of which he had refused to advance by the better road in the first place. On the 14th he was joined by General Stevens with seven hundred Virginia militia; but on the same day Lord Cornwallis reached Camden with his regulars; thus golden moments for crushing the British in detachments were gone forever.[341] This was very regrettable in view of the British forces scattered widely over the state.

The British cavalry commander, Banastre Tarleton, who played an important part in the Battle of Camden, speaks of Gates' strategy while encamped opposite the British on Lynch's Creek:

> The American commander discovered that Lord Rawdon's position was strong, and he declined an attack; but he had not sufficient penetration to perceive that by a forced march up the creek, he could have passed Lord Rawdon's flank and reached Camden, which would have been an easy conquest and a fatal blow to the British.[342]

Lord Rawdon on August 13th fell back to Camden, calling all the scattered British contingents to join him there, including those from Clermont. Colonel Sumter of the South Carolina militia at this point reported to Gates that an escort with clothing, ammunition and other stores was en route from Charleston for the troops in Camden. In order to capture this prize he needed reenforcements; he therefore requested Gates to send him some infantry and two small pieces of artillery. The General ordered a detachment of one hundred regular infantry and two small pieces of artillery, under Lieutenant Colonel Woolford, to join Colonel Sumter. Thus on the eve of battle Gates weakened his forces by giving up a hundred of his best soldiers in a useless enterprise – if he lost the battle he would lose the supplies, and if he defeated Cornwallis he could readily capture the wagon train.[343]

Williams says that in the opinion of many, Gates, now at Clermont, would have done well to take a secure position with his army and wait only a few days. By that time, abundant provisions would have flowed into his camp, and volunteers from the westerly section of the Carolinas would have given him numerical superiority over the British:

> On the 15th of August Gates sent the sick, the heavy baggage and all the camp equipment that could be spared, to Washaw. This order was unfortunately not executed in time, so that the baggage wagons fell into the hands of the enemy after

the loss of the battle. On the same day the order for the march to Camden was issued, which was to be taken up at ten o'clock in the evening in the following order: The advance was formed by a part of Armand's Legion, then came the cavalry under Colonel Armand himself, whose right and left flanks were covered by Colonel Porterfield and Major Armstrong with the light infantry, marching in Indian file at a distance of two hundred yards from the road. They were followed in regular order by the First and Second Maryland brigades and the North Carolina and the Virginia divisions, each command being preceded by its artillery. The rear was again covered by volunteer cavalry. In case of an attack by the enemy's cavalry in front, the light infantry on either flank were directed to advance immediately and open a heavy fire, under cover of which Colonel Armand was to resist the attack, and if possible to drive off the enemy. The troops were commanded, on pain of death, to march in profound silence.[344]

At the time Gates issued these orders, he did not know that Cornwallis had arrived in Camden to support Rawdon. Furthermore, he believed that he had 7,000 men in his command. He called a council of the officers, informing them of his plan, based on the erroneous estimate of his actual force. Meanwhile, the deputy adjutant General, Colonel Williams, checked carefully with each corps and found that the men fit for duty numbered exactly 3052. When Williams submitted his figures to the General, the latter's reply was: "These are enough for our purposes." He added that when he read his orders to the council there had not been a dissenting voice. Naturally, Gates had read orders, but had not called for comments or a vote.[345]

On August 9th, when General Caswell had joined the forces under Gates, giving the American army great superiority over that of General Rawdon, de Kalb, as related above, advised a smashing attack on the British army entrenched on the opposite side of Lynch's Creek. A few days later, when Gates had marched to Clermont, de Kalb advised their continuance at Clermont to strengthen a naturally good position, awaiting at least more reliable intelligence than they now had. And if attacked, it would better suit the composition of the American army to be on the defensive than to risk a combat in open field, on a force so largely consisting of raw militia. Besides, the enemy might have been reenforced, and if so might possibly have such an excess as "to render our attempts either useless, or fatal to the expedition."[346]

When Gates on August 15 again scorned de Kalb's and Williams' advice, and without asking for comment, read his orders for an attack that night, the Baron naturally remained silent.[347]

With the reenforcements brought by Cornwallis, the British forces numbered fully three thousand men, most of them well-disciplined veterans, supported by a strong body of cavalry under Tarleton, and six heavy cannon. Adjutant General Williams' report put the American army at three thousand and fifty men, of whom more than half were militia, many for the first time facing the enemy, and uninstructed in the use of bayonets just issued to them. In addition there were seven pieces of artillery and Lieutenant Colonel Armand's sixty cavalrymen. Numerically the armies were about equal, but in fighting experience the Americans were outnumbered about two to one, even after the arrival of Brigadier General Stevens with his Virginians.

It seems incredible that Gates remained ignorant of the arrival of Cornwallis. On August 15 an inhabitant of Camden came, as if by accident, into the American encampment and was conducted to headquarters. He affected ignorance of the approach of the Americans, pretended great friendship for his countrymen, the Marylanders, and promised the general to be out again in a few days with all the information the general wished to obtain. The information which he gave was the truth, but not the whole truth, as events afterward revealed; yet so plausible was his manner that General Gates dismissed him with many promises if he would faithfully observe his engagements. Suspicions arose in the breasts of some of the officers about headquarters that this man's errand was easily accomplished; the credulity of the general was not arraigned, but it was conceived that it would have been more prudent to have detained the man for further acquaintance.[348]

The Battle of Camden is noted for some very tragic decisions by the American commander, but one of them certainly borders on the ridiculous. It was customary to serve the troops an allowance of one gill of rum when they were about to fight the enemy; but no spirits were at hand. Gates therefore conceived the bright idea that molasses, of which a supply had just been received, would serve as an acceptable substitute. Probably few soldiers thought so. In Gist's order book "rum," first written in, was crossed out and "molasses" substituted.[349] Accordingly, one gill of molasses per man, and a full ration of corn and meat were issued to the army previous to their march, which commenced according to orders at about ten o'clock on the night of August 15th.

> The troops of General Gates' army had frequently felt the consequences of eating bad provisions, but at this time a hasty meal of quick-baked bread and fresh beef with a

> dessert of molasses mixed with mush or dumplings, operated so cathartically as to disorder many of the men, who were breaking ranks all night and were certainly much debilitated before the action commenced in the morning.[350]

Gates had "read his orders to the council;" he had called neither for a vote nor for discussion. The other generals had no doubt by this time learned to know their commander well enough to be convinced of the futility of offering suggestions. As soon as the meeting was over, the officers expressed their shock at the sudden offensive planned by Gates, seemingly without intelligence as to the enemy's plans or position. Colonel Armand was probably the most indignant because he, with his cavalry, was ordered to the front of an advancing column "to march in profound silence" in the depth of the night—let no horse neigh!

Lord Cornwallis arrived in Camden on August 15, and judged immediately that delay was dangerous in view of Gates' superiority in numbers, and especially because his own brutal conduct toward the Americans was causing great numbers to join in fighting the British. He therefore decided to attack the newly constituted American army in their open, irregular encampment at Clermont. He started on the march at ten o'clock. Both armies bent on a surprise attack, but ignorant of each other's plans, started at the same hour of the night on the same road, in opposite directions. About half way between their respective camps, they met near midnight.

> The first revelation of this new and unexpected scene was occasioned by a smart mutual salutation of small arms between the advanced guards. Some of the cavalry of Armand's legion were wounded, retreated, and threw the whole corps into disorder – which, recoiling suddenly on the column of infantry, disordered the whole line of the army. The light infantry under Porterfield, however, executed their orders gallantly; and the enemy, no less astonished than ourselves, seemed to acquiesce in a sudden cessation of hostilities. Some prisoners were taken on both sides. From one of these the deputy adjutant general of the American army extorted information respecting the situation and numbers of the enemy. He informed that Lord Cornwallis commanded in person about three thousand regular British troops which were in line of march about six hundred yards in front. Order was soon restored to the corps of infantry in the American army, and the officers were employed in forming a front line of battle, when the deputy adjutant general

communicated to General Gates the information which he had from the prisoner. The General's astonishment could not be concealed. He ordered his deputy adjutant general to call another council of war. All the general officers immediately assembled in the rear of the line. The unwelcome news was communicated to them. General Gates said, "Gentlemen, what is to be done?" All were mute for a few moments, when the gallant Stevens exclaimed, "Gentlemen, is it not too late *now* to do anything but fight?" No other advice was offered, and the general desired that the gentlemen would retire to their respective commands.

The Baron de Kalb's opinion may be inferred from the following fact. When the deputy adjutant general went to call him to council, he first told him what had been discovered. "Well," said the Baron, "and has the general given you orders to retreat the army?" The Baron, however, did not oppose the suggestion of General Stevens, and every measure that ensued was preparatory to action.[351] It is usual, in such a desperate situation, that the council of the boldest prevails, especially if he speaks up first. No one likes to argue for retreat or other moderate course at such a moment.

Only about eight miles north of Camden, the armies had met in a narrow space between two wide swamps, growing narrower behind the British and wider behind the Americans. The American line was formed before daybreak; Gist's second brigade, composed of one Delaware and three Maryland regiments on the right; in the center the North Carolina militia; and Stevens' Virginians on the left, together with Armand's corps. In reserve was Smallwood's first Maryland brigade, held in the rear. The artillery was stationed in front of the center. De Kalb was in command of the right wing and took his post with it in the line. Gates and his staff took a position six hundred yards back of the line.[352]

On the British side, Lord Rawdon commanded the left wing opposite Gist, and Lieutenant Colonel James Webster the right. There was a second line composed of Highlanders, while Tarleton's cavalry was in reserve. Six cannon were posted in the British center. The flanks of both armies were protected by the swamps.

As darkness lifted, Colonel Williams noted the dim outline of British infantry advancing. He ordered the artillery to open fire and then rushed to the rear to report to General Gates: "The enemy are deploying on the right, Sir. There's a good chance for Stevens to attack before they're formed."

"Sir, that's right. Let it be done," said Gates. And that was the last order he gave in that battle or any other.[353]

But it was too late for Stevens to attack. The British were upon them, fired one volley, and then rushed forward in a bayonet attack. The militiamen had never been under fire, nor had they ever been instructed in the use of the bayonet. Weak and terrified as they were, they cast away their muskets and ran for their lives. In their panic they threw the first Maryland reserve into complete confusion. General Gates was swept away in the general rout, and did not stop until he reached Charlotte, sixty miles from the battle field. Of course, as the proverb has it, whoever suffers misfortune is sure to reap ridicule; for example, General Wayne said, comparing him to a famous military leader of antiquity, "Gates' retreat was like that of Xenophon, only a little faster."[354]

For the further account of the battle, I shall quote the eloquent and well documented description of Christopher Ward.

> Now both the center and the left were gone – hopelossly gone. The right wing of Marylands and Delawares, under General Mordecai Gist and dauntless de Kalb, its own left wide open to the enemy, alone held the field against Rawdon's repeated attacks.
>
> De Kalb called for the reserve, the First Maryland Brigade. It had recovered from its confusion, but had so far had little part in the battle. His aide sought its commander, to give him the message: but Smallwood was not with his troops – had, in fact, left the field. Otho Williams took charge and brought the brigade forward in line with the American right wing. It was immediately hotly engaged. Williams tried to bring it up to the left of the Second Brigade, but the British were between them. In spite of his efforts, the enemy held a gap of six hundred feet between the two.
>
> Cornwallis saw his chance. He swung Webster's regulars against the front and flank of the First Maryland Brigade. The Marylanders gave ground, rallied, were driven back, rallied again, but at last were overcome and routed.
>
> Now there were only Gist's Marylands and Delawares left to fight or fly. They fought. "Firm as a rock the phalanx of de Kalb and Gist remained."[355] They had stood off Rawdon's Volunteers of Ireland, the Legion infantry, the Royal North Carolina Regiment, and Bryan's Tory volunteers, more than a thousand men against their possibly six hundred – not only had held them off, but had driven them back. With one bayonet charge, they had broken through the ranks of their attackers and taken fifty prisoners. Then their left was turned, and they were forced back. De Kalb and Gist reformed them. Again they charged, and again they were driven back. Yet once more they attacked.

It was at this point that their companion brigade was broken and swept away. The smoke and dust hung in clouds in the air, so thick that one could see but a little distance. De Kalb and Gist knew nothing of the retreat of the other brigade, were not aware of the fact that they and their few men stood alone on the field. They knew that *they* were winning their fight and thought the battle was going as well for the rest of the Americans; otherwise they would have seen that a further contest was hopeless and would have retreated as best they could, with no further sacrific of their men. They had had no orders from Gates to retire. So they fought on, and "never did troops show greater courage than those men of Maryland and Delaware."[356] With the same unflinching obstinacy which they had shown at the Gowanus and on Chatterton's Hill in 1776, the Delaware and Maryland troops contended with the superior force of the enemy for nearly an hour.

De Kalb's horse was shot under him. "Long after the battle was lost in every other quarter, the gigantic form of de Kalb, unhorsed and fighting on foot, was seen directing the movements of his brave Maryland and Delaware troops. His head had been laid open by a saber stroke. Peter Jaquett, adjutant of the Delawares, fighting by his side, hastily bandaged the wound and begged him to retire. But no orders had come from Gates, now miles away and in full flight. De Kalb still thought victory was in sight. He refused.[357]

The fighting was hand to hand, terrific in its fierceness. Sabers flashed and struck, bayonets lunged and found their meat, clubbed musket fell on cracked skulls. But Cornwallis, as vigilant as Gates was not, had now thrown his entire force on these last remaining foemen, 2,000 men on no more than 600.

Overwhelmed by numbers that almost entirely surrounded him, de Kalb called for the bayonet again. All together his men answered. De Kalb in their lead, they crashed through the enemy's ranks, wheeled, and smote them from the rear. But ball after ball had struck their heroic leader. Blood was pouring from him; yet the old lion had it in him to cut down a British soldier whose bayonet was at his breast. That was his last stroke. Bleeding from eleven wounds, he fell.[358]

The brigade had lost its leader, yet the worse than decimated ranks closed, advanced once more, repelled another charge – but that was all. Tarleton's cavalry, returned from pursuit of the fugitives, swept down upon them, broke their ranks, and the battle was over.

BATTLE OF CAMDEN - DEATH OF DE KALB

Major Archibald Anderson of Maryland rallied a few men of different companies of the Continentals; Colonel John Gunby, Lieutenant Colonel John Eager Howard, Captain Henry Dobson, all of Maryland, and Captain Robert Kirkwood of Delaware collected about sixty men. All these preserved a compact body in the retreat. Such of the rest as had not fallen or been captured scattered and fled to the swamps.

Prostrate in the field lay de Kalb. It was only when the Chevalier Dubuysson, his aide, threw himself on his general's body, crying out his name and rank, that the thirsty bayonets were withheld from further thrusts into his body. Some of the enemy, British or Tory, carried him off and propped him against a wagon so that they might more easily appropriate his gold-laced coat. There he stood, gripping the wagon with both hands, his head in weakness bowed on his chest, bleeding to death from all his wounds, when Cornwallis came riding by, rescued him from the despoilers, and caused him to be cared for by the British surgeons. His great bodily vigor kept the life in him for three days before he died in Camden.

But where was Gates? From the time he gave the first order to Stevens, not a word of any sort had come from him to his fighting men. He had been "swept away" in the torrent of fleeing militia in the very first minutes of the battle, as some of the historians kindly describe his flight. "Swept away" he was – on the fastest horse in the army, a noted racer, "the son of Colonel Baylor's Fearnaught, own brother to His Grace of Kingston's famous Careless," a fit charger for General Gates. And that gallant steed never stopped sweeping him away until he landed his master at Charlotte, sixty miles from the field of honor. There Gates slept that night.[359]

Rupert Hughes has given us a fitting judgment of General Gates at the Battle of Camden: "No writer of fiction, no writer of fairy stories, could have contrived for a hero's vindication or a villain's downfall a more incredible revenge than fate inflicted on Gates."

De Kalb's *noblesse oblige* served to inspire nobility in others. It would not be easy to find greater devotion than that shown by the Baron's aide, the Chevalier Dubuysson, who protected the fallen general with his own body, sustaining four wounds, among them a bayonet thrust in the chest, from which he never recovered. He was forced to leave the service and returned to France; he died March 27, 1786.[360]

On his deathbed de Kalb was attended by the faithful Dubuysson, who had crossed on the "Victoire" and had been the Baron's friend and companion at Valley Forge and Morristown, down to the Battle of Camden. The dying hero asked him to express to the two Maryland generals, Smallwood and Gist, as well as to the brave soldiers of the Maryland line, his thanks for their valor in battle, and to bid them an affectionate farewell. From Charlotte on August 26, 1780, Dubuysson wrote the two generals:

> Dear Generals: Having received wounds in the action of the 16th instant, I was made prisoner, with the Honorable Major General the Baron de Kalb, with whom I served as aide-de-camp and friend, and had an opportunity of attending that great and good officer during the short time he languished from eleven wounds, which proved mortal on the third day.
>
> It is with particular pleasure I obey the Baron's last commands, in presenting his most affectionate compliments to all the officers and men of his division. He expressed the greatest satisfaction in the testimony given by the British army of the bravery of his troops; and he was charmed with the firm opposition they made to superior force, when abandoned by the rest of the army. The gallant behavior of the Delaware regiment and the companies of artillery attached to the brigades afforded him infinite pleasure. And the exemplary conduct of the whole division gave him an endearing sense of the merits of the troops he had the honor to command.[361]

Another request made by de Kalb shows how deeply attached he had become to the Americans and the cause of freedom. He asked that Dubuysson request the Pennsylvania Supreme Executive Council to grant his two sons, aged fifteen and thirteen, commissions in the army of that state. The request was granted September 10, 1781.

> September 10, 1781
> Supreme Executive Council
>
> Whereas Lieutenant Colonel Dubuysson, aide-de-camp to the late Major General Baron de Kalb, who fell at the Battle of Camden, gallantly fighting in the defence of America, has represented to this Board that it was the earnest desire of the Baron de Kalb that his sons should bear commissions in the American service in the Pennsylvania Line, without pay or the emoluments of command, unless in case of actual service;

whereupon, out of respect to the memory of the brave officer, and as a tribute of esteem to his family, Resolved, that the said request be complied with, and that the Honorable Board of War be requested to issue commissions of Ensigns to Pierre Baron de Kalb and to John Baron de Kalb. (Minutes, Vol. XIII, page 516).[362]

Neither of the sons, (whose names were not as given above, but Frédéric and Elie) ever came to America. Frédéric died a victim of the guillotine, and Elie ended his days on the family estate, Milon la Chapelle.

To a British officer who condoled with him in his misfortune, de Kalb replied: "I thank you for your generous sympathy, but I die the death I always prayed for – the death of a soldier fighting for the rights of man."[363]

De Kalb was buried by his victorious adversaries, among whom were many Freemasons, with military and Masonic honors. Down to the year 1825 a solitary tree was all that marked his resting place. On September 2, 1780, Dubuysson reported to Congress on de Kalb's death:

> Hillsborough, September 2, 1780
>
> Sir:
>
> The Baron de Kalb, taken by the British and mortally wounded, desired me to repair immediately to Philadelphia to give in his name to Congress a full account of his transactions relative to his command of the Maryland and Delaware Line, since his departure from Pennsylvania, to clear his memory of every false and malignant insinuation which might have been made by some invidious person, but as my wounds do not permit me to travel as fast as I could desire, I thought it convenient to prevent (sic) you, Sir, of my repairing to Congress with all the Baron's papers and accounts, that no measure be taken for this affair before my arrival in Philadelphia, which will be as speedily as possible.
>
> The Baron de Kalb, deserted by all the militia, who fled at the first fire, withstood with the greatest bravery, coolness and intrepidity, with the brave Marylanders alone, the furious charge of the whole British army; but superior bravery was obliged, at length, to yield to superior numbers, and the Baron, having had his horse killed under him, fell in the hands of the enemy, pierced with eight wounds of bayonets and three musket balls. I stood by the Baron during the action and shared his fate, being taken by his side, wounded in both arms and hands. Lord Cornwallis and Rawdon treated us with the greatest civility.

> The Baron, dying of his wounds two days after the action, was buried with all the honors of war, and his funeral attended by all the officers of the British army. The doctor having reported to Lord Cornwallis the impossibility of curing my wounds in that part of the continent, he admitted me to my parole, to go to Philadelphia for effecting an exchange between me and Lieutenant Colonel Hamilton, prisoner of war at Philadelphia. But, Sir, being informed by Governor Nash, that this Mr. Hamilton is a man of very great influence among some Indian tribes, and that this exchange may prove of dangerous consequences, I submit in that case to drop the matter altogether, being unwilling that my exchange should be attended with the least injury to our cause, and should I not be able to negotiate another exchange, I will fulfill the tenor of my parole.
>
> With the highest esteem and consideration, I have the honor to be, Sir, your most obedient and humble servant.[364]

General Gates, in his defeat and humiliation, rose to a fine gesture by according generous praise to the better man and soldier. He wrote to Washington, September 3, 1780: "Too much honor cannot be paid by Congress to the memory of the Baron de Kalb; he was everything an excellent officer should be, and in the cause of the United States he sacrificed his life." To the President of Congress on the same day he was equally the gentleman: "Here I must be permitted to say how much I think is due to the Baron de Kalb, and I am convinced Congress will declare to the world the high estimation they have for his memory and services.[365]

Among de Kalb's friends, the most dashing soldier was François-Louis Teissèdre de Fleury. He accompanied Lafayette and de Kalb on the Canadian expedition, had a horse shot down under him at Georgetown, and at Stony Point he seized the enemy flag. For his bravery Congress rewarded him with a rare honor – a medal picturing his Stony Point exploit, – and Washington urged him to return to France for a nine months' vacation. On this occasion he made the acquaintance of Mme. de Kalb.

On September 10, 1780, from Newport, Colonel Fleury wrote a letter whose addressee is unknown:

> I have promised the Baroness de Kalb to send her news about her husband. It is so sad that I must ask you to prepare her for the blow. You were a friend of General de Kalb; you were his man. The consolations of friendship are a much needed resource after irreplaceable losses.

> The Baron de Kalb was mortally wounded at the Battle of Camden. He died two days afterward. Lord Cornwallis, whose prisoner he was, supplied him with the very best of care during his mortal agony, and after his death offered all the honors due to an officer of his rank and merit. The French, to whom his wise, moderate conduct did great honor, united with the Americans to mourn him. He is praised widely in America, where the good patriots are not always the best of friends. The rank M. de Kalb held sets him off in a class by himself, and his high sense of honor and his high merit gained him the esteem and friendship of all who knew him.
>
> As for me, Monsieur, I regret him all the more profoundly because I knew him best; I feel his loss as keenly as you do. Please assure Mme. de Kalb that I share deeply her grief.[365]

The supreme praise came from Washington in a letter to Dubuysson of October 10, 1780: "I sincerely lament the loss of Baron de Kalb. The manner in which he died fully justified the opinion which I ever entertained of him, and will endear his memory to the country."[366]

Congress, on the 14th of October, 1780, resolved to commemmorate the glorious example given by General de Kalb to his troops by erecting at Annapolis, the capital of the state whose division he had commanded, a monument with this inscription:

> Sacred to the memory of the Baron de Kalb, Knight of the Royal Order of Military Merit, Brigadier of the Armies of France, and Major General in the service of the United States of America. Having served with honor and reputation for three years, he gave at last a glorious proof of his attachment to the liberties of mankind and the cause of America, in the action near Camden, in the State of South Carolina, on the 16th of August, 1780, where, leading on the troops of the Maryland and Delaware Lines against superior numbers, and animating them by his example of deeds of valor, he was pierced with many wounds, and on the 19th following expired, in the 48th year of his age. The Congress of the United States of America, in gratitude for his zeal, services and merit, have erected this monument.

More than a century elapsed before the monument was erected and dedicated in 1886. It consists of a more than life-size bronze statue of the General, shown charging with his sabre as he had again and again done at Camden. It is the work of a Baltimore sculptor, Ephraim Keyser. It stands appropriately in State House Circle in Annapolis, the capital of the state whose soldiers had distinguished themselves under de Kalb's leadership. There is one error in the inscription: de Kalb fell not in his forty-eighth but in his fifty-ninth year.

In several letters de Kalb mentions his bitter disappointment over the lost opportunity of a good visit with Lafayette on the latter's return from France early in 1780. He had a hundred questions, as he put it, to ask of his old friend, who could bring news from home, familial and political. But his sense of duty compelled him to avoid the slightest delay in proceeding on his march south with the army placed under his command by Washington. It was only by a few days that he missed the reunion with the companion of many adventures.

Yet in a manner of speaking, the two met once more. In the course of his triumphal tour of the United States in 1825, Lafayette accepted the invitation to lay the cornerstone of a monument to de Kalb about to be dedicated at Camden, South Carolina, a granite obelisk fifteen feet high, with appropriate inscriptions, one of which reads:

> Here rest the remains of Baron de Kalb, a German by birth, a cosmopolitan in principles.

Another states:

> His love of liberty induced him to leave the Old World to aid the New in their struggle for independence.

The ceremonies were conducted with military honors and Masonic rites on March 8, 1825. The chief speaker, addressing himself to the septuagenarian Lafayette, said:

> Your visit to Camden excites sublime emotions; we live over, in fancy, the scenes of its early history... monuments of the Revolution on all sides remind us of the deeds of our fathers. In its bosom reposes Baron de Kalb, your friend and companion in arms. Inspired with a holy enthusiasm in the cause of freedom and mankind, he buffeted with you the storms of the perilous ocean. With you, he first touched American soil in Carolina, and doubly sanctified it by his first visit and his last sigh; and you are now, in your old age, to deposit a stone over his ashes, which will speak to coming years. I know, Sir, it will afford you a melancholy pleasure to

pause and drop a tear at the hero's grave; his spirit and Washington's will commune with you there.

Lafayette replied:

> The congratulations of my friends on this happy visit to the State of South Carolina cannot at any time or place be more affecting and honorable to me than when offered by you, Sir, in the name of the citizens of Camden and its vicinity, on this classic ground where, in several battles, my revolutionary brethren have fought and bled; and where, even on unlucky days, actions have been performed which reflect the highest praise on the name of which we are so justly proud, the name of an *American soldier*. Such have been, Sir, the able conduct as a commander, the noble fall as a patriot, of General de Kalb. Among my obligations to you, I gratefully acknowledge your kindness in associating me to the tribute paid to the memory of a friend who, as you observe, has been the early confidant and companion of my devotion to the American cause.[367]

APPENDIX I

Officers Sailing on the "Victoire"

To sail on "La Seine" (S)		Age	Rank Given by Deane	By Congress	
Marquis de Lafayette		19	Major General	do	
Baron de Kalb	S	56	Major General	do	Fell in action
Vicomte de Mauroy	S	42	Major General		Refused; returned
M. de Valfort		27	Colonel		Refused; returned
M. de Lesser		25	Colonel		Refused; returned
M. de Fayolle	S	27	Lt. Colonel		Refused; returned
M. de Franval	S	26	Lt. Colonel		Refused; settled in U.S.
Chevalier Dubuysson		25	Major		De Kalb's Aide
Dubois Martin	S	32	Major		Refused; to San Domingo
M. de Gimat		22	Major	Lt. Colonel	Lafayette's Aide
M. de Vrigny	S	36	Captain		Lafayette's Aide
M. de Capitaine		38	Captain		Lafayette's Aide
M. de Colombe		22	Lieutenant	Captain	
M. Candon		26	Lieutenant		Refused; returned
Leonard Price		22		Major	Lafayette's American Aide
M. Bédoulx		25		Lt. Colonel	Served with Pulaski

Expected to sail on the "Seine"	6
Refused and returned to France	5
Refused and remained in U.S.	1
Refused and returned to San Domingo	1
Fell in action	1

APPENDIX II

De Kalb's portrait in Independence Hall, Philadelphia, is by Charles Wilson Peale. The Maryland Historical Society has a copy by James Lambdin. Another copy is in possession of the family at Milon la Chapelle. The illustrations, "Baron de Kalb Introducing Lafayette to Silas Deane," and "Battle of Camden – Death of de

Kalb" are by Alonzo Chappell of New York (1828-1887), an illustrator of historical scenes.

APPENDIX III

The United States Department of Interior, Board of Geographic Names, informs me that there are nine towns and villages in the United States named "de Kalb." There are also six counties bearing this name – in Alabama, Georgia, Illinois, Indiana, Missouri and Tennessee.

In the de Kalb County Court House in Auburn, Indiana, there is a painting representing "De Kalb Crowned by the Goddess of Victory, as one of the bravest heroes of the Revolution. His horse being killed under him, he has regained his feet and, although badly wounded, is setting a fine example to his soldiers in attacking the enemy again until mortally wounded." (Courtesy of Walter C. Manon, County Clerk.)

PRINCIPAL AUTHORITIES
With Key Words Used in the Notes
(Unless otherwise specified the place of publication is New York)

ADB	Allgemeine deutsche Biographie, Leipzig, 1876
AHNENTAFEL	*Deutsche Geschichte in Ahnentafeln* (Heinrich Banizza and Richard Mueller, Berlin n.d.)
AHR	American Historical Review
ANON.	*Relation de la campagne en Brabant et Bergen-op-Zom*, The Hague, 1748
ARCHENHOLTZ	J. W. Archenholtz, *Geschichte des siebenjährigen Krieges*, Leipzig, 1911
AG	Archives Générales, Bibliothèque Nationale, Paris
ARETZ	Gertrud Aretz, *Die Marquise von Pompadour*, Dresden, 1921
ARGENSON	Marquis d'Argenson, *Journals et Mémoires*, 8 vols., Paris, 1866
BALCH	Thomas Balch, *The French in America during the War of Independence, 1777-1780*, 2 vols., Philadelphia, 1891
BANCROFT	George Bancroft, *History of the United States*, 6 vols., 1887
BARBIER	E. J. F. Barbier, *Journal Historique et Anecdotique du Regne de Louis XV*, 4 vols., Paris, 1849-1856
BAURMEISTER	Bernhard Alexander Baurmeister, *Letters from Major Baurmeister to Colonel Junckenn. Written during the Philadelphia Campagne*, edited by Bernhard Uhlendorf and Edna Vosper, Philadelphia, 1937
BELCHER	Henry Belcher, *The First American Civil War*, London, 1911
BILL	Alfred Hoyt Bill, *Valley Forge, the Making of an Army*, 1952
BIOGRAPHIE	Biographie Universelle (Dezos de la Roquette on de Kalb)
BLANCHARD	Amos Blanchard, *The American Biography, Sketches of the Officers of the Revolution*, Wheeling, 1833
BLUMENTHAL	Walter H. Blumenthal, *Women Camp Followers of the American Revolution*, Philadelphia, 1952
BOUTWELL	G. A. Boutwell, "Silas Deane and... Lafayette," New England Magazine VIII (1895 N 5)
BREITNER	Erhard Breitner, *Jeanne du Barry*, Leipzig, 1938
BROGLIE "ARCHIVES"	Letters to and from the Comte de Broglie, Vicomte de Mauroy, Baron de Kalb; also "Mémoire du Vicomte de Mauroy" etc., in Archives Générale, Bibliothèque Nationale, Paris, Carton "Broglie"
BROGLIE "DUC"	Victor François de Broglie, *Correspondance Inédite*, 4 vols, Paris, 1903
BROGLIE "SECRET"	*Secret Correspondence of Louis XV with his Diplomatic Agents*, 2 vols., London 1879
BURNETT "CONGRESS"	Edmund C. Burnett, *The Continental Congress*, 1941
BURNETT "LETTERS"	Edmund C. Burnett, *Letters of Members of the Continental Congress*, Washington, 1926

CARLYLE	Thomas Carlyle, *History of Friedrich II of Prussia*, 4 vols., London, 1858
CARRÉ	Henri Carré, *La Marquise de Pompadour*, Paris, 1937
CHARDIGNY	Louis Chardigny, *Maréchaux de France, 1185-1941*, Paris, 1941
CHIDSEY	Donald R. Chidsey, *Valley Forge*, 1959
CHINARD	Gilbert Chinard, "George Washington as the Europeans Saw Him," Report of Washington Association of New Jersey, February 22, 1946
CLARK	George Clark, *Silas Deane*, 1913
CLOSEN	Ludwig von Closen, *The Revolutionary Journal of Ludwig von Closen*, ed. by Evelyn M. Accomb, Chapel Hill, 1958
COLLEVILLE	Ludovic, Comte de Colleville, *Les Missions Secrètes du Général Major Baron de Kalb...* Paris, 1885
COURCELLES	Chevalier de Courcelles, *Dictionnaire Universelle*, 8 vols. Paris, 1823
CUNZ	Dieter Cunz, "De Kalb and Maryland," Society for the History of the Germans in Maryland, XXV, 18 ff.
DEANE	*The Deane Papers*, New York Historical Society Collection, 1887-1891
DENEKE	Otto Deneke, "Carl Grosse," Goettinger Tageblatt, June 25, 1937
DICTIONNAIRE	*Dictionnaire Historique et Biographique Français*
DONIOL	Henri Doniol, *La Participation de la France à l'Etablissement des Etats-Unis d'Amérique*, 5 vols., Paris, 1886-1890
DUBUYSSON	Chevalier Dubuysson, "Mémoire d'un des officiers français passés en Amérique avec le Marquis de Lafayette" in Doniol III 215-222 or in Stevens VI no. 808. (Original in archives des affaires étrangères, Paris, Correspondance politique, Etats-Unis IV, 425-428)
DUPUY	R. Ernest and Trevor N. Dupuy, *The Compact History of the Revolutionary War*, 1963
EELKING	Max Eelking, *Die deutschen Hilfstruppen*, Hannover, 1863
FAUST	Albert B. Faust, *The German Element in the United States*, 1927
FAY	Bernard Fay, *The Revolutionary Spirit in France and America*, 1927
FAYOLLE	Rousseau de Fayolle, "Journal d'une Campagne en Amérique," 1777-1779, ed. by General L. Segretain in Bulletins et Mémoires de la Société des antiquaires de l'ouest. Poitiers, XXV, 1901
FIEFFÉ	Eugène Fieffé, *Histoire des troupes étrangères*, 2 vols, Paris, 1854
FISKE	John Fiske, *The American Revolution*, 2 vols., Boston, 1901
FITZPATRICK	John C. Fitzpatrick, *George Washington Himself*, 1933
FORD	Worthington C. Ford, *The Writings of George Washington*, 1889
FRANKLIN	*Writings of Benjamin Franklin*, Smith edition, 10 vols., 1912
FRAUENHOLZ	Eugen von Frauenholz, *Die Eingliederung von Heer und Volk in dem Staat Bayern, 1597-1815*, Munich, 1940
FUNCK	Funck et d'Illens, *Plans et Journaux des sièges de la dernière guerre de Flandre*, Strassburg, 1750

GORDON	Alexander Gordon, *Anecdotes of the American Revolution*, 3 vols., Brooklyn, 1865
GIST	Mordecai Gist, *Order Book*, in possession of Maryland Historical Society, Baltimore, Md.
GOTTSCHALK I	Louis R. Gottschalk, *Lafayette Comes to America*, Chicago, 1935
GOTTSCHALLK II	Louis R. Gottschalk, *Lafayette joins the American Army*, Chicago 1937
GREENE, G.	George Washington Greene, *The German Element in the War of American Independence*, 1876
GREENE, H.	George Washington Greene, *Historical View of the American Revolution*, 1865
HECKENWELDER	John Heckenwelder, *History, Manners and Customs of the Indian Nations*. Philadelphia, 1819.
HEROLD	J. Christopher Herold, *The Swiss without Halos*, 1918
HORRY	Peter Horry and L. M. Weems, *The Life of Francis Marion*, 1860
HOYER	Johann Friedrich Hoyer, *Geschichte der Kriegskunst*, 2 vols., 2 parts each, Goettingen, 1797
HUGHES	Rupert Hughes, *George Washington*, 3 vols., 1930
IVES	Mabel Lorenz Ives, *Washington's Headquarters*, Upper Montclair, 1933
JEFFERSON	*The Papers of Thomas Jefferson*, ed. by Julian Boyd, Princeton, 1951
JOHNSON, D.	"De Kalb, Gates and the Camden Campaign," MAH, VIII, No. 7
JOHNSON, S.	*Sketches of the Life and the Correspondence of Nathanael Greene*, 1822
JOMINI	Baron Henri de Jomini, *The Art of War*, 1892
JOURNALS	*Journals of the Continental Congress*, 1774-1789, 34 vols., Washington, 1904-1937
KAPP	Friedrich Kapp, *The Life of John Kalb*, 1884
KAPP, G.	Friedrich Kapp, *Leben des amerikanischen Generals von Kalb*, Stuttgart, 1862
KAPP, S.	Friedrich Kapp, *Der Soldatenhandel deutscher Fürsten nach Amerika*, Berlin, 1874
KAPP, ST.	Friedrich Kapp, *The Life of Frederick William von Steuben*, 1859
KITE	Elizabeth S. Kite "Lafayette and his Companions on the "Victoire," "Records of the American Catholic Historical Society," XLV (1934)
KNOLLENBERG	Bernhard Knollenberg, *Washington and the Revolution*, 1940
LAFAYETTE	*Memoirs, Correspondence and Manuscripts of General Lafayette*, London, 1837
LAMETH	Theodore de Lameth, *Mémoires*, Paris, 1913
LANCASTER	Bruce Lancaster, *From Lexington to Liberty*, 1955
LANDERS	H. L. Landers, *The Battle of Camden*, Government Printing Office, 1929
LASSERAY	André Lasseray, *Les Français sous les treize étoiles*, 2 vols., Paris, 1935

LEE	Richard Henry Lee, *Memoire of the Life of Richard Henry Lee and his Correspondence*, by his Grandson Richard H. Lee, 2 vols, 1825, (At end of Vol. I, Letters by de Kalb.)
LENEL	Edith Lenel, *Friedrich Kapp*, Leipzig, 1935
LEONARD	Emile Leonard, *L'Armée et ses problèmes au XVIIIe siècle* Paris, 1958
LEROY	Alfred Leroy, *Madame de Pompadour et son temps*, Paris, 1936
LEVERING	Joseph M. Levering, *A History of Bethlehem*, Bethlehem, 1903
LOCHEMES	Sister M. Mary Lochemes, *Robert Walsh, his Story*, Washington, 1941
LOSSING	Benjamin J. Lossing, *Pictorial Field Book of the American Revolution*, 2 vols. 1850-1852
LOWELL	E. J. Lowell, *The Hessians and Other Auxiliaries of Great Britain in the Revolutionary War*, 1884
MAH	Magazine of American History
MARSHALL	Cristopher Marshall, *Extracts from the Diary of Cristopher Marshall*, 1774-1781, Albany, 1877
MARYLAND	Maryland Archives, Vols. 43-45, July 27 – August 15, 1780
MAUROIS	André Maurois, *Adrienne, the Life of the Marquise de Lafayette*, 1961
MAUROY	Vicomte de Mauroy, *Mémoire*, see Broglie, "Archives."
MILON	Items from the de Kalb family papers from his estate, Milon-la-Chapelle, now in safe deposit of M. Soulange-Teissier, a descendant of the General
MONTROSS	Lynn Montross, *War through the Ages*, 1944
MOORE	Frank Moore, *Diary of the American Revolution*, 2 vols., Hartford, 1858
MORISON	Samuel Eliot Morison, *John Paul Jones*, Boston, 1959
MUHLENBERG	Henry A. Muhlenberg, *Life of Major General Peter Muhlenberg*, Philadelphia, 1849
NACHTMANN	J. Nachtmann, *Un Chapitre de la vie de Kalb*, Paris, 1859
NOLAN	J. B. Nolan, *Lafayette in America Day by Day*, Baltimore, 1934
PMHB	Pennsylvania Magazine of History and Biography
PAINE	*The Writings of Thomas Paine*, ed. by Moncure Daniel Conway, 1894
PALLESKE	Emil Palleske, *Schiller, Leben und Werke*, 2 vols., Berlin, 1859
PALMER	John McAuley Palmer, *General von Steuben*, New Haven, 1937
PATTERSON	Samuel W. Patterson, *Horatio Gates, Defender of American Liberties*, 1941
PERKINS	James Breck Perkins, *France in the American Revolution*, 1911
PETTENGILL	Ray W. Pettengill, ed. *Letters from America* (letters of Brunswick, Hessian and Waldeck officers, – 1924
PHILIPS	Edith Philips, *The Good Quaker in French Legend*, Philadelphia, 1932
PRESER	Carl Preser, *Der Soldatenhandel in Hessen*, Marburg, 1900
ROSENGARTEN	J. G. Rosengarten, *The German Soldier in the Wars of the United States*, Philadelphia, 1890

SCHM	South Carolina Historical Magazine
ST. PAUL	De Kalb's letter to M. de St. Paul, November 7, 1777, published in the American Historical Review, XV (1910) 562-567
SAXE	Maurice de Saxe, *The Art of War, Reveries et Mémoires*, London, 1811
SCHLOSSER	Friedrich C. Schlosser, *Weltgeschichte* (especially Vol. 14) Leipzig, 1873
SCHLOEZER	August Wilhelm Schloezer, *Briefwechsel*, Goettingen, 1770-1782
SCHROEDER	John F. Schroeder, *Washington und die Helden der Revolution*, 1857
SCHUMACHER	Karl von Schumacher, *The du Barry*, 1932
SEGUR	Louis Philippe Segur, *Mémoires, ou Souvenir et Anecdotes*, Paris, 1842
SEUME	Johann Gottfried Seume, *Sämmtliche Werke*, Leipzig, 1853
SEYMOUR	William Seymour, "A Journal of the Southern Expedition," Historical Society of Delaware, Vol. II, (1846)
SHEEAN	Vincent Sheean, *A Day of Battle*, 1938
SIMMS G	W. E. Simms, *Life of Nathanael Greene*, 1849 (Otho H. Williams' "Narrative of the Campaign of 1780" is printed in the appendix)
SIMMS M	W. E. Simms, *The Life of Marion*, 1857
SINETY	Le Marquis de Sinety, *Vie du Maréchal de Lowendal*, 2 vols., Paris, 1867
SKRINE	Francis Henry Skrine, *Fontenoy*, London, 1906
SMITH	J. Spear Smith, "Memoir of the Baron de Kalb," Maryland Historical Society, Baltimore, 1858
SMOLLETT	Tobias G. Smollett, *Humphrey Clinker*, 1771
SPARKS	Jared Sparks, *The Writings of George Washington*, 12 vols., Boston, 1834
STAEDTLER	Erhard Staedtler, *Die Ansbach-Bayreuther Truppen im Amerikanischen Unabhaengigkeitskrieg* (Gesellschaft für Familienforschung in Franken, Nuernberg, 1956)
STEDMAN	Charles Stedman, *History of the Origin, Progress and Termination of the American War*, 2 vols., Dublin, 1794
STEVENS	B. J. Stevens, *Facsimiles of Manuscripts in European Archives Relating to the United States*, 25 vols., Dublin, 1794
STEVENS, J.	John Austin Stevens, "The Southern Campaign," MAH, V no. 4 (October, 1880)
STILLÉ, B.	Charles J. Stillé, "Comte de Broglie, the Proposed Stadtholder of America," PMHB XI 4, 1887
STILLÉ	Charles J. Stillé, *Major General Anthony Wayne*, Philadelphia, 1893
STONE	William J. Stone, ed. *Letters of Brunswick and Hession Officers during the Revolution*, Albany, 1891
STOUDT, F.	John B. Stoudt, *The Feu dejoie*, Norristown, 1928
STOUDT	John Joseph Stoudt, *The Ordeal of Valley Forge*, 1963
STRYIENSKI	Casimir Stryienski, *The Eighteenth Century*, Putnam n.d.
SYDNEY	William C. Sydney, *England and the English in the Eigteenth Century*, 2 vols., 1892
TAILLANDIER	St. René de Taillandier, *Maurice de Saxe*, Paris, 1870
TARLETON	Banastre Tarleton, *History of the Campaign of 1780 and 1781*, Dublin, 1887.
TELFER	J. B. Telfer, *The Strange Career of the Chevalier d'Eon*, London, 1895

TERCIER	Claude Augustin de Tercier, *Mémoire Politique et Militaire de General de Tercier*, 1770-1816, Paris, 1891
THACHER	James Thacher, *Military Journal during the American Revolutionary War*, Boston, 1823
THAYER	Theodore Thayer, *Nathanael Greene, Strategist of the American Revolution*, 1960
TOWER	Charlemagne Tower, *The Marquis de Lafayette in the American Revolution*, Philadelphia, 1895
TREACY	M. F. Treacy, *Prelude to Yorktown*, Chapel Hill, 1963
TREVELYAN	George Otto Trevelyan, *The American Revolution*, 6 vols., London, 1909-1914
VAGTS	Alfred Vagts, *A History of Militarism*, 1959
VATEL	Charles Vatel, *Histoire du Madame du Barry*, 3 vols., Versailles, 1883
WALDO	Albigence Waldo, "Diary of Surgeon Albigence Waldo." PMHB XXI (1897), 299-323
WARD	Christopher Ward, *The War of the Revolution*, 2 vols., 1952
WARD, D.	Christopher Ward, *The Delaware Continentals*, 1941
WASHINGTON	*The Writings of George Washington*, ed. by John C. Fitzpatrick, 39 vols., 1933
WHARTON	Francis Wharton, *The Revolutionary Diplomatic Correspondence of the United States*, 6 vols., Washington, 1889
WILDES	Harry Emerson Wildes, *Valley Forge*, Oaks, Pa., 1920
WILLIAMS	Williams refers to Otho Holland Williams, "A Narrative of the Campaign of 1780," printed as an appendix to William Johnson's Sketches of the Life and Correspondence of Nathanael Greene, 1850, pp. 359-383. (Quotations are from Simms' text.
WINSOR	Justin Winsor, *Narrative and Critical History of America*, 8 vols., 1884-1889
WOODMAN	Henry Woodman, *The History of Valley Forge*, Oaks, Pa., 1920
WOODWARD	W. E. Woodward, *George Washington, the Man and the Image*, 1920

NOTES

INTRODUCTION

[1] Perkins 204 f
[2] Herold 43 f
[3] Skrine 28
[4] Schloezer XIV 103-107
[5] Herold 58
[6] Smollett, Letter of July 10; Vagts, Chapter 1
[7] Frauenholtz 26
[8] Ward I 25
[9] Seume I 55 f
[10] Carlyle I 585
[11] Fieffé I 306
[12] For Marshals of France, cf Leonard; Courcelles; and Chardigny
[13] Sinety II 133
[14] Sinety I, 1

CHAPTER I

[15] Kapp 310
[16] Kapp 2
[17] Archives of French Ministry of War
[18] ADB Fischer, Johann Christian
[19] Sinety 373-377
[20] Kapp in "Schroeder" Appendix
[21] Kapp 267; Kapp St. 459
[22] Milon
[23] Morison 311
[24] Palmer 13-15; Ahnentafel "Steuben"
[25] Staedtler 34 f
[26] Leonard 128
[27] Argenson quoted in Carré 81
[28] Carré 12
[29] Argenson VIII 362
[30] Hoyer 494
[31] Tercier VII
[32] Courcelles (alphabetical listing)
[33] Preser 69
[34] Leonard 164 f
[35] Wharton I 397
[36] Kapp 254
[37] ADB
[38] Kapp S; E. J. Lowell; Preser
[39] Ley 1-10, tells the story of Lady Craven and cites some of her literary works.
[40] Kapp 132

CHAPTER II

[41] Stryienski 146-148
[42] For Saxe see Taillendier; Skrine; Courcelles; Chardigny
[43] Saxe 9; 21; 48; 90; 95; Leonard 129
[44] Skrine 361
[45] Sinety's *Vie de Maréchal Lowendal*
[46] Kapp 7
[47] Kapp 9
[48] Washington, IX 130 and XII 128
[49] Sydney I 329
[50] Milon, quoted by Kapp 40-42
[51] Montross 423

CHAPTER III

[52] Barbier II 488
[53] On Pompadour Carré; Aretz; Leroy; Archenholtz
[54] Aretz 239
[55] Carré 123, 197
[56] Carré 128

241

[57] Carré 159
[58] Carré 203
[59] Montross 390
[60] Archenholtz; Carré 188; 200
[61] Archenholtz 296
[62] Montross 383
[63] Montross 396
[64] Archenholtz 218f
[65] Kapp 266
[66] Kapp 29
[67] Broglie "Duc" IV 600
[68] Kapp 32
[69] Kapp 309

CHAPTER IV

[70] Letter quoted by Kapp 309, dated August 31, 1779
[71] Kapp 33
[72] De Kalb's marriage: Kapp 35-37; Doniol III 204; marriage certificate
[73] Kapp 38
[74] Kapp 285
[75] De Kalb – Choiseul correspondence in Ministry of Foreign Affairs. Copies in Pennsylvania Historical Society; University of Maryland etc. Kapp (selections) 39-51
[76] Kapp 47
[77] Lochemes 182

CHAPTER V

[78] On du Barry Vatel; Breitner; Schumacher
[79] Reports to Choiseul Kapp 53-73
[80] Specimens of de Kalb's code Kapp 308. Cf also Stevens for many coded letters.
[81] Marshall frequent mention of Dr. Phile
[82] Heckenwelder in Lossing II 41
[83] Milon
[84] Shipwreck Kapp 59; Colleville 62-68; Nachtmann 41-48; New York Gazette February 8, 1768
[85] Archives of Ministry of War quoted by Kapp 71
[86] De Kalb's summarizing report of August 8, 1768 given in Kapp's Appendix, 286-292

CHAPTER VI

[87] Kapp 75-78
[88] Broglie "Secret"
[89] Le Chevalier d'Eon J. B. Telfer
[90] Story of the brick, Broglie, Le secret du Roi, II 230
[91] Kapp 80
[92] De Kalb letter in U.S. Archives
[93] Journals VII 174
[94] Beaumarchais letter to Deane I 342
[95] Deane 342
[96] Deane I, 343
[97] Doniol II 52
[98] Lafayette I 6 ff
[99] Deane I 409 ff
[100] Lameth 105-107
[101] Lameth 107
[102] AHR XV (1910) 563
[103] Kapp 86
[104] AHR XV (1910) 564
[105] Lafayette I 8

CHAPTER VII

[106] Deane 1 163
[107] Deane I 113
[108] Wharton II 74
[109] Journals VII 174
[110] Kapp 94 ff
[111] Deane I 426; Stevens 603-604
[112] Wharton 394 f
[113] Chidsey 86
[114] Deane I 404
[115] Kapp 92
[116] Paine I 428
[117] Deane I 344
[118] Deane I 431
[119] Kapp 127; Doniol III 226; Stevens VIII 755; Stillé 369

CHAPTER VIII

120 Lafayette I 9
121 Kapp 101; Doniol III 207
122 Lafayette 112
123 AHR XV (1910) 564; Kapp 106
124 Doniol III 206
125 Kapp 104; Doniol III 207
126 Fayolle 3
127 Kapp 104
128 Maurois 12
129 Kapp 104; Doniol III 306
130 Kapp 105
131 Doniol II 420
132 Kapp 108; Doniol III 211
133 Stevens VII no. 686
134 Lafayette I 13 note
135 Lafayette I 13 note
136 Tower I 58
137 Broglie "Archives" 304 f
138 Data on the officers on the "Victoire" Kapp 296; Deane I 407; Kite; Doniol; Lasseray; Balch
139 Doniol II 393 note

CHAPTER IX

140 Lafayette 191
141 Doniol III 212; Kapp 109
142 Lafayette I 14 note
143 Broglie "Archives" 441
144 Broglie "Archives" 442; Doniol III 215
145 Lafayette I 14f; Doniol III 215
146 Lafayette 15; Doniol III 216
147 Lafayette I 94 ff; Doniol III 216
148 Lafayette I 96
149 Lafayette I 98
150 Broglie "Archives" 441 f
151 Broglie "Archives" 442
152 Doniol III 215-222
153 Doniol III 217 ff
154 Lafayette I 15; Fayolle 1 ff
155 Mauroy's Mémoire; Broglie "Archives" 304-325
156 Philips 105

CHAPTER X

157 Broglie "Archives" 334A
158 Deane I 342
159 Burnett II 31
160 Burnett II 259
161 Journals VII 174
162 Journals VII 174
163 Burnett II 304
164 Journals VII 185
165 Burnett II 394
166 Journals VII 605
167 Burnett II 430
168 Journals VII 605
169 Doniol III 218
170 Burnett 497
171 Kapp 304
172 Kapp 113; Doniol III 220
173 SCHS VII 182 f
174 Kapp 113 ff
175 Journals VIII 721
176 Milon, dated Bethlehem, September 19, 1777
177 Journals VIII 746
178 PMHB 384
179 Burnett II 513
180 Kapp 302
181 Kapp 118
182 Rosengarten 107; Kapp 119
183 De Kalb letter, recipient unknown, courtesy Pierpont Morgan Library
184 Marshall 135
185 Levering 462, 468
186 Clark 133
187 Franklin VII 77

CHAPTER XI

188 Milon, October 11, 1777; Stevens VIII 755
189 Washington X 94
190 Washington IX 388
191 Kapp 121; Journals IX 762
192 SCHM VII 58
193 Lasseray 160; 348
194 Washington X 71
195 Washington X 233
196 Lafayette 21
197 Thayer 198
198 Marshall 159

[199] Burnett "Congress" 283
[200] Washington X 75 f
[201] Ward 379
[202] Kapp 127
[203] Kapp 134
[204] Kapp 137
[205] Stillé 114
[206] Kapp 145
[207] Marshall 152
[208] Lafayette 39
[209] Kapp 151
[210] Lafayette quoted in Kapp 56
[211] Stevens VIII 808
[212] Kapp 156
[213] Chidsey 128
[214] Kapp 178
[215] Data on de Kalb's moves are from Washington's *Writings* and de Kalb's letters

CHAPTER XII

[216] Gordon 278
[217] Washington X 133
[218] PMHB XX 234
[219] Pennsylvania Executive Council
[220] Stillé 53
[221] Hughes 221 quoting Gordon
[222] Washington X 471
[223] Kapp 137
[224] Stevens VIII 761
[225] Washington X 171
[226] Lafayette I 142
[227] Kapp 136
[228] Thayer 220
[229] Washington X 196
[230] Thayer 221
[231] Kapp 139
[232] Ward 543
[233] Lafayette I 35
[234] Wildes 134
[235] Kapp 143
[236] Washington X 377
[237] Kapp 141
[238] Kapp 140
[239] Washington X 184 note
[240] Washington X 193
[241] PMHB XXI 299-321
[242] Washington X 471
[243] Washington X 183
[244] Chidsey 23
[245] PMHB XXI 305
[246] Kapp 142
[247] Chidsey 47
[248] Baurmeister 41
[249] Kapp 142
[250] Kapp 142
[251] Lafayette I 142
[252] Milon, March 30, 1778
[253] Thayer 221
[254] Kapp 142 f
[255] Kapp 143 f
[256] Faust I 330
[257] Woodman 66-69
[258] Letter in possession of the Stephens family
[259] Kapp 159
[260] Washington X 354
[261] Stoudt F 14 f
[262] Sparks V 356
[263] Kapp 160
[264] Kapp 307
[265] Ives 177

CHAPTER XIII

[266] Washington XIII 352
[267] Washington XIII 364
[268] Kapp 172 f
[269] Stevens XIII 1988
[270] Stevens XIII 1988
[271] Stevens XIII 1988
[272] Kapp 163
[273] Kapp 164
[274] Kapp 167
[275] Kapp 169
[276] Ward 598
[277] Washington XV 396 f
[278] Ward 603
[279] Kapp 176
[280] Kapp 176 f
[281] Kapp 177
[282] Kapp 177
[283] Kapp 179
[284] Kapp 280 f
[285] Kapp 183
[286] Kapp 182
[287] Washington XVIII 60
[288] Kapp 186
[289] Washington XVIII 199; 200; 205; 215; 265
[290] Wharton I 423
[291] Kapp 180
[292] Kapp 106

[293] Kapp 113
[294] Sparks 531
[295] Kapp 163
[296] Wharton I 421
[297] Kapp 302

[298] Kapp 319
[299] Wharton 421
[300] Kapp 316
[301] Moore 310 ff

CHAPTER XIV

[302] Washington XVIII 199
[303] Washington XVIII 197
[304] Kapp 194
[305] Washington XVIII 251
[306] Kapp 195
[307] Document in Pennsylvania Historical Society
[308] Kapp 196 f
[309] Kapp 198
[310] Kapp 198
[311] Washington XVIII 263
[312] Jefferson III 433
[313] Jefferson III 463
[314] Jefferson III 465
[315] Saxe 95

[316] Kapp 200
[317] Kapp 200
[318] Horry, Chapters XI to XIII
[319] Maurois 62
[320] Broglie "Archives" 326 A
[321] Woodward 336
[322] Lancaster 392
[323] Jefferson III 496
[324] Kapp 204
[325] Kapp 206
[326] Williams 361
[327] Maryland Archives XLIII 325
[328] Williams 361
[329] Horry 102
[330] MAH V 293

CHAPTER XV

[331] Kapp 214
[332] Jefferson III 524
[333] Kapp 213
[334] Kapp 216
[335] Williams 366
[336] Kapp 218
[337] Ward 913 note 20
[338] Blumenthal 62
[339] MAH V 496 (October 1880)
[340] Stedman II 228 ff
[341] Fiske II 193; Moore II 310
[342] Tarleton 99
[343] Williams 368
[344] Williams 369
[345] Smith 17
[346] Williams 367
[347] Smith 17
[348] Williams 367 f
[349] Gist August 15, 1780
[350] Williams 371
[351] Williams 372
[352] Ward 726
[353] Ward 726

[354] Thayer 279
[355] Lossing II 467
[356] Bancroft V 388
[357] Fiske II 196
[358] Williams (eye witness) 374 f; Gordon III 443; Lossing II 467; Dubuysson note XV 34
[359] Ward 728-732
[360] Lasseray 191-194
[361] Kapp 237
[362] Pennsylvania Supreme Executive Council, Minutes Vol. XIII 516
[363] Rosengarten 114
[364] Wharton, I 420
[365] Gates' letters to Washington and to Congress quoted by Kapp 237
[366] Lasseray I 150
[367] Washington XX 144
[368] Lafayette at de Kalb's monument: Kapp 237-239; Masonic Intelligencer (Boston) April 9, 1825

INDEX OF NAMES

Abzac, Raymond de Baudière, Vicomte de (De Kalb's descendant), 4, 5
Abzac, Leonore, Vicomtesse d' (De Kalb's granddaughter), 22
Adams, John, 71
Adams, Samuel, 2
Alden, Professor Douglas W., 5
Anderson, Major Archibald, 225
Anna, Czarina of Russia, 16
Anna Ivanovna, Duchess of Courland, 16
Anne, Queen of England, 103
Antin, Duc d', 41
Appony, M., 60
Argenson, Antoine René, 2, 25, 26
Ariovistus, 195
Aristotle, 122
Armand, Colonel Charles (assumed name of Armand-Charles Tuffin, Marquis de la Rouërie), 196, 201, 208, 219, 220, 221, 222
Armstrong, Major John, 162, 214, 219
Augustus II, King of Poland and Saxony, 15
Aurora, Countess of Königsmarck, 15
Auteroche, Comte de, 31

Balsamo, Giuseppe, see Cagliostro, 23
Bamford, Dean Ronald, 5
Bancroft, George, 107
Barbier, Edmund Jean François, 46
Barry, Jean, Comte du, 66, 78
Barry, Jeanne, Comtesse du, 65, 66
Beaumarchais, Pierre-Augustin Caron de, 24, 26, 87, 89, 94, 148
Bécu, Anne (du Barry's mother), 65
Bédoulx, Charles de, 113, 115, 125, 126
Berkeley, Earl of, 28
Bernadotte, Jean Baptiste, King of Sweden and Norway, 103

Bernis, François-Joachim, Cardinal de, 48, 49, 65
Berwick, James Fitzjames, Duke of, 15, 17
Bingham, William, 132
Biron, Duc de, 31
Bischoff, Rudolf (collateral descendant of de Kalb), 5
Boucher, François, 46
Boursier, Captain de, 109, 111, 115
Braddock, Samuel Edward, 17, 40
Brent, John Carroll, 22
Brinckerhof, Colonel, 184
Broglie, Comte de, IX, 2, 3, 19, 53, 54, 57, 58, 59, 82, 83, 84, 85, 87, 88, 89, 90, 91, 94, 95, 102, 103, 104, 105, 106, 107, 108, 125, 145, 147, 153, 154, 163, 166, 168, 169, 184, 185, 206
Broglie, Duc de, Maréchal de France, 50, 51, 53, 55, 57, 58, 59, 82, 83, 104, 145
Brunswick, Charles, Prince of, 19, 49, 50
Buford, Colonel Abraham, 196, 208
Burgoyne, General John, 151, 206
Burnett, Edmund C., 152
Burr, Aaron, 204

Cadwalader, General Thomas, 158
Cagliostro, Alessandro (born Giuseppe Balsamo), 23
Candon, Lieutenant, 232
Capitaine, M. de, 118, 126, 127
Carlyle, Thomas, 14
Casanova, Giovanni Giacomo "de Seingalt", 23
Castries, Marquis de, 56
Caswell, General Richard, Governor of North Carolina, 124, 126, 196, 202, 207, 208, 214, 215, 219
Chappell, Alonzo, 233
Charles II, King of Spain, 28, 86
Charles VI, Emperor of Austria, 8

Charles VII, Elector of Bavaria, 8
Charles XII, King of Sweden, 16
Charlie, Bonnie Prince (The Young Pretender to the English Throne) 32, 39, 40
Chavannes, Comte de, 31
Chevert, François du, 25
Chidsey, Donald R, 103
Chinard, Gilbert, 1
Choiseul, Etienne François, Duc de, 49, 55, 59, 60, 61, 62, 63, 65, 67, 68, 69, 70, 74, 75, 76, 77, 78, 79, 82, 92
Churchill, Arabella, (mother of the Duke of Berwick), 15
Clairon, Mlle, 28
Clarke, George L. 147, 148
Clausewitz, Karl von, 25
Clerke, General Robert, 57, 58
Clinton, General Henry, 109, 182, 183, 201, 215, 219
Cochran, Dr. John, 184
Coenen, Dr. Frederic E, 5
Cohorn, Menno, 36
Coigny, Vicomte de, 110, 113
Colbert, Jean Baptiste, 56
Coligny, Marshal, 50
Colomb, Pierre de, 118, 126, 127
Condé, Louis II de Bourbon, Prince de, 51
Conway, Thomas, 94, 136, 150, 151, 152, 156, 157, 158, 170, 193
Cornwallis, Lord Charles, 215, 216, 217, 218, 219, 220, 221, 223, 224, 225, 227, 228, 229
Courcelles, Chevalier de, 26
Crates, Greek philosopher, 129
Craven, Lady, née Berkeley, wife of Lord Craven, 28, 29
Cumberland, Duke of, 30, 31, 49
Cunz, Professor Dieter, VII, 5

Dean, Colonel James, 216
Deane, Silas, 24, 84, 86, 87, 88, 90, 91, 92, 93, 94, 95, 97, 98, 102, 104, 105, 106, 108, 109, 110, 113, 114, 119, 125, 126, 132, 134, 135, 136, 137, 138, 139, 140, 141, 144, 147, 148, 150, 175, 192,
Defoe, Daniel, 24
Diderot, Denis, 88
Dobson, Captain Henry, 225
Donop, Carl von, 29
Doniol, Henri, 4, 5, 57
Don John of Austria, 103

Dryden, John, 187
Dubois, M., chief clerk of the minister of war, 59, 60
Dubois-Martin, François Auguste, "Little Dubois", 97, 108, 109
Dubois-Martin, M., (Comte de Broglie's secretary), 59, 60, 61, 95, 96, 104, 105, 108
Dubuysson, Charles François, Chevalier de, 118, 122, 125, 126, 135, 137, 141, 142, 146, 154, 164, 194, 195, 217, 225, 226, 227, 229
Du Coudray, Philippe, 88, 135, 136, 137, 138
Dumonceau, Billard, 65, 66
Du Ponceau, Peter, 2, 8, 174, 193
Duportail, General Louis Le Begne, 88, 135, 139, 162, 163

Eden, William, 114
Edward VIII, King of England, 28
Elizabeth Czarina of Russia, 45, 83, 84
Elizabeth, Queen of England, 103
Emerson, Ralph Waldo, 91
Eon, Chevalier d', 82, 83, 84
Estaing, Charles Henri Theodat, Comte d', 148
Estrées, Duc d', Maréchal de France, 49
Eugene, Prince of Savoy, see Savoy

Faneuil, Peter, 133
Fayolle, Pierre de Rousseau, Chevalier de, 124, 126, 131
Ferdinand, Duke of Brunswick, 97, 99, 103, 104, 105
Fischer, Johann Christian, 19, 26, 54, 118
Fleury, François Louis Teissêdre, 8, 187, 228
Folard, Jean Charles, Chevalier de, 34
Ford, Colonel Benjamin, 215
Franklin, Benjamin, 33, 77, 98, 102, 104, 105, 106, 126, 135, 136, 137, 138, 148, 175, 204
Franval, Captain, 148
Frederick II, King of Prussia (Frederick the Great), 1, 8, 12, 23, 25, 29, 34, 37, 44, 45, 49, 50, 52, 62, 67, 99, 103
Frederic III, King of Denmark, 16
Freeman, Douglas S., 3

Garibaldi, Giuseppe, 78

247

Gates, Horatio, IX, 3, 151, 152, 155, 156, 195, 196, 206, 207, 208, 209, 210, 211, 213, 214, 215, 216, 217, 218, 219, 220, 221, 222, 223, 224, 225, 228
George II, King of England, 44
George III, King of England, 70, 71, 74, 76, 89, 109, 180
Gerard, Conrad, 72, 175, 192
German and Girardot, (commercial firm) 98
Gervais, John Lewis, 144
Gimat, Jean Joseph Sourbader de, 118, 122, 125, 126, 184
Gist, Mordecai, 190, 220, 222, 223, 224, 226
Gloucester, Duke of, 89, 94
Glover, John, 42
Gneisenau, Neidhart, Graf von, 24, 25
Gottschalk, Louis T. 2, 3
Gouvion, Jean Baptiste de, 88
Greene, George Washington, 3
Greene, General Nathanael, 135, 138, 141, 151, 162, 165, 168, 169
Gun, Captain, 209
Gunby, Colonel John, 225

Hamilton, Lieutenant Colonel Henry, 204, 228
Hancock, John, 2, 86, 133, 135
Harrison, Benjamin, 137
Hasenburg, Captain, 95
Hay, Lord Charles, 31
Hay, Major Samuel, 166
Henry, Joseph, Governor of Pennsylvania, 133
Henry, Patrick, 204
Hill, Dr. Robert W., 5
Holtzendorf, Louis Casimir, Baron de, 92
Hommet, Captain, 63
Horry, Captain Daniel, 204, 205, 211
Hortales and Company, 89
Howard, Lieutenant Colonel John Eager, 225
Howe, General Robert, 123, 147, 153, 156, 198
Howe, Major General Sir William, 217
Hoyer, Johann Friedrich, 26
Huger, Major Benjamin, 121, 123
Hughes, Rupert, 225
Huntington, General Jedediah, 168

Irvine, General William, 162
Ives, Mabel Lorenz, 180

Jackson, General Thomas ("Stonewall"), 206
James II, King of England, 40
Jamison, Major, 201
Jaquett, Captain Peter, 224
Jefferson, Thomas, 132, 199, 201, 202, 207, 209, 213
Johnson, Samuel, 194
Jones, John Paul, 23
Julius Caesar, 40
Junot, Androche, Duc d'Abrantes, 23

Kalb, Johann (or Jean), Baron de, I, V, VIII, IX, 1, 2, 3, 4, 5, 8, 9, 11, 18, 19, 20, 21, 23, 26, 29, 30, 35, 37, 38, 39, 40, 41, 42, 43, 48, 50, 52, 53, 54, 55, 56, 57, 58, 59, 60, 61, 62, 63, 64, 67, 68, 69, 70, 71, 72, 73, 74, 75, 76, 77, 78, 79, 80, 81, 82, 84, 85, 86, 87, 88, 90, 91, 92, 93, 95, 98, 102, 103, 104, 105, 107, 108, 109, 110, 111, 112, 114, 115, 116, 118, 119, 120, 121, 122, 124, 125, 126, 130, 131, 132, 133, 134, 136, 137, 138, 141, 142, 144, 145, 146, 147, 148, 150, 151, 153, 157, 158, 159, 160, 162, 163, 164, 165, 166, 168, 169, 170, 171, 172, 173, 174, 175, 179, 180, 182, 183, 184, 185, 186, 187, 188, 189, 190, 191, 192, 193, 194, 195, 196, 197, 198, 199, 200, 201, 202, 203, 204, 205, 206, 207, 208, 209, 210, 211, 212, 214, 215, 216, 217, 219, 220, 221, 223, 224, 225, 226, 227, 228, 229, 230, 231, 232, 233
Kalb, Mme. de (née Anne Elisabeth Emilie van Robais), 3, 22, 63, 69, 72, 113, 124, 146, 153, 174, 179, 183, 185, 187, 193, 203, 228
Kalb, Anna Maria Caroline de (de Kalb's daughter, married Captain Luke Geymueller), 56
Kalb, Charlotte von, née von Ostheimb, 22
Kalb, Elie de (de Kalb's younger son) married Elise Signard, 56, 226, 227

Kalb, Frederic de (de Kalb's elder son, died a victim of the Revolution), 226, 227
Kalb, George (collateral descendant of de Kalb), 5
Kalb, Henry de (Major in a French regiment), 21
Kalb, Johann Leonard (de Kalb's father), 18, 20, 22
Kalb, Leonore de (married Vicomte d'Abzac, de Kalb's granddaughter), 22
Kalb, Margaretha (de Kalb's mother), 18
Kapp, Friedrich, 4, 19, 21, 22, 23, 57, 106, 189
Karl Alexander, Margrave of Ansbach-Bayreuth, 24, 25, 28
Karl Friedrich Wilhelm, Margrave of Ansbach-Bayreuth, 26
Kaunitz, Prince Wenzel Anton, 44
Keall, Henry, 86
Keyser, Ephraim, 230
Kirkwood, Captain, Robert 225
Klingelhofer, Dr. Herbert E., 5
Knox, General Henry, 135, 138, 141, 153, 162
Königsmarck, Marie-Aurore, Comtesse de, 15

Lafayette, Marquis de, VIII, 1, 8, 86, 90, 91, 92, 93, 94, 105, 108, 109, 110, 111, 112, 114, 115, 116, 117, 118, 119, 120, 121, 122, 123, 124, 125, 126, 130, 131, 132, 133, 134, 136, 137, 138, 139, 140, 144, 146, 148, 150, 152, 156, 157, 158, 162, 164, 165, 169, 176, 177, 184, 192, 193, 199, 200, 201, 206, 217, 228, 230, 231
Lafayette, Mme. de, 110, 113, 124, 169
Lafayette, George Washington de, 231
Lambdin, James, 232
Lameth, Theodore de, 91
Lannoy, M., 88
Laurens, Henry, 138, 144, 155
Learned, General Ebenezer, 150
Le Boursier, Captain, 109, 111, 115
Lecouvreur, Adrienne, 16
Lee, Arthur, 87, 94, 148, 175
Lee, General Charles, 182, 206
Lee, Colonel Richard Henry, 145, 147, 150, 152, 155, 193, 194
Lee, General Robert E. 206
Leicester, Earl of, 103
Lenel, Edith, 4
Le Normant, Charles (Mme. Pompadour's husband). see Tournehem
Leonard, Emile, 26
Lesser, le Theyet de, 118, 122, 125, 126, 142
Lessing, Gotthold Ephraim, 88
Lincoln, General Benjamin, 192
Livingston, William, Governor of New Jersey, 167
Louis IX (St. Louis), 32
Louis XIV, King of France, 10, 48, 56
Louis XV, King of France, 28, 32, 34, 42, 44, 47, 50, 66, 67, 79, 80, 82, 83
Louis XVI, King of France, 51, 65, 84, 88, 116, 126, 175, 176
Louvois, François Marquis de, 10
Lovell, James, 3, 105, 133, 134, 135, 136, 148
Lowendal, Maréchal de, IX, 15, 16, 17, 20, 21, 26, 30, 32, 35, 36, 37, 50, 53, 55, 216. List of officers in his regiment, 20, 21.
Lupton, George, 114
Luzerne, Marquis de la, 23, 192

McDougall, General Alexander, 157
McLane, Captain Allen, 186
Maintenon, Françoise, Marquise de, 48
Manon, Walter C., 233
Maria Theresa, Empress of Austria, 8, 44, 45, 51, 65
Marie Antoinette, Queen of France, 75, 104, 109
Marion, Francis, 204, 205, 211
Marlborough, Duke of, 7, 15, 103
Marshall, Charles, (son of Christopher Marshall), 71
Marshall, Christopher, 71, 74, 147, 151, 152, 155, 159, 195
Maurepas, Jean Frédéric Phélypeaux, Comte de, 91, 112
Mauroy, Chevalier de, 4, 105, 116, 118, 124, 125, 126, 130, 131, 132, 136, 141, 206
Maximilian, Emperor of Mexico, 103
Maxwell, General William, 162
Mease, John, 156
Meinières, M. de, 48
Mersereau, M., 73

Meyer, Georg, 18
Meyer, Johann, (de Kalb's godfather), 18
Mifflin, General Thomas, 165
Mills, Walter, 31
Monroe, James, 202
Montbarey, Prince de, 19, 54, 55
Monteynard, Marquis de, 80
Morison, Samuel Eliot, 23
Morris, Gouverneur, 118
Morris, Robert, 86, 132, 133, 135
Moultrie, General William, 123
Muhlenberg, General Peter, 162

Nachtman, M., (tutor of de Kalb's great-grandchildren) 22
Napoleon Bonaparte, Emperor of France, 23, 25, 30, 40, 51, 118
Napoleon III, Louis, 103
Nash, Abner, Governor of South Carolina, 202, 213, 214, 228
Nassau, Prince of, 96
Nelson, Major Thomas, 208
Neuhof, Teodor von, 24
Noailles, Louis Marc Antoine, Vicomte de, 90, 91, 113, 118

Orange-Nassau, Prince William of, 102, 107
Oyeras, Comte d', 58

Page, John, 132
Paine, Thomas, 105
Paoli, Pasquale, 78
Parish, Betsy, see Phile
Parma, Duke of, 36
Paterson, General John, 150
Peale, Charles Wilson, 232
Peter the Great, Czar of Russia, 16
Phile, Dr. Frederic, 70, 72, 74, 84, 85, 86, 95, 133, 159, 195, 200
Phile, Betsy Parish, 70, 72, 141, 200
Philip V, King of Spain, 15
Pickering, General Timothy, 151, 168
Pitt, William, Earl of Chatham, 128
Poisson, François, Pompadour's father, 45
Poisson, Mme. François, Pompadour's mother, 45
Poisson, Jeanne Antoinette, see Pompadour
Pompadour, Marquise de, 42, 44, 45, 47, 48, 49, 50, 51, 53, 59, 65, 67, 78, 82
Poneza, Major de, 177
Poor, General Enoch, 162

Porterfield, Lieutenant Colonel Charles, 213, 219, 221
Prahl, Dean Augustus J., 5
Preser, Carl, 26
Price, Leonard, 113, 119, 120, 121, 122, 125, 126
Pulaski, Count Casimir, 8, 119

Radière, M., 88
Rawdon, Lord Francis, 109, 215, 216, 217, 218, 219, 222, 225, 227
Raynal, Guillaume Thomas François, 131
Reed, John, 5
Reed, Joseph, 161
Renouvin, Professor Pierre, 4
Richelieu, Louis François Armand, Duc de, 50, 66, 189
Rittenhouse, Mr. 104
Robais - see van Robais
Rogers, Colonel Nicholas, 3, 174, 194
Rousseau, Jean Jacques, 46, 88, 117
Rozière, M., 81, 82
Rutherford, General Griffith, 202, 212
Rutledge, John, Governor of North Carolina, 201, 207

St. Clair, General Arthur, 153, 191
St. Evrard, Abbé Simon, 98
St. George, Chevalier, a name assumed by James, the "Old Pretender" to the English throne, 40
St. Germain, Claude Louis, Comte de, 84, 85
St. Julien, M., 98
St. Louis, see Louis IX
St. Simon, Comte de, 15
Salles, General de, 53
Sartines, Gabriel de, 97
Savoy, Prince Eugene of, 7, 15, 26
Saxe, Maurice de, 15, 16, 17, 30, 31, 32, 33, 34, 39, 49, 50, 51, 84, 202, 216
Saxe, Prince Xavier de, 53
Scharnhorst, Gerhard David von, 25
Schaumburg-Lippe, Count William 57, 59
Schiller, Friedrich von, 29
Schuyler, General Philip, 133
Schwarzenberg, Austrian General, 36
Scott, General Charles, 162
Ségur, Louis-Philippe, Comte de, 70, 93

250

Seitz, see Kalb, Margaretha
Seume, Johann Gottfried, 12
Sinety, Marquis de, 16
Smallwood, General William, 162, 189, 222, 223, 226
Smollett, Tobias, 11
Solomon, 167
Soubise, Charles, Prince de, 49, 50, 51, 53, 55, 59, 92, 189
Soulange-Teissier, R., 4, 5
Southey, Robert, 7
Sparks, Jared, 89, 193
Stark, General John, 156
Stedman, Charles, 42, 217
Steinmetz, Karl Friedrich von, 25
Stephens, Abijah, 170, 174, 175
Steuben, Baron von, 8, 22, 23, 59, 119, 148, 177, 179, 193
Stevens, B. F., 206
Stevens, General Edward, 202, 214, 218, 220, 221, 225
Stewart, Major John, 187
Stillé, Charles, J., 107, 155
Stirling, General (Lord) Alexander William, 151, 162, 177
Stormont, Viscount, 92
Stuppa, Swiss General, 10
Sullivan, General John, 135, 138, 141, 162
Sumter, Thomas, 217, 218

Tammany, Indian Chief, 71
Tarleton, Lieutenant Colonel Banastre, 218, 220, 222, 224
Tercier, Claude Augustus de, 26
Tessé, Comtesse de, 112
Thackeray, William Makepeace, 17
Thomson, Charles, 144, 145, 147, 193
Tilghman, Lieutenant Tench, 168
Timoleon, 117
Tournehem, Charles François Paul le Normant de, 45
Trevelyan, George Otto, 3
Trumbull, Joseph, 134
Turenne, Maréchal Henri de, 51

Vagts, Alfred, 5
Valeroissant, M. de, 81
Valfort, Louis de, 106, 118, 122, 125, 126, 142, 144, 145
Valous, Marquis de, 5
Van Robais, see Mme. de Kalb
Van Robais, Peter, father of Mme. de Kalb, 56
Varnum, General James, 153, 162, 166

Vergennes, Charles Gravier, Comte de, 79, 119, 148, 165
Virgil, Roman poet, 187
Vogue, General de, 53
Voltaire, François Marie Arouet, 12, 25, 46, 49, 51, 55, 88, 112, 117
Vrigny, Cloquet de, 118, 126
Vrillières, Duc de, 80, 81

Wadsworth, Jeremiah, Colonel, 195
Waldo, Dr. Albigense, 167, 168
Walker, Captain Benjamin, 177
Wallenstein, Albrecht, Duke of Friedland, 103
Walpole, Horace, 28
Walsh, Robert, 64
Ward, Christopher, 216, 221, 223
Wartenburg, Yorck von, 25
Washington, George, 1, 39, 42, 48, 93, 94, 99, 105, 106, 107, 108, 118, 129, 133, 135, 137, 144, 146, 147, 150, 151, 153, 154, 155, 156, 157, 158, 161, 163, 164, 165, 166, 167, 169, 170, 176, 179, 180, 182, 183, 186, 187, 188, 191, 195, 196, 197, 198, 199, 201, 204, 206, 216, 228, 229, 230
Washington, Colonel William, 196, 208
Wayne, General Anthony, 153, 155, 162, 186, 187, 216, 223
Webster, Colonel James, 222, 223
Weedon, General George, 162, 170, 171, 172
Weems, Parson Mason Locke, 204, 211
Weymouth, Lord, 92
Wharton, Francis, 103, 105, 192
Whipple, William, 134, 144
White, Colonel Anthony, 195, 208
Wilkinson, General James, 152
Williams, Colonel Otho Holland, 195, 210, 211, 214, 215, 218, 219, 220, 222, 223
Woodford, Brigadier General William, 163, 177
Woodman, Henry, 170, 174
Wolff, Peter, 146
Woolford, Lieutenant Colonel Thomas, 218

Xenophon, 223

Zucker, Dr. Lois M., 6

251

www.ingramcontent.com/pod-product-compliance
Lightning Source LLC
Chambersburg PA
CBHW020748160426
43192CB00006B/281